Nazis to the Core

J. Botman

Nazis to the Core

The Sassen brothers and their anti-Bolshevik crusade in Latin America

Aspekt Publishers

Nazis to the Core
© J. Botman
© 2015 Uitgeverij ASPEKT
Amersfoortsestraat 27, 3769 AD Soesterberg, The Netherlands
info@uitgeverijaspekt.nl – http://www.uitgeverijaspekt.nl

Picture on cover:
Wim (left) and Alfons (right) Sassen in 1944. Source National Archive, The Hague (The Netherlands) NL-HaNA, Justitie/CABR, 2.09.09, inv.nr: 87844 and 31614.

Cover: Mark Heuveling
Inside: Thomas Wunderink

ISBN: 9789461538239
NUR: 680

All rights reserved. No reproduction copy or transmission of this publication may be made without written permission.

Contents

Foreword	7
Chapter I Wim Sassen	11
The German invasion	20
War over	69
Reunion in Ireland	107
Refuge in Argentina	111
Adolf Eichmann	117
Working for Secret Services	123
Wim Sassen in peace	139
Chapter II Alfons Sassen	173
Liberation of Holland	192
In Spain	212
Ecuador	221
Epilogue	251
Abbreviations	255
Family tree of the Sassen	259
Notes	263
Documentary Sources	297
Archives	297
Bibliography	298
Magazines and papers	306
Internet	308
Audio	309
Index	311

Foreword

Much has been written about SS reporter Wim Sassen. Always referring to the famous interview with Adolf Eichmann, his implication in the kidnapping of Eichmann by the *Mossad,* and his criminal trial in Jerusalem. The main focus was Eichmann, but who was this unknown low ranking Nazi Wim Sassen who acted as his ghost writer? And why was he chosen to interview Eichmann?

Wim Sassen is mentioned in numerous publications over the last 50 years. Usually the authors refer to unverified sources and rumours. A lot about Wim Sassen was just hearsay. One could even speak of some mystification about this SS reporter in order to justify the cloak and dagger (conspiracy) theories about Nazi fugitives in Latin America; the escape organisation *Odessa* or resurrection of the *Fourth Reich,* etc. Both Sassen brothers were interrogated and interviewed many times in the post war period (in particular during the seventies and eighties) by British, American, Belgian and Dutch investigative judges, intelligence services and international journalists.[1] They were usually interviewed about the *"bureaucrat of the Endlösung" Adolf Eichmann, Josef Mengele* or friend *Klaus Barbie*, but they were never subjected to an in-depth interview concerning their own past. When asked, they boasted of their Nazi friends, their war time experience and their innocence. No questions were asked about their motivation or the ideology which led them to collaborate with the Germans or their true past.

Similarly, the Sassens' offspring in Latin America created their own truth about their fathers' past. Some of them even glorified it. Others like the well known political-sociologist daughter Saskia stated in several interviews that her father detested the Nazis and was solely driven to join the SS so as to pursue his journalistic career. My research will show that this is hardly a reflection of the real truth. The whole Sassen family, their father, the two brothers, sisters and other relatives where active members of extreme right wing movements before and during the war. They collaborated heavily with the Nazi regime both in the Netherlands and in Belgium. No matter what the next of kin state about their fathers, the truth is that they were Nazis through and through. They had no part in the physical persecution of the Jews but they did create and propagate an anti-Semitic sentiment among the occupied population via their broadcasts during the war. These clever boys always evaded detection. The clever strategies of deception ensured that whatever trick they played, they always managed to escape persecution, fool their superiors, double cross intelligence services, and make a handsome profit out of war mongering countries or military dictatorships. Even the best espionage thriller could not keep up with these scoundrels.

This book, which in the original Dutch version was first published in 2013, has sought to re-examine the past of Willem (Wim) Sassen and his younger brother Alphons. Thorough archive research has brought to light new revelations about Wim Sassen and his family. Not only did the whole family collaborate with the Nazis, the majority of them, the two known brothers and two sisters, managed to escape to Latin America. While the two sisters had, in the meantime, abandoned their Nazi affiliation, the two brothers ended up regrouping with expat Nazis in Latin America out of anti communist zeal, to assist military juntas in crushing leftist movements. Their closest partners (and friends) were the well known *"Butcher of Lyon"* Klaus Barbie, *Luftwaffe* Ace *Hans Ulrich Rudel* and counterfeiter *Friedrich Schwend*.

The Sassen boys were no shrinking violets during the war. In their position as reporters they were known spokesmen for the German propaganda war machine with their anti-Semitic and communist speeches broadcast over the radio. At the end of the war they participated in the Nazi-underground movement *Werewolf* which prepared for sabotage, as well as hit and run strikes against the Allied forces. After the collapse of the Third Reich they were recruited by the Allied intelligence agencies in order to dismantle other *Werewolf* networks in the Netherlands and Germany. The Dutch interrogators soon realized, however, that these two had no intention of abandoning their Nazi-ideology, and were actively seeking a way out of Europe to reunite with their fellow comrades in Latin America.

Through several Dutch ratline organisations, and with the assistance of the clergy, a total of four Sassen family members managed to reach Latin America safely. There the sisters kept a low profile, while the Sassen boys joined a network of Nazi-diehards. With the backing of international intelligence services they became notorious arms dealers and military advisors to right-wing governments in Argentina, Bolivia, Chile, Ecuador and Paraguay.

This book has focused solely and entirely on the Sassen family. It is not an additional study on the Eichmann case, about which much has already been written. This research is aimed at clarifying the misconceptions which still exist in the present media (and publications) about Wim and his brother Alfons.

This work contains many citations of interviews that have been conducted with the Sassen brothers, family members and friends. Lately, more personal stories of "common" volunteers have been published to tell their version of their exploits during WWII; why they became members of affiliate parties, joined the SS or fought as volunteers on the Eastern Front. This research is based on documents from the National Archive in The Hague Holland, NIOD in Amsterdam, regional archives like the BHIC (Brabant), the Jesuit (Nijmegen) and the Belgian archive ADVN (Antwerp).

In 2015, I discovered new information at CEGESOMA in Brussels (Belgium), which has been added in this last edition. It deals with additional material concerning the Sassen brothers' ideological perceptions on entering the war, and helps to explain their war and post-war exploits. In order to stay as close to the original statements, interviews or intelligence reports some translations from British, German, French, Spanish or Dutch sources might have suffered. The author apologizes in advance for any such unintentional errors.

Chapter I
Wim Sassen

Wilhelmus (Wim) Antonius Maria Sassen was born on 16 April 1918 in Geertruidenberg, born into what he would say was "a long line of magistrates". His father *Jan Sassen* originated from Caberg, south of Holland. He had a commercial background and started his first business in Geertruidenberg, Company *De Zon* which specialized in beds, furniture and wallpaper. There he met the daughter of the local grocer J*ohanna Margaretha van Bavel* and they married in September 1910. Soon business expanded to the neighbouring villages of Raamsdonk and Kaatsheuvel, where he also represented a company from Antwerp specialising in mineral oils. In 1912 their first daughter *Maria*, nicknamed "Mies" was born. Business flourished until the First World War broke out halting all commerce with neighbouring countries. Even though neutral Holland did not formally participate in the war, Sassen senior was mobilised. Two years into the war, on 24 August 1916, their second daughter *Georgette* was born. Willem, usually referred to as Wim was their third child, born at the end of the First World War.

According to old Catholic tradition, Wim was to be a priest. Father Jan Sassen was a god-fearing Catholic and wanted to make Wim a man of God. At eleven years of age, Wim was sent to the Dominicus College in Neerbosch (Nijmegen). Sassen senior was convinced he would follow in the footsteps of his three prominent reverend Dominican uncles. Two of them, *Jan*[2] and *Willem Sassen O.P* were from the nearby village of Dongen. The seminary would be young Wim's first step. It soon turned out, however, that priesthood was not Wim's cup of tea. He discovered that he had an attraction to women. Too much so to dedicate his life and love solely to God. So Wim was sent to the more disciplined environment of Canisius College in Nijmegen – the College of Jesuits. There he was under the scrutiny of his Jesuit uncle, the famous Dutch philosopher *Ferdinand Sassen.* Ferdinand was an old member of the College and taught philosophy at the Catholic University of Nijmegen. The time spent at Canisius had a substantial influence on Wim: "*the hereby followed courses and human development had a deep impact throughout my life. Because of my rebellious nature and my lack of any compromise with the world around me I became a strong-minded and driven young man. The first elements of my strong anticommunist sentiment and sporadically pro-nationalistic thoughts originated here. The conflicts with the board of the College coupled with my parents' financial troubles lead to my voluntary expulsion of the Canisius College and our moving to Breda, where I resumed and finished my studies at the Lyceum.*"[3] Where his parents' financial troubles are concerned, Wim is referring to the burdening years of the Great Depression of the 1930s.

Wim grew up in the political environment of his father. From the early 1920's his father harboured an ambition of a political career for him. Over a period of twenty years he had become Counsellor of Geertruidenberg, alderman, loco-burgomaster, chairman of the Dutch retailers' movement, honorary president of the Roman Catholic Workers Union (*Roomskatholieke*

Werklieden Vereniging) and foremost a member of the *Roomskatholieke Staatspartij* (RKSP: Roman Catholic State Party). During that time his father became a sympathiser of the Flemish Movement and at the same time, a proponent of the *Greater Netherlands Movement*.[4] After the big depression of the 1930s, his father started to radicalise his ideals with anti-Jew, anti-communist and –anticlerical sentiments referring to the latter as the "parasites of the poor". To Sassen senior the clergy (especially bishops) had done nothing to alleviate the harsch conditions of the workmen and the poor during the years of depression. He advocated vehemently against the exploitation of a cheap labour force and their miserable living conditions, doing his utmost to represent them in unions and trying to improve their living conditions by offering them education and art. His radicalisation so far had not had any implications on his political career as a councillor for the RKSP. Sassen senior was, however, not considered a threat by all. On the contrary, he was quite a popular propaganda-leader for the retailers in Flanders and the southern Dutch provinces. He was even invited to speak on the Dutch and Belgian radio (KRO and KVRO, respectively) about his beloved Brabant, to fulminate against the rural depopulation, the dangers of the total industrialisation of the economy and the abandonment of the church by the youngsters with the resulting vacancy of churches nationwide.

Already in 1933/34 Sassen senior publicly stated that the current democratic system was not going to represent the wishes of the tradesmen. Only a corporate system would be able to conceal the growing influence of the industrial state. Only a strong uniform authority could halt the post-war enrichment of the whole sale traders and the great industrialists, the enormous unemployment, poverty and the "perverted" Godless youth. In short he was absolutely pro-corporatism, anti-liberalism and -socialism. His ideal world would be the participation of the population in a uniform economic life.

Wim's father was a devout Catholic. He often consulted with his Dominican cousins who lived in Dongen. They had introduced the Sassen family to the Neo-Thomistic philosophy, one that completely coincided with his father's political vision based on a harmony-orientated, classless and organic society, and against any form of individualistic liberalism or domineering Marxism. Wim's uncle Ferdinand Sassen SJ was at this time one of the evangelizers of this philosophy.[5]

Wim Sassen grew up amongst a mixture of right-wing politics and modern Catholicism. The foundations of the *Greater Netherlands Movement*, his anti-Semitism and his admiration for Flemish and German leaders was germinated. Wim's belief in *Dietschland* (the Greater Netherlands Movement) became more and more coloured by the principles of National Socialism, in which he saw a means for building up a new Western Europe, with improved social and economic conditions.[6]

While his father visited the Rally in Nurnberg in 1936, Wim went to Berlin. During his stay, his admiration for Hitler and Nazi Germany increased: *"The second event that had a huge impact in my life was my visit to Berlin during the Summer Olympics of 1936. I was struck by the all-surrounding energising spirit of the young and by the European solidarity among the adolescents which reached its apotheosis during the Summer Olympics. During private talks with other young Germans, and especially a Referent (Spokesman) of the Ministry of Propaganda, Dr Mauer, I was warned of the resurgence of Prussian materialism, for which National Socialism could be a camouflage; I was, however, too young and inexperienced to see this danger at the time. In order to get my head around it I decided to stay longer and found work in a factory in Wedding, the industrial part of Berlin, where I lived among the workers. I realised that the "system" had rooted deeply in the workers' environment, although I took notice of the fact that there was only a scant difference between achieving a National Socialist ("NS") or Communist dominance among the workers. On the one hand the Partei (Nazi Party) could win these "Red Masses" in order to achieve complete victory, but on the other hand loyal communists prevented them from joining the Partei....The clergy also had my interest, and I could see the young clergymen were enthusiastic, while the older ones took a more neutral position regarding the NS. I found this situation very helpful in order to gage my position, politically. It was of great importance to my future "faits et gestes"."* [7]

In an interview with Belgian journalist and author *Stan Lauryssens* Wim said the following: *"I was seventeen when I travelled for the first time to Italy and interviewed Benito Mussolini. When I was eighteen, I went to Berlin. Minister of propaganda Josef Goebbels knew of my visit to Mussolini and asked me if I wanted to interview him. Of course I wanted to do so. At the end of the interview Goebbels introduced me to the Führer. The most powerful man in Europe, and maybe of the whole world. I was eighteen... By the time I returned from Berlin to Holland I was a convinced Nazi."*[8]

All of Sassen senior's children followed in their father's footsteps. They were immersed with contemporaneous rightist ideologies and movements, but did not join them. Not yet. Some of them joined these movements at a later stage. Besides the influence of the Dominican uncles living in Dongen, father Sassen was more Catholic than the Pope. He feared the effect of the modernisation and the urbanization upon his own children and others. "*The youth would turn against God, lead a libertine and uncontrolled life dedicated solely to individual pleasures.*"[9] He was not going to allow that!

Wim's father was not adverse to the *Zwart Front* or the Dutch version of the Flemish rightwing movement of *Verdinaso, Dinaso*. As a Councillor of the RKSP, however, he and his family members were prohibited from joining any right-wing movement either in the Netherlands or abroad. Neither Wim nor his younger brother Alfons could become member of the fascist youth movements like *Jeugdstorm* or the *Hitlerjugend*. Wim's uncle *Ad Sassen* did end up joining the Zwart Front at one stage despite Sassen senior's admiration for Hitler and visited the *Reichsparteitag* (Rally) in Nurnberg. He remained a member of the RKSP until the WWII broke out.[10]

University years in Holland and Belgium

After returning from Berlin in 1936 Wim started his law studies at the Catholic University of Nijmegen. His uncle *Ferdinand Sassen SJ* was *rector magnificus*. Like in all Dutch or Flemish university towns the student life in Nijmegen was a hub of political activity. Local historian *A.P. van der Wiel* described this as follows: *"Italian fascism had an enormous attraction among the Catholic students, especially the new students, writers and poets. In the 1930s the moderate influence of the family and church upon youngsters diminished considerably, thus opening the way for the young bustling, romantic and adventure driven boys like Willem Sassen.*"[11]

Wim was indeed to be found in the extreme rightwing Catholic (political) corner. Like his father he soon became involved in politics, but never joined a movement. During his study Wim got more and more indoctrinated by the popular nationalist and fascist movements. At student-rallies, rightwing parties did their utmost to recruit new members. It was during these meetings that Wim met the Dutch student *Anthony Mertens,* also a law student from Nijmegen. Mertens was at that time one of the spokespeople advocating the Greater Netherlands and the Dutch affiliate of the Flemish Verdinaso, Dinaso. This encounter was to mark the beginning of a strong friendship between the two young men.

The next time they met Mertens had left *Verdinaso* for *Zwart Front*, and was recruiting new members. Wim was to become one of his recruits. From that moment onwards, they would not lose sight of each other.

In the following years Wim switched from one university to the other. Nijmegen, Tilburg (Catholic School of Economics and Business) and Leuven (Belgium): "*When my financial troubles continued to burden me I decided to go to Leuven to renew my studies in Law.*"[12]

Not surprisingly, Wim was sent to study where his father's political ideals were best represented, namely in Leuven and Ghent. His older sisters Maria and Georgette already had gone to Belgium. Father Jan Sassen knew some very prominent members of the Flemish Nationalistic Movement, among which were the founding fathers of the Flemish activism movement and who were teaching at the Flemish universities. They included Professors *Frans Daels*, *Adrian Martens*, *Edward Herreweghe* and *Reimond Speleers*: all nationalist to the core.[13]

Wim felt strongly for those student-fraternities who were much influenced by the Flemish nationalism movement. In a political sense, he didn't differ much from his father, although he still did not become a member of Verdinaso or the VNV. It remains unclear whether he was restricted by his father from doing so.

In 1935 he did become a member, like his sister Maria, of the *Algemeen Vlaams Studentenverbond* and *Duitsch-Vlaamsche Arbeidsgemeenschap* (DeVlag). This last organisation committed itself to improving the cultural relationship between Flanders and Germany, enabling exchanges of students between its universities. In secret, the organisation continued to support the Flemish activists in their desire of independence like it had done during the WWI. Anyone was able to become a member; it was not a political organisation. It was within this organisation that both Wim and Maria were indoctrinated even more into the National Socialistic ideology. Like their father they were convinced that a better world would be created through adherence to the principles of National Socialism and that Flanders and Holland would, under the same ideological banner, be unified and follow Nazi Germany's example.

A year later, at the age of nineteen, Wim finished his studies in Political and Social Science at the University of Leuven. Wim already knew that his professional future would be as a journalist.

Starting back in his university years, he had earned some extra money by providing "opportunity correspondence" for Flemish and Dutch newspapers like the *Neerlandia* group and the Flemish nationalistic paper *De Schelde*. The senior editor of the Dutch daily *Dagblad voor Noord Brabant en Zeeland*, a subdivision of the *Neerlandia* group, *Josephus Eugenius Albertus van der Poel*, lived in Breda and was a known figure to the Sassen family. He was not only known as a former Flemish activist, but had a huge influence in North-Brabant through the media concern Neerlandia. In his newspapers he openly favoured a pro-German course.

Wim was pro-Nazi and did not hide it. His first public appearance was in Ghent. In front of a gathering of students Wim loudly advocated Nazi doctrine. His pro-Nazi propaganda immediately drew the attention of the local Belgian authorities, who started to keep an eye on him. Following his next public appearance Wim was expelled from Belgium*:"At the University of Leuven I had many Flemish friends. I was busy with cultural and artistic work (theatre) and far from local party politics, because I was an alien in Belgium. I never adhered to any political formation in Holland nor would I aspire to become one in Belgium. It nevertheless did not mean that in conversations I took a resolute anti-communist position and defended certain parts of the National Socialistic ideology. Around 20 April 1939 I was ordered by a Belgian police constable to leave the country. I did not know why, unless it was because of my choice of words expressed in a very intoxicated state, which resulted in my arrest and retention at the police station in Leuven. I cannot quite* *remember what I said, but it could be that I had uttered some political "axioms" in my drunken state of mind."*[14]

The German invasion

Dutch mobilisation

In 1938 Wim received his first call to fulfil his military service obligations. Recruit Wim was trained as an artillerist within the 7th Field Artillery Regiment near Utrecht. In August 1939 every able-bodied man was mobilised; Wim first reported to his unit in Bergen op Zoom, and then at the 2nd Battery LUA. He quite liked the army: "[m]*y service time so far hasn't been hard. I get along with my superiors. They just let me do what I want... I might even be promoted.*" Like his father during the First World War Wim entertained the soldiers with theatrical performances: *"The commanders of the 3*[rd] *artillery division asked me to participate in the organisation of the company playgroup to entertain the 3*[rd] *Regiments troops. With the support of my direct superiors, I asked at the headquarters to create a central theatre and film-unit within the army, which would visit all regiments in the country. If I succeed I might be promoted to CC Sergeant Major and with even more luck, officer for special services."*[15]

On the other hand: "*In the meantime my way of thinking had changed. During student rallies and encounters with German delegations my fear for a new camouflaged German imperialism was confirmed again. The Germans had approached me. At the beginning I was fine with these encounters, but then I started to realise they tried to win me over for the idea of a political Pan-Germanism. I ab-*

solutely refused it, because it was completely against my own thoughts, which were more nationalistic coloured, and therefore against all forms of violent dominance or peaceful penetration by a foreign power. It was because of this I lost contact with German students. Though the idea was tempting because of my financial limitations; they had even offered to pay for my studies at a German university. When I was mobilised and after the hostilities with Poland, I was convinced of Germany's good intentions and was not afraid to hide my point of view. I took a resolute position. To me, the border incident at Venlo in November 1939 [the case in which British agents with help of the Dutch high command were to be smuggled into Germany] seemed a justified casus belli for Germany."[16]

The imminent threat of war did confuse Wim. On the one hand he was convinced of Germany's good intentions. Did the *Venlo incident* (9 November 1939) trigger the war between Germany and Holland? No. But when the Nazi war machine did rush into Holland, Wim Sassen found himself in Geertruidenberg. Sassen senior had gone to Belgium and his mother was alone at home with her three daughters and little Alfons.

Wim found himself confronted with a serious moral dilemma. He was utterly disappointed, and Germany had in his eyes no justified casus belli this time.... *"Sassen claimed that he underwent a severe mental torture then as to what he had to do according to his conscience. On the one hand he saw that as a Dutchman he would have to fight against a nation for whom he had the greatest sympathy, and who was the exponent of his political belief. On the other hand he saw his own country brutally raped and attacked by another nation (militaristic imperialists), and that, he saw irrespective of any political beliefs. This second view triumphed, and Wim decided to report to his Regiment which at the time was located in Utrecht.*

On a bicycle Wim arrived in Den Bosch, where he and many other soldiers were trying to get across the rivers, as the bridges had already been blown up. All the military personnel were advised by the local police commissar to wait there until the Germans arrived. Deciding that this was not the right spirit, Wim commandeered a car and made his way to Breda, only to be advised to do the same there. He finally made his way to Bergen op Zoom and later Middelburg, realizing that if the Dutch army made a stand anywhere at all, it would be in Zeeland."[17]

As a Second Lieutenant Wim acted as an interpreter for the French troops who took their positions in Zeeland. The German advance was too strong, and pushed the auxiliary forces southwards: "*On 15 May "1940 [the province of] Holland capitulated, and the battle continued in Zeeland. On 16 May the Rear Admiral H.J. Van der Stad together with his staff abandoned Middelburg. On 18 May the Battle of Walcheren Causeway started between the French troops and the German Standarte Deutschland der Waffen SS. Together with the French I took part in the counterattack on the German positions with success. The French commanding officer even recommended me for the Croix de Guerre for my brave performance during the counterattack. [...] The next day I was taken prisoner by the Germans.*" On 19 May 1940 Wim was taken as a POW to Middelburg and later to his former army quarters in Bergen op Zoom. Shortly afterwards his demobilisation followed.[18]

Wim's father had, in the meantime, been dismissed (by telegram) as loco burgomaster of Geertruidenberg by the provincial governor of North Brabant because of his outspoken pro-Nazi views. Sassen senior wasn't in Geertruidenberg when his dismissal arrived. He was on a business trip to Antwerp, Belgium, to visit his oldest daughter Maria who like him was a commercial agent for the Belgian oil factory Luysen and Pauwels in Deurne (Antwerp). In contrast to his brother *Ad* (who was arrested with the likes of many other known Nazi-sympathisers, communists, suspicious foreigners and undesirables), Sassen senior was lucky. The authorities had taken Ad to the provisional prison *De Krententuin* in Hoorn (province of North Holland) as a precaution for possible *Fifth Column* activities, in order to prevent possible sabotage acts by pro-Nazi underground groups.

While Wim was in the process of being demobilised, father and Maria mounted a rescue operation for their ideological Flemish friends in need.[19]

What to do? Turbulent days
The confinement of Dutch POW's wasn't very strict. Wim was able to leave the barracks unnoticed. Once on his way to his parents he realized that without his demobilisation papers he would run the risk of being arrested, and imprisoned for a longer period. He returned to Bergen op Zoom and asked the German military administration to release him in order to continue his work as a journalist. They agreed and Wim set off with an *Entlassungschein* for Geertruidenberg. This document stated that its keeper, W. Sassen, by profession journalist of the Dutch Catholic newspaper *De Avondster*, was permitted to freely leave and return to the city of Bergen op Zoom. He was however bound

by *Sperr-*(curfew) time. Wim also wanted to continue his work for Belgian newspapers and needed a visa to enter Belgium. He got on a train in Breda and made his way to the 2nd Parkstraat, in The Hague. There at the *Passierscheinstelle* he got into a conflict with the Sicherheitsdienst representative and was subsequently jailed: "*After a brief interrogation I was locked up, because I did not know the answer to who was the greatest Flemish man. And therefore I was a suspect. From The Hague I was sent to Hertogenbosch where I was interrogated again. After three days they released me, but without a visa for Belgium.*" It didn't stop him. He tried and reached the Belgian frontier unhindered, where he continued his work as a journalist for Belgian nationalistic newspapers such as *De Schelde, Nieuw Vlaanderen, Candide* and the Dutch weekly *Vrijdag*. For some time, he commuted between Geertruidenberg and St. Gilles, Brussels.[20]

The rescue mission

Wim's father and oldest sister Maria had been prevented from returning home since the outbreak of the war. As long as the German advance into France was taking place, no one was allowed to travel without special travel permits. They heard the most awful rumours about their comrades who had been taken away in so-called "spooktreinen" (ghost-trains) to France. Like in Holland, many Belgian pro-Nazi friends and other unfortunates had been arrested out of precaution. Some of them had apparently been executed. One of their family friends *Edgar Lehembre* was gone too. So they planned a rescue mission together with their remaining Flemish friends: "*Eight days after the war started, when everything was in complete chaos, and most friends concocted all sorts of plans with a pint of beer in their hands, father Sassen, as the Flemish would call him, decided to take action in order to free their comrades".*[21] On 21 May 1940 they started their search for their missing friends. Most likely they were in France, but they did not know where. His father, together with *Eduard van den Hemel*, who had become head of mission to repatriate political prisoners aged 16–35 to Belgium, decided to combine their efforts in order to localize their friends in the French concentration camps. On 10 June Sassen senior and Maria left for the concentration camp in Sedan where 12.000 Belgians were imprisoned. They got permission from the German authorities to travel through the *Sperrgebiet*. And they departed in their own car.

Their activities were intensified when news came that Verdinaso-leader *Joris van Severen* was brutally executed by panicked retreating French troops when the German army advanced rapidly. Fortunately not all prominent Flemish rightwing leaders suffered the same fate. The leader of the *Vlaams Nationaal Verbond* (VNV, Flemish National Union) *Staf LeClerq* was released quickly. Soon after the French capitulation the VNV-leaders established a committee to find and repatriate their comrades and fellow Flemish nationalists from French detention centres.[22]

While father returned to Geertruidenberg daughter Maria intensified her efforts within this organisation to free fellow Flemish nationalists. The wife of Lehembre put her into contact with a certain *Fraulein "Eber"*, the leader of the women's section of the *Nationalsozi-*

alistische Volkswohlfahrt (NSV) in Antwerp. Due to her contacts within the *Passierscheinstelle* (travel permit office) she obtained the necessary visa to travel through France. Her official acknowledgement by the Flemish repatriation committee was confirmed by the chairman of the *deported political delinquents commission, René Lagrou,* as being an active member in the find and search organisation of political delinquents. On her third trip she carried a letter signed by Lagrou for the *Deutsche Gefangenen und Befreiungskommission* (German Prisoner and Release Commission) to ask for their assistance in her search: *"An die Deutsche Gefangen und Befreiungskommission..., Bevollmachtigen Fraulein MJJ Sassen das Notwendige zu tun um die internierte Flamen in das besetzte Gebiet zuruck zu fuhren. Sie bitten die Deutsche Gefangenen und Befreiungskommission ihr ein Befehl zur Freilassung der folgende Personen zu übermitteln.."*[23]

Maria carried a search-list of persons of interest to the Flemish nationalist party; among those on the list were *Ward Hermans, Heyst ten Berg, Dr. Edgar Lehembre* and many others. Like other members of this rescue operation, Maria visited all the French detention centres in France and negotiated the release of prominent members. On one of her trips she received information that more political prisoners were to be found at Le Vernet d'Ariege (French midi Pyrenees). [Maria :] *"After a couple of days we managed indeed to locate our imprisoned Flemish leaders Dr Lehembre, Ward Hermans, and others"*.[24]

In July 1940, their father had returned to Geertruidenberg. Even though he was a pro-Nazi by conviction, he did not become a member of the Dutch *National Socialist Union* (National Socialistische Bond: NSB) when the opportunity arose. First he tried to become a member of the recently created new political moderate party *Nederlandse Unie*, which was an alternative to the pro-Nazi parties like the *Nationaal Front* (NF) and the unpopular NSB. But he was rejected because of his pre-war activities and his known admiration for Hitler. His brother Ad Sassen advised him instead to become a member of the NF. Ad had a prominent role within the movement and Sassen senior could start right away as a spokesman for the party.[25]

The radicalision
Alongside his journalistic activities Wim decided to continue his unfinished law studies, this time at the University of Utrecht. That year, on 27 September 1940 he married *Paula Fisette*.[26] They moved to Professor Spronklaan 10 in Zeist. Resuming his studies was hard for Wim even with the assistance of repetitor *Meester Ravenswaaij*. It turned out to be a less than successful attempt and therefore he decided to proceed with his journalistic work. In December 1940 Wim finally received his *Passierschein* to travel to Belgium. This time the document stated that W. Sassen, trader by profession, lived in Zeist. With this *laissez passer* Wim was free to travel in Belgium and France. It is unclear if he also represented his father's firm at that time. In any case until the summer of 1941 the young Sassen family led a discrete life.

His father on the other hand had set off in February 1941 to Berlin to represent the NF. He considered that the NF should serve as a substitution for the unpopular NSB of *Anton Mussert*. Berlin said it would reconsider this substitution. In the meantime, his father was asked to forge a union of Dutch and Flemish parties who could seriously be considered an alternative to the NSB. Two weeks after his visit to Berlin, Sassen senior went for a five day reconnaissance trip through Flanders to see if he could unify his Flemish comrades with a political alliance between Verdinaso and VNV. The thinking behind this was if united, the realisation of Dietschland (Greater Netherlands) might still be possible under German dominance.

Between 17 and 21 February 1940 his father met up with all the major leaders of the Flemish movements: *August Borms, Cyriel Verschaeve, Frans Daels, Hendrik Borginon* and *René Lagrou*. The opinions were divided. Not all were sure the Germans would be willing to unify all Dutch speaking countries into one and to let it operate as a vassal state thereby keeping its own identity. However no compromise could be established and Sassen senior went back to Holland without success or hope for the fulfilment of the Greater Netherlands.

When questioned about the early stages of the war in Belgium, Wim Sassen explicitly stated: "*As of 10 May 1940 until 21 June 1941, I refrained from any pro-German activity, simply because I was not convinced that the Germans were driven by ideology, or rather plain imperialism and therefore despite my ideological affinity, after their invasion of the 10th of May 1940, I saw them technically as my enemy.*" But then something happened which turned him completely.[27]

Waffen SS Kriegsberichter

Eidesformel in SS Ausbildungslager: "Ich schwöre Dir, Adolf Hitler, als germanischen Führer Treue und Tapferkeit. Ich glaube Dir und den von Dir Bestimmten Vorgesetzten Gehorsam bis in den Tot, so war mir Gott helfe." (Oath of loyalty to the Führer)

At six in the morning on 22 July 1941 the minister of propaganda Josef Goebbels announced on the radio the declaration of war with Russia. Not even an hour later the 23 year old Sassen reported himself to the recruitment office as a volunteer to the Waffen SS: "*My whole anticommunist education, social environment, religion and the tendency to react on instinct were enough reason for my volunteering to take action within a Dutch formation deployed to the Eastern Front. I made absolutely clear in my conscription that I could only take up arms against the Soviet Republic, and not against the Allies of the West. These conditions were accepted by the German authorities. After much bureaucratic work it had been decided they would place me as a war correspondent (Kriegsberichter) in the Dutch voluntary army.*"[28]

Two weeks later he received his call to have his physical check at the medical examiner in The Hague. On 14 August 1941 Wim Sassen was on his way to Debica in Poland with the first contingent of the recently created Dutch Propaganda Company (*Propaganda Kompagnie*: PK). There, he received his military instruction. Whereas all Dutch and Flemish recruits had to renew their pledge of oath to Hitler, most volunteers for the Eastern Front refused. Wim was one of them.

In order to tie them down by some kind of oath, the SS authorities devised an alternative oath which seemed to satisfy all concerned. The general SS oath demanded the total subordination of all units to Hitler's command. For the volunteers, this oath would mean not only that they would be participating in the crusade against the Bolshevists, but also that they could be deployed against Allied forces and even their own people. It was this very possibility of action against their own population which caused serious objections. An agreement was made with the German high command and as a result, an exception was made especially for these volunteers. They would be solely deployed in action on the Eastern Front.

[Wim :] *"I tried to hasten my training as much as possible, because I feared the war with Russia would be over soon. I, of course, was of the opinion that my former aversion to Germany, because of the invasion on 10 May, was no longer justified. We now shared now a common enemy from the East, which automatically neutralized our dispute between Germany and Holland."*[29]

Wim's continuation of schooling took place at the Cadet Training Centre, the *Kadettenantstalt Lichterfelde unter den Eichen*, in Berlin. There, he met another trainee, the Dutch known film director *Vitus de Vries*. Together they successfully started to write propaganda news for the German broadcasting station *Deutsche Europa Sender* (DES) and Friesland.

Instead of finishing the whole course at *Lichterfelde* (which normally lasted for approx 6 months) Wim and de Vries left after four weeks. They were exempted on account of the fact that they as the chief-editors for the Dutch broadcasting were already supplying articles to the radio station Bremen.

Lichterfelde Berlin, 2 September 1941: *"Dearest Paula-After preparation lasting nearly two weeks we have arrived at our training quarters. The training days last from four thirty am until nine at night. It is thorough and I didn't think it would be that intense. We are drilled to the extreme, and not even the slightest protest is allowed, it's in short the reshaping of individuals into a body of men. Individualism is not tolerated, which apparently is the secret of the German war machine. On top of that we also received technical instruction. As a journalist, cameraman, etc, we participated in all sorts of exercises in order to comprehend the workings of the German army. I have of course found something new to do. Occasionally I get to prepare shortwave radiobroadcasts. Five in total now, of which in three, I am the speaker. As you know I most definitely enjoy this, especially because my famous friend Vitus de Vries is able to get me a position with radio Bremen and maybe even for the ultra short wave. Most likely I will be broadcasting in English too..."*[30]

Together with De Vries, Wim made a propaganda movie about Dutch legionnaires and volunteers who were being prepared for service at the Eastern Front. In autumn 1941 Wim Sassen and De Vries themselves were sent to the southern part of the Eastern Front, in the sector Rostov (Ukraine). Wim was ordered to report at the 5th *Kriegsberichterzug* (platoon for war correspondents) a section within the *SS Wiking* division. Wim's mission was to report on the progress of general field marshal *Walther von Reichenau's* Sixth Army group in the direction of Bjelgorod and Charkov. At the end of December 1941 Wim and De Vries had reached the southern front. There the 5th *Kriegsberichterzug* was quartered in Amwrosijewka, a small town of 30.000 inhabitants just above Rostov.

In May 1942, after a short break in Berlin, they were sent again eastwards to report on the German advance during the *Battle of the Caucasus* (*Fall Blau*). In June 1942 while accompanying the attacking forces, Wim was wounded for the first time.

When talking about his Eastern Front experience in an interview with the Belgian journalist *Stan Lauryssens*, Wim revealed little about the horrors behind the frontline. On only one occasion he referred to the murder of Jews by the special *Einsatzgruppen*. He stated that in the locality of Dnjepropetowsk, his Company Commander ordered 28 Jews to beat each other to death with bats. The four strongest men –or better said the survivors– would get mercy. Sassen's unit watched. After half an hour all Jews were dead.

Rising star Maria
While Wim was at the front his father and oldest sister Maria gradually got more involved in the Nazi movement. As father grew disappointed with the NF (they were too pro-British), he and his brother Ad turned to the NSB in autumn 1941. He had made the transition at the right time. Not much later both the *Nederlandse Unie* and NF were declared as forbidden political parties. That summer the German administration prohibited all *Greater Netherlands* activities. No other option remained.

In the summer of 1941 the Sassen family moved to Breda (Brabant), 30 Rustlandstraat. At that time his sister Johanna and his youngest brother Alfons stayed at home. Soon their home was called the "moffenhuis", a place known to be frequented by German officers and Nazi party members. The war, so far, did not change much. Normal pre-war life was resumed. *Johanna*, nicknamed *Hansi*, switched from being a dentist's assistant to secretary and translator at the *Ortskommandantur* in Breda. The other sister *Francisca*, nicknamed *Franzl*, had just moved out to Utrecht in order to work for the NSB office for propaganda. Indeed, both *Hansi* and *Franzl* followed their father's example and joined the NSB. Georgette was still working as a *Vortragskünstlerin* (recitress) for the Belgian radio NIR, and Wim's little brother Alfons was busy finishing school.[31]

Wim's oldest sister Maria remained in Belgium. She had contacts with the Flemish German cultural organisation *Deutsch-Vlämische Arbeitsgemeinschaft* (DeVlag), led by *Jef van de Wiele.* As the spokeswoman of several Flemish organisations, she represented the interest of Belgian companies working for *Organisation Todt.* Due to her contacts within the Flemish nationalistic movement, she had access to the highest German circles in occupied Belgium: "*Once back in Antwerp I headed to Brussels to celebrate the return of the deported Flemish nationalists. There I met the Obersturmführer of the German Sicherheitsdienst (SD) (German secret police) in Brussels, Otto Desselman. To make a bit of money out of the war situation, Desselman gave me money to acquire luxury products from abroad. In return for this favour he helped me out with providing travel permits/safe conducts (Reisbescheinigung) to do business for the Sassen firm in France. Desselman asked me to work for the SD, which at first, I refused. Some months later he asked me again. This time, the purpose would be to gather information on the morale within the occupied territory of Flanders. As a reward I got many permits to travel freely to Breda to see my parents.*"[32]

Maria was in close contact with the SD organisation in Antwerp and Brussels. In Antwerp, she was frequently seen at the SD quarters at 21 Della Faillelaan, where she reported to *Desselman* and *Hauptscharführer Hulmann*. In Brussels she reported to a certain *"Maas"*.[33] According to her she wasn't on the SD's payroll, but she did receive all sorts of permits to travel within Belgium, Holland and France, from which the Sassen firm benefited. Business was flourishing; wine, brandy, cognac, champagne from France, perfume and crèmes (toiletries) from Belgium. All luxury goods were sold to the barracks and cantinas of the *Wehrmacht* in Holland. Business during the early days of war time was quite profitable.

Maria started to become more drawn into the Nazi ideology. *"Some months later I received news about a course in Berlin at the Deutsche Auslandswissenschaftliches Institut (DWI), which was called "Um das Neue Europa".*[34] With help of the aforementioned Desselman, she received permission to travel to Berlin and to participate in this course, held at Berlin University. The course was held in June 1941 and was especially designed to further the integration of the occupied territories into the German *Reich*. The study focused on the development and realisation of this *New Europe* in all its facets, within the National Socialist ideology. In fact the DWI was part of the *Reichssicherheitshauptamt* (RSHA), the German Secret State Police, which dedicated its efforts entirely to the Nazi-indoctrination of all occupied territories. Maria became an active member of the *Ausländerkreis*, a circle that organised meetings of artists, professors, and spokesmen in the foreign departments of DWI, so as to smooth the transition to the Nazi doctrine within the occupied territories. In November 1942 she would leave again for Berlin to start her new course *Ausländerkursus 'Fragen der neuen Ordnung'*. This course dealt with the development and progress of the New Order under the Nazi administration.[35]

Then the first setbacks started to occur. Wim's uncle Ad suddenly died after a short sickness in May 1942, at the age of 36.

Casualty

On 26 July 1942, Wim was heavily injured during a street fight nearby Rostov. A bullet had entered his chest and exited through his left armpit. His tattooed SS blood group was unrecognizable because of the wound. His recovery took place in different army hospitals. First he was treated in Krakow, Poland, then in Munich and finally Berlin.

His injury made it into the Dutch newspapers. SS war correspondent *Anton van Breugel* wrote: "*A raw painful scream. The Dutch war correspondent Willem Sassen became a casualty. His Norwegian colleagues patched him up in an armoured car; poor lad you won't make it to Rostov. You wanted to be the first to wander the streets of Rostov, but now you have to recover for weeks from your wounds in a field hospital. Carefully Willem Sassen is being transferred to a Red Cross ambulance. Then the armoured vehicle continues its way in the direction of Rostov, the SS marches onwards, the SS continues, steadfast and tough. Up to Rostov.*"[36]

In Berlin the Sassen family finally got to see him. Sassen senior was the first. On 13 August 1942, father

Sassen wrote to the home front: "*Dear Mother, Mies and Fonske, What a joy it was to have found our son Wim in the SS field hospital in Berlin. He was enormously happy about my visit and wanted to know all the details from home. His arm has been bandaged and I saw where the bullet bounced off his breastbone. He wanted so badly to be present at the seizure of Rostov and write a good story about it. He was right there in the frontline, driving with an armoured car. He jumped off because he wanted to confirm whether he did in fact take out three Russian soldiers, when suddenly one of them rose up and shot him. Wim felt a short but painful jerk and noticed his arm dangling loosely on his back. His chest was also covered in plaster cast. He just arrived yesterday from Munich and he realized he had been terribly lucky. He called his wife Paula to tell her he was fine, and that he wanted her to come over with sister Lieveke (Godelieve). We are at the Hotel Alexander, 9 Deutschmark per night. Tomorrow I will write again. He still has a fever but he is strong physically and mentally. According to the doctor, Wim will be released in December. Wim says, however, that he considers himself lucky and unlucky at the same time. Yes, he survived which is good but he so wanted to be present at the capitulation of Rostov. He had a narrow escape...*" [37]

The NSB propaganda-leader in Utrecht was notified of Wim's recovery on Sassen senior's return to Holland. Breda, 26 August: "*I am back again and left Wim in good health behind. God is merciful. He had been lucky, because in such inferno no one gets through unscathed. You have to realise that during two hours a Norwegian volunteer – who did not get hurt – stayed with him under severe enemy fire, no less than twenty yards away. These Bolshevists would have cold-bloodedly slain them to death if they had had a chance. Their hatred for the SS is enormous. They were kept at bay by friendly fire until some SS tanks came to their aid. Then they removed him from the battlefield. His chest wound is slowly healing, and his left arm is bandaged, but he is in good spirits which will enable him to recover soon. And I may say so myself, he is a brave chap. I have seen and heard a lot, and I am even more convinced that we are fighting for a good cause. Well, we will discuss this at a later stage. Yours faithfully, Sassen senior.*"[38]

During his recovery Wim kept himself busy. As a very productive war correspondent he became a known and popular propaganda specialist. He was asked to write about his experience at the Eastern Front for German, Flemish and Dutch newspapers. On top of that he was invited to NSB rallies and radio stations to talk about his adventure and his comrades at the Eastern Front. As a war correspondent he had developed a unique talent for engaging the public with his vivid, nearly theatrical and romantic description of the battle field, the surrounding scenery and the heroic effort of their sons confronting the Bolshevik enemy as they themselves were participating in the advance in the East: "*In a nearly whispered tone the order goes out in the pitch black night, Panzer Marsch. They have come from the woods, an endless column of armoured vehicles. Like silent creatures with only the muffled humming of the engines they roll over the dark fields.*"[39]

Besides the glorification of the crusade against the communists, Wim Sassen wanted to improve the image of the Eastern Front soldier, especially about their own (Dutch volunteers) lads who participated in this crusade. He wanted to make clear that these boys had left and fought for their country: *"...what would become of him when he returns home, will he still find the reasons for why he left and took up arms against the Bolsheviks? Will he see his family, return to his former job, his country and people? All these uneasy thoughts will cross the mind of the Dutch volunteer while travelling back in a D-train from Osnabruck to Bentheim and then onwards, homebound. All Dutch volunteers had this inner battle of questioning whether they had done the right thing, and whether their patriotism would be understood by those back home. Because they did fight for their beliefs, they did sacrifice blood, sweat and tears or even an eye or a limb to fulfil their mission. Damned it should be said, these volunteers differed from the men or politicians who speak light-heartedly about their commitment to the cause but actually did pursue their cause, and fought for the values of our people...without thinking of their own personal gain."*[40]

Wim was allowed to recover in the Netherlands. The section-head of the propaganda company *H. Sternberg* informed the *Höhere SS und Polizeiführer Niederlande Hanns Albin Rauter* that Wim Sassen was going to work for the Dutch transmitter, *Radio Hilversum*: "*Der SS Rottenführer Willem Sassen wird mit wirkung von 18-11-1942 zum Sender Hilversum abkommandiert. Er hat die Erlaubnis der Abteilung in Breda zu wohnen und ist dem Lazarett in Breda zur ambulanten Behandlung zugewiesen worden. Sassen hat neben seiner Mitarbeit beim Sender in Hilversum der Auftrag auch Wortberichte ze schreiben.*"[41]

His sister *Georgette* had already started at *Radio Hilversum in* September that year. She took part in radio drama before she left for Stuttgart where, in September 1943, she ended up as a recitress for the *Deutsche Europa Sender.*

In April 1943, war correspondent Wim Sassen was officially released from hospital. Newly appointed to the rank of *Untersturmführer*, Wim was sent again to report on the German advance in Russia. He arrived in sector Charkov. This time he was tasked to realise audio-recordings *in situ*. It was in Charkov where, for the first time, he got in trouble with the German authorities. Instead of sending the recordings firstly to the office of censorship in Berlin, he had sent them directly to the *Reichs-Rundfunk-Gesellschaft* for broadcasting. *SS Oberscharführer L.C. Kruithof,* the head of the censorship office of the Dutch section which coordinated all Dutch radio broadcasting material passing the *Kriegsberichterzentrale,* reprimanded him for his impulsive behaviour. The restrains of the German censorship would impact his initial journalistic drive. This lack of freedom influenced his narrative work. Wim started to lose his interest as war correspondent. This was confirmed in a letter he wrote to his wife Paula. He no longer wanted to be a correspondent, but a soldier at the frontline: *"5 June 1943. Vitus remained in Berlin to work for the broadcasting company. There is only one other young man from Hilversum, Wybrands. My leave for the battlefield is no punishment of some sort, but just an order which I had received and had to execute without questioning it. It is not within my power to decide whether I will or will not go to the frontline as you might understand. Besides I volunteered to fight as a common soldier. The commander however did not grant my request and I was sent again as a war correspondent. I will of course do my best to be more of a soldier than a reporter. My enthusiasm for my profession has been diminished by my superior Rundfunkchef Stenzel. He obstructs me in every sense, and deprives me of my broadcasting work for the Dutch people."*[42]

Wim still believed in the German triumph. A month later he wrote to Paula: *"Dearest... I am on leave now not far from the frontline. I want to remain alive for you...also for our children, but also for me to enjoy my life to the fullest. The nearby future, whatever it holds, may not be easy. War is a funny thing, but then again I will never lose my faith in my Führer. Nevertheless I am undoubtedly sure that in the end we will reach happiness for all..."*[43]

In the summer of 1943 Wim was sent to do a refreshment course at the *Kriegsberichterlehrgang* (war correspondent school) in the Austrian Kärnten, near Villach. Participating correspondents were instructed in the finesses of war correspondence and propaganda. This *Arbeitstagung* which lasted for approximately a fortnight was a conference for propagandists during which general and political views and problems were discussed. A particular point of study was the relationship then and in the future between Germany, Great Britain and the USSR, and the propaganda-strategy with regards to this relationship.[44]

At the end of the conference Wim was ordered by Kurt Eggers to resume further training at a *Führer Schule*, an officers-candidate school, which he refused. He was called to Berlin by *Günther D'Alquin*, the Commander of Kurt Eggers, to explain his attitude. In his defence Wim stated that as a Dutchman he did not feel the need to bind himself politically to another nation, which he would do if he became an officer. However he expressed his loyalty to the SS and convinced

Standartenführer D'Alquin of his commitment in the battle against the Bolsheviks. At the same time he was considered to be one of the best journalists of the Propaganda Company (PK), which prevented this matter being taken higher up. Instead of going to a *Führer Schule*, Wim was ultimately sent to Brussels to organise the Dutch and Flemish broadcasts of radio Brussels at the NIR.

Wim's father's career within the NSB had reached its peak. In the summer of 1943 he was assigned as Chief Special Affairs for the Department of Propaganda and Press. In July 1943, he was appointed as honorary member of the *Waffen SS*, and on 25 August, he accepted his position as NSB mayor of the small town of Veghel.[45]

On 1 September 1943, Wim's father moved into a house that was confiscated by the Germans. Its previous Jewish owners had gone. It was only father who moved to the NCB-laan in Veghel; his wife Johanna and daughters remained in Breda. Except for fathers resignation from the NSB later that year, not much happened in rural Veghel.[46]

Radio Brussels

Together with his Flemish colleague *Jef Desseyn*, Wim became part of the broadcasting board of the SS Propaganda Company, although he never got on the payroll of the *Deutsche Europa Sender*. As a war correspondent, he was still a member of the *Waffen SS*, and was only temporarily deployed. Wim thoroughly enjoyed his time there. There was enough room for his creativity. Due to his love for theatre he knew how to captivate his listeners. Through his work, he became a well known broadcaster. His broadcasts were a popular diversion within the Flemish and Dutch occupied zone. His recordings were heard in Vienna, *Die Deutsche Europa Sender* (DES), *Kurzwellensender* (KWS) Bremen, Calais, etc. His superiors at the *Gruppe Rundfunk SS Standarte Kurt Eggers* were extremely happy with his performance. *"Mit 73 gefertigten und auch gesendeten Berichten steht Sassen an der Spitze aller Berichter. Er hat zwar Zeiten gegeben, an denen die Sassen – Produktion noch eifriger und reichlicher war, aber auch dies Ergebnis ist übveraus zufriedenstellend. Es werden mit Sassen – Berichten die Sender Brussel, Luxemburg und zu einem geringenTeil auch Stuttgart versorgt."* Even the minister of propaganda Goebbels complimented him on his outstanding work as a propaganda journalist.[47]

Wim stayed in Brussels until the Allied invasion in June 1944. Most talks around that time were concentrated on one topic; the possible invasion, when, where and how it could be that nobody knew anything. One thing was sure; it was going to happen. And when it did happen, it would have a devastating impact on all of them. This new front would affect them personally, their friends and their family. It would be a fierce battle.

A couple of days before *D-Day*, Wim reported on the impregnable Atlantic wall defences: Radio bulletin number 6623, on 6 June 1944…*"Here speaks Wim Sassen… the grand inspection tour of Field Marshal Erwin Rommel just finished along the Atlantic Ocean on the West coast of Europe, reaffirmed Rommel's unquestionable belief that whatever Allied powers may have gathered in front of these defences and how ever big its resources will be, it will never be strong enough to gain a serious foothold on the West coast. Anyone who has seen the fortifications on its coast, the enormous floating caissons, the gun barrels of thousands of artillery batteries pointing at the enemy, with defence works after defence works stretching for miles into the hinterland, the many miles of anti-tank ditches that would cause havoc and death, the endless redoubts, bunkers, trench lines, battery positions, aerodromes and hidden secret weapons, could only say let them have it, we are waiting for you..."*[48]

And indeed the Allied forces arrived on 6 June 1944. To their own astonishment the allied landings were an unbelievable success. As war correspondent, Wim visited the newly created Western Front and reported: "*Blazing flames, Caen burns, Bayeux burns, Saint Lô burns, Trouville burns, the whole of Normandy is a burning accusation to those that do not care for cathedrals or for culture but instead who could only admire an electric razor or a fridge. Caen burns. The Cathedral of Rouaan, the Basilica of Lisieux are burning remnants of their destruction. Will the next victim be the main church of Antwerp? Poor people who had to be liberated of this Nazi terror. When the Allies will approach, they will also sound a warning signal of the anticipated death of the hundred thousand who will perish during the advance.*"[49]

In Normandy, Wim nearly was taken prisoner, but since he was working in civilian clothes, he managed to escape during the confusion of the battle. He followed the retreating German army up to Brussels. There, he broadcasted his experiences on the frontline of Northwest France. Radio Brussels, broadcast on 23 July 1944, at 13.15 hours, headed "*Flanders*

Voice on the European Frontline"; the program began with fanfare music, before announcing its speaker Wim Sassen: "*In Normandy the fierce battle continues. For every step onwards the Allies pay a heavy price in the face of numerous guns. The Brits and Americans will bounce off our wall of comradeship that our young European lads have built. There is not a single country in Europe that doesn't embody this wall of solidarity. Germany sent its SS-Panzer-Division to Hitlerjugend. When the Brits heard of their presence they laughed and nicknamed them as "The Baby Division". But it soon got serious and they learned that these "babies" were the toughest of soldiers, fighting for their idealistic dreams. The army bulletin kept a close eye on the outstanding performances of these young men, our war correspondents who accompanied the HJ division will describe their actions on the front: "Our banner means more to us than death! That is the banner song of the HJ Division and with that spirit they, the German and European soldier, confront the enormous supremacy of war equipment that the uncoordinated and destructive Allies unleashed upon our soldiers. A war industry, supremacy in weapons versus heroism. This is the character of the battle on the invasion of Western Europe and the Allied forces. Great Brittany had turned her back on Europe. Its weapon is fratricide and treason. This miscall of judgement cannot be washed away with compensation in any form, money or goods. The youth of Europe, loyal to the European thought, will defy this storm from the West, as a dam against an upcoming tide from the East. We, the Flemish, will also stand our ground in this battle. We soldiers of Langemark will sacrifice ourselves for the Flanders of tomorrow. It will be what it once was, a pearl in the crown of Europe. This is why we soldiers of the SS Storm brigade Langemark fight and are prepared to bite the bullet.*" The radio bulletin ended with the battle song of the Flemish legion.[50]

On 1 September, the order came to evacuate *Sender Brussel*, and to move its staff to Herkenrath, near Cologne, Germany. Wim took command of a mobile broadcaster unit (*Kampfsender*); *Radio Flanders Free*. The live recordings at the front were over. Instead the German propaganda machine placed all its efforts into deceiving the population. The broadcasting station acted as an Allied station. On 20 April, the Dutch communist newspaper of the Resistance, *De Waarheid*, gave a warning about *Radio Flanders Free*: "*Only those who are still in possession of a radio transmitter can, as of recently, listen to a Flemish broadcaster, which seems to voice the Belgian communists. The communist leaders within the Belgian exile government are being praised openly, but at the same time the local population is instigated to plunder the stocks of farms and allied forces, propaganda is made against enlisting in the Allied forces, and the Catholics are being scoffed at – nobody and nothing is good except for the communists. Of course the broadcasts, time and time, again fulminate against the Allies. This broadcaster is controlled by the Nazis. You are warned though, that these broadcasters will operate even after our liberation, and that the Nazis will broadcast in the Dutch territories too.*"[51]

Two weeks later Wim moved to Holland. His colleague *Oberscharführer Jef Desseyn* took over and kept Radio Flanders Free in the air until March 1945.

Old friend Mertens and the Resistance
The Allied invasion of Normandy shook the Nazi regime at its foundations. For the civilians in the occupied territories the end of war was near. Collaborators panicked. All seemed lost as the allied forces advanced rapidly northwards. Would Hitler's secret weapons stop them in time?

New Resistance groups rose and many joined to the already existing groups. With the anticipated defeat of the Nazis, more men were brave enough to contribute to the liberation of the country. Doubt was struck amongst the collaborators. It was time to take precautions. Maybe the Allies would get the upper hand.

Wim was no different. In order to find a way out after a possible Allied victory, he approached his old friend Anthony Mertens.

Mertens knew the Sassen family well. They had mutual friends. When the German administration finally prohibited the NF as a political party, Mertens realised that the creation of Dietschland was never going to materialise. He did not want to join the NSB. In 1942, as Mertens decided to cease his studies at the University of Nijmegen and return to his birthplace in the village of Grathem in Limburg. There he joined in the local Catholic Resistance which operated in Venlo and Roermond: the National Organization for Aid to those in hiding *Landelijke Organisatie voor hulp aan Onderduikers* (L.O.).

Limburg was a transit zone for prisoners of war that managed to escape; Jews, people in hiding, and crashed-landed allied pilots. Mertens was active in the so called air pilot and navigators escape network to England via Switzerland and Spain and Portugal.

In 1943 the L.O. suffered a heavy blow. Treason had caused the arrest of many L.O. leaders participating in a meeting during a SD raid. The German secret police SD also kept an eye on Mertens. They knew he was somehow involved but lacked proof. Twice he had been interrogated by the *SS Hauptscharführer Richard Nitsch*, *Kriminal Oberassistent* (criminal investigator) of the SD headquarters in Maastricht. So far Mertens had been lucky, the SD had found nothing to incriminate him.

Nonetheless, as time passed, the situation for Mertens became too precarious. His luck soon ran out. In June 1944, Mertens decided to leave for Alkmaar (province of North Holland) to stay with his fiancée *Valentine Marie Louise Conijn*. He met her in Nijmegen. Her brother *Fritz Conijn* was the founder of the resistance group *KP Alkmaar*. In the meantime, some members of the *Landelijke knokploeg (*L.K.P., National organisation of Armed Squads, or in short *KP* (*knokploeg:Action Group) Roermond Pierre De Bie, Jacobus Frencken* and *Albert Reulen* had joined *KP Alkmaar*. The SD had been too successful in Limburg, and soon they would be on their trail too. On 25 June 1944, *KP Alkmaar* was nearly entirely wiped out (Frencken and Reulen were arrested in May of 1944). *Fritz Conijn*, together with Pierre de Bie, went into hiding in Amsterdam. Around that time Mertens lived in the capital too. He had just accepted a job at the publishing house *Urbi et Orbi*. Whether he was still involved in resistance work at that time remains unclear. Notably, his brother in law Fritz and De Bie reorganised themselves into a new resistance group, *KP Noord Holland*. The group was headed by Fritz. Two police investigators of the Amsterdam police force joined their team; *Piet Elias* and *Arend Jaspin*.[52]

Again misfortune struck. On 28 August, Fritz Conijn, in the midst of a secret meeting about the release of resistance member *Henri Scharrer*, was arrested by the SD in a café, *De Gekroonde Valk*. Scharrer's friend *Jan Lowey Ball Scharrer's* wife and *Ton Yardin Millord* tried to negotiate the release of Scharrer from the SD through a mediator called Pons, in exchange for 10.000 Dutch guilders. The middleman *Willy Pons* was a known *V-mann* (*Verträungsmann*, an infiltrator), who had set a perfect trap for his SD superior *Herbert Oelschlägel*. Fritz just happened to be there. He wasn't the object.[53]

It wouldn't be long before the SD officials realised that with the arrest of this group they also had laid their hands on the wanted *"Fritz von Alkmar"*. Again no stone was left untouched to free Fritz. Mertens: *"In order to prevent his execution during the hectic days of September 1944, we tried everything that was possible to free him. Bribes, enticements, blackmail, looking for resistance members, civilians or collaborators it didn't matter, anything or any person who could help us in any way to get access to Fritz. We were hunting down corrupt SD thugs who could be pressured or bribed. All contact with the South of Holland was frozen, even before Operation Market Garden took off or the General Railway Strike (September 1944) started. Within this chaos the only thing we wanted was to free my brother-in-law. Family and the underground movement were willing to pay a fortune for his release. Everybody knew that the end of the occupation was near, and that there would be a reasonable chance of success."*[54]

Anthony Mertens at that time lived in an attic at the Stationskade in Amsterdam. Fritz Conijn is said to have spent the night there before this fatal meeting.[55]

Mertens' fiancée, Fritz' sister Valentine, even paid a visit to *SS Hauptsturmführer Hans Carl Blumenthal* at this Gestapo office at the Euterpestraat in Amsterdam. On 11 September, she even managed to speak to the SD chief *SS Sturmführer Willy Lages* in person. But to no avail, he informed her that her brother was executed in Vught on 6 September.[56]

Resistance colleague Pierre de Bie wanted to know who was behind the "treason" of Fritz. Via his informant, Blumenthal's secretary *Thea Hoogesteijn*, he received the news that SD agent Herbert Oelschlägel had coordinated the arrest. On 23 October, a month later, Oelschlägel was liquidated by the Resistance.

Pact

In the midst of this turmoil, Mertens and Wim Sassen met again. Mertens: *"On one of these September days of 1944, I met in civilian clothes the SS man Wim Sassen who was in civilian clothes, a degenerate member of the well known Brabant family, but in essence a man of talent and style, as a student immersed in Wein, Weiber, und Lieder (wine, women, and songs), and as a SS, also an outcast. I knew him well as a study mate at the university and in Belgium. At the Flemish universities he was a well received entertainer, a sentimental fascist, chauvinist, ultranationalist, etc, you know there were dozens of these characters in God's and Hitler's kingdom. During the war I read he had become a Kriegsberichter on the Eastern Front, an obvious place for him to end up. Please do understand me: these characters rise in wartime as scum of the earth, but if they have had as such heart as talent they could have also become brave partisans, as they had be-*

come SS...Already at that time there were these rebellious SS men with the German Volunteers who used their wartime experience on the Eastern Front to claim their rights in the homeland. The strange thing was that among these men were intellectuals with an activist student-fraternity background in Leuven, Ghent, Leiden, Utrecht, who tried to save a bit of the former Dietse (Greater Netherlands) ideology on the basis of their prestige on the battlefield. When these stubborn hotheads lost their drive even on this front, they really got completely disillusioned with their German superiors. Their embitterment and resentment only grew. Under these circumstances I met, "by accident" this former student Willem Sassen, dressed in civilian clothes, standing beside a black French Citroën without military number plates on the Kalverstraat in Amsterdam. I was just about to enter a German bookstore when I saw him. We talked and from that moment on we maintained contact. Amsterdam in September was the time of Operation Market Garden, the crisis and chaos of Dolle Dinsdag a city on alert, and a vacuum at the same time. The Hunger Winter did not start yet, and nobody knew how long it would take before the war would come to an end. Was it going to be days or weeks? The short talk gave me enough insight into his political affiliation. Our pre-war friendship reinforced my belief that he could be trusted with the information about my activities for the resistance during the war without endangering my family, friends and comrades within the Amsterdam underground movement."[57]

Has Wim turned?

The Flemish editor in chief of the Flemish VNV paper *Volk en Staat* (People and State), *Jeanne de Bruyn,* predicted the forthcoming hunt for collaborators after the Allied Victory just before 3 and 4 September (*Dolle Dinsdag*) 1944: "*Dietschland, Hou Zee, we will be put in prisons and concentration camps, forced to lifetime labour, shot, hanged, tortured, skinned alive and rubbed down with salt. With our scornful downfall the patriots will sing their Bracançonne (Belgian national Hymn), a God save the King and a Yankee Doodle; the devout will sing their hymns to thank the Lord, because we are the guilty ones of this war.*"[58]

Did *Dolle Dinsdag* drive Wim into the arms of the Resistance? Could it have been a turning point for him? Wim: "*In the meantime my inner predisposition had changed a lot. Slowly I saw the economic and political imperialist goals of Germany, leading me to internal moral conflict, which in the end, just made me stay, and to save what could be saved. My remaining hope was a compromise peace which would defeat Russia for once and for all, but at the same time would force the Germans to concede to the West and Europe. Their wish for more national independence and to reinstitute the dynasties (royalties) to assume power, though under the economically and most probably also military German order, which would find its equal in the maritime and colonial world-organisation of Great Brittany and other Western European powers. The efforts of all Dutchmen, like those of other European peoples should concentrate on this goal; and a special role should be given to those fighting in Holland; on either side of the frontline of political beliefs, but bound by the same patriotism. This is why in my opinion the volunteers for the Eastern Front were as valuable as the Dutch soldiers fighting in Allied forces or those members of the Resistance. These thoughts I defended in my articles in De Telegraaf* *when I started working as chief editor on the 5 October 1944."*⁵⁹

Was Wim truly doubting, and did he foresee the end of the *Reich*? Was he looking for a way out?

[Wim:] *"Throughout the war I maintained contact with some friends, who, even though they thought politically different and some of whom were very active in the national Resistance movement, nevertheless respected my point of view as I did their's. As soon as I was released from prison they tried to convince me to turn sides. As of July 1944, my case had been put before Dutch government in exile. They would make sure that once I got through the frontlines, I would be able to speak to my fellow Dutch volunteers in German divisions by radio, to convince them to lay down their arms...after this broadcast I would be pardoned of my crimes. However, I declined this proposition. I did not like to be seen as a rat abandoning a sinking ship and leave my brothers in arms to themselves. My resistance friends did ask me, in case of a German capitulation, or whatever might succeed in the nearby future, to surrender to them. They would be authorised to arrest me and conduct an investigation into my crimes....under favourable conditions of course. In October 1944, I had a meeting with friends and members of the underground movement of Fritz Conijn (executed in September by Willy Lages). Present at this meeting were also Anthony Mertens and others of whose names I have forgotten. Fritz Conijn was a very active member of the underground movement, and in spite of his complete opposite political vision, he respected me and my convictions. He informed his closest colleagues of our mutual understanding and told me what he could do. When he was executed his friends, in full confidence, approached me. They tried to convince me that by now it should be clear what the Germans were up to. I had been ordered to leave my country. The only country I was willing to fight for. In spite of an enormous moral conflict I decided to decline their advice and not to desert. Their propositions were kind but ludicrous, and I did not want to leave my friends, or cause any adverse repercussions to my family."*[60]

Wim's downfall

At the end of September 1944, Wim lived in a *Kriegsberichter* home that was located above the bookstore (*Bücherei*) of the German newspaper (*Deutsche Zeitung*) on the Kalverstraat in Amsterdam. A number of war correspondents worked for the Dutch newspaper *De Telegraaf*. In the building of *De Telegraaf* at the Nieuwezijdsvoorburgwal Wim met an old acquaintance, *Hakkie (H.A.C.) Holdert*, also a veteran of the Eastern Front and now working as the director of *De Telegraaf*. They first met in Klagenfurth at a meeting of radio-reporters. Holdert was assigned by the *Pressereferent Dr. Walther Wilhelm Dittmar* to make this pro-German newspaper more attractive to the public. Wim, with his outstanding reputation (as a correspondent), seemed to be the perfect candidate. So Holdert asked him to become his chief-editor of the Dutch newspaper *Courant Nieuws van den Dag* (De Telegraaf). Wim accepted the offer and two weeks later he started his new job.

As editor-in-chief Wim wanted to pursue a different independent political course with the newspaper, a direction that the German Propaganda Office was not very keen on. They considered Sassen to be a trouble-maker and an 'enfant terrible', on whom a close eye should be kept.

Sassen's colleagues started to notice his increasing indifference with the wartime situation. This indifference translated into endless parties with jenever and women. It did not take long before Wim went too far.

On 23 October 1944, Wim wrote an article ("Licht": Light) that marked the end of his career at *De Telegraaf* and nearly got him imprisoned... In the article, he called upon the hungry and cold of Amsterdam to steal food and fuel in the quarters of the more rich and wealthy people. The underground press responded immediately. On 27 October 1944, Sassen was being accused of inciting riots and a state of anarchy in the capital by exploiting the difference between the haves and the have-nots during these times of hardship. He was playing on the sentiments of the needy; young mothers with babies, who had no money to buy the basic necessities: soap, oil, fuel, wood, etc. During these last weeks or months of the war everything was rationed, and even then nothing was available. Sassen was just making things worse in an already critical situation. The Resistance knew that with a possible uproar, the German authorities would have an excuse to carry out reprisals and tighten the control over the city.

Another underground newspaper *"De Baanbreker"* wrote an article entitled "False light"*(15-12-1944): "A certain Sassen who seems to be the chef editor of the 'Nieuws van den Dag',... now that he has heard the liberators at the gate, he senses his hour has come. Darkness has fallen upon those who have persecuted us. And now they claim to have seen the light. Sassen has seen this light. He, the preacher of hate and disunity, is trying to instigate an uproar to claim our basic needs...our people are suffering because of these Sassens; they have been robbed of everything by the Germans and their followers, to the enjoyment of all Sassens… The Sassens are reaching for our darkest instincts hoping to give the final coup de grace to our people in the wake of liberation.*"

In the meantime the Resistance groups from the left became aware of Wim's contact with Mertens' resistance contacts. The underground newspaper *De Wegwijzer* (1 November 1944), no. 84, headed: *Warnings against agitators: "SS soldier Wim Sassen, chief editor of Nieuws van den Dag, is trying to gain access to the underground movement. He is an idealist, who will betray anyone as soon as he has infiltrated into the organisation."* The leftist opposition (Resistance) groups were warned about this two-faced man, and took precautions against his possible attempt to approach them.

However Mertens was convinced of Wim's loyalty. *"I have during our meeting in autumn 1944 never doubted Wim Sassen's loyalty when asked for help. He, at his own risk, offered to help us any way that he could. When he was briefed by my fiancée on the Resistance activities of her brother Fritz Conijn Wim was deeply impressed. The two different worlds of Wim Sassen and Fritz Conijn shocked him: two different idealists on opposite sides. His confidence had taken a blow after talks with the Dutch Resistance. His romantic view to either commit suicide or fall into battle was shattered. As a broken man he asked what he could do to enlighten the day of judgement when Holland was liberated. If Wim was to help us, we would return this favour when he was in trouble. Shortly afterwards Wim handed us some Abwehr "soldbücher" he stole from a booth of a car; out of a cellar of a flat on the Velazquezstraat he removed machineguns of deserted*

SS soldiers; he gave us the telephone numbers of German lines, and told us how to make use of them. His willingness to help us went so far that he even handed in the daily reports of the Kriegsberichter unit of the freed province of Brabant, with allied propaganda, photos, maps and small newspapers. The assassination of the much feared V-mann of the Gestapo, Herbert Oelschlägel, on an evening in October in the Apollolaan in Amsterdam, however, had put the SD on high alert and our contact became too dangerous and therefore less intense. Just before he was banned from the city he had handed us over a document stating that the carrier was employed by the SD. Just in case of emergency…and then we lost sight…"[61]

Instigating people to rebellion was most definitely a step too far, also for the Germans. The *Pressechef Reichskommissar Dittmar* immediately dismissed Sassen. The SD was asked to conduct an internal investigation into the redaction of the Dutch newspaper. According to Dittmar these kind of articles would not only have a negative influence on the morality of the people, but also increase the defeatism among the *Wehrmacht* troops and NSB. Dittmar completely misunderstood the purpose for publishing these articles. Did Sassen use *De Telegraaf* as a means to cause confusion? Or was Wim transferred to Amsterdam to fulfil his task as a black-propaganda operator, as he did with *Radio Flanders Free*?

Wim Sassen had to report at the SD headquarters at the Apollolaan in Amsterdam. There, he was received by SD police-officer *Heijtink*. He had to explain the contents of his articles. An argument followed. Wim Sassen was pressed by *Heijtink* and SD chef Willy Lages to sign a statement in which he would declare never to participate in journalistic activities again. If he didn't sign it, he would immediately be sent to a concentration camp. Wim refused to give in and ripped the document to pieces. Lages didn't hesitate, and took Wim into custody at the Weteringschans. After two days, Wim was out again.

The *Sicherheitsdienst* (SD) kept a close eye on *Oberscharführer* Wim Sassen following his release from detention. On 28 October, only five days after the publication of the inflammatory article, he got into trouble again. He was arrested by the *Feldgendarmerie* because of his participation in the raid of the *Café Berry's* wine cellar. The liquor and wine was looted for a party of his former SS comrades of the *Hohenstaufen* division that he met a year ago in Normandy.

The *Generalkommissar für das Sicherheitswesen und Höherer SS und Polizeiführer Nordwest* (SS chief of police) *Hanns Albin Rauter*, sent a telegram to the commander of Kurt Eggers, Günther D'Alquin, explaining what had happened and suggesting two alternatives; either Sassen would be liquidated, or he would be banished from Holland. In return D'Alquin deployed *Kriegsberichter Obersturmführer Joachim Fernau* as a mediator with special authorizations to Amsterdam, in order to negotiate Sassen's release from prison.[62] They came to an agreement. Wim would be kept under tight control of the Propaganda Company (PK). Two days later Wim was again released from prison, and received an order to report to *Hauptscharführer Sternberg* of the PK in Holland, who was in charge of ensuring that Sassen would actually leave the Netherlands.

Wim says, about this event: *"After working for about four months, a big conflict broke out with the SD (Sturm-*

bahnführer Lages, Untersturmführer Heytink). After a brief period of imprisonment, I had to sign a declaration that I would never again speak over the radio or write in Dutch newspapers. At the request of Reichskommissar Obergruppenführer Rauter, *given to me by my direct chief (Hauptscharführer Sternberg), I was ordered to leave Holland immediately because my politics could no longer be tolerated. Since I had connections with the underground, I contemplated going into hiding. This would mean deserting, and this I would not do as it would cause severe repercussions for comrades and family members who had been evacuated to Germany.*"[63]

Wim was lucky again.

Black propaganda

Wim did not want to leave Holland. With the intent of being sent to a front line coy and be subjected to the authority of the army, thereby evading Rauter's civilian authority, Wim contacted *Obersturmführer Beisel*, the head of the Propaganda Company of *Heeresgruppe H*, the *Wehrmacht*. The commander of Army Group H was General *Kurt Student* and he had set up his quarters in Zellem, located between the river Weser and Arnhem. Wim had met Beisel in the residence of the *Kriegsberichter* house above the *Deutsche Zeitung*. The former chief of the black propaganda section *Skorpion West* regularly visited *Hauptsturmführer* Heinrich Sternberg. Wim knew if he succeeded in being deployed within the *Wehrmacht*, the SS would no longer have any control over him.[64]

His contacts within the propaganda division paid off. As of October 1944, the press and propaganda were under complete control of the SS subversive propaganda unit (disinformation unit) *Skorpion West* and with it, *SS Standarte Kurt Eggers*. This was a unit that worked together closely with the armies in the field on the Western frontlines.

Wim was allowed to stay in Holland. He had to report to *Hauptsturmführer* Sternberg, chief of the *Kriegsberichter Abteilung* (Battalion) Holland in Doetinchem. From now on Sternberg was responsible for the troublemaker Wim Sassen. Officially Wim had left Holland. His editorship was kept secret. If Dittmar would have heard of his presence in the east of the country, serious sanctions would have followed. Wim had to promise his superior Sternberg to keep a very low profile and stay away from *Festung Holland* (Western Part of Holland).

In Doetinchem, Wim was once again to participate in the *Abteilung Aktivpropaganda* of the *Rijkscommissariaat* (Department of active propaganda of the Reich Commission). This was a department under the command of *SS Sturmbahnführer Dr. Hans Damrau*, which dealt exclusively with psychological warfare over public announcements (radio), posters, banners, propaganda brochures, leaflets and faking illegal or resistance publications. With the mobile transmitter *Flanders Free* acting from Klagenfurth, Wim had already been involved in the practice of black propaganda. It might have been the case that Wim continued this strategy during his time at *De Telegraaf*.

Wim was ordered by the army authorities to start a paper intended for the civilians in the army controlled area. At the same time it was suggested to him that he might also start a secret radio station for the purpose of broadcasting to the liberated parts of Holland. At first, he simply copied the enormously popular satirical weekly, the propaganda newspaper *De Gil* (The Yell). On 20 November 1944, the first issue of *Het Laatste Nieuws* (The Latest News) was printed. Its contents hardly differed from *De Gil*; a satirical magazine full of anti-German black humour, in which the precarious future of Dutch collaborators after "the liberation" was being mocked. A lot of emphasis was put on the alleged abuses in the "liberated areas", the Roman Catholic fear of post-war Bolshevistic domination. [Mertens]: "*He called it 'Het Laatste Nieuws', which originally intended to keep the local population quiet, but which was also used by Sassen as a propaganda paper, allegedly published by the underground. In this paper, 40 % of the articles were against Germany, 30 % against the Allies and the remaining 30 % in favour of Holland, but always tinted Dietsch flavour... By tacit agreement of the German military authorities Sassen was allowed to use his own methods with regard to the articles in the paper and radio, and he was not censored. He claims that the population actually did think that the paper was a new illegal organ, and that it sold in very great numbers.*"[65]

In Doetinchem, Wim met *Miep van der Voort.* His marriage with *Paula Fisette* never really went well. Paula could not and did not want to go along with Wim's political views. Even her parents eventually took their distance from the notorious propagandist for the German cause. On top of that, Wim accused his wife of having extra-marital affairs with German officers while he was at the front. The married Miep van der Voort was a stenographer She left The Hague together with her superior Sternberg. At the end of 1944, she started working in Wim's editorial office. [Miep van der Voort :] *"Wim Sassen was the chef of the so-called illegal newspaper Het Laatste Nieuws. I worked out the copies of the weekly. This weekly was printed at Misset in Doetinchem. I not only did secretarial work, but in order to be near Wim, which was forbidden, I also acted as a cleaner for the whole editor team. I never took part in the distribution of the weekly."*[66]

When Dittmar realized, after a visit to the editorial office, that Wim never had left the country, all hell broke loose. Dittmar was by now a sworn enemy of both Wim and his colleague *Willy van den Hout*; the brain behind *De Gil*. Both had, in a way, fallen victim to the ongoing battle between Dittmar and the head of *Hauptabteilung Volksaufklärung und Propaganda* (an institution modelled on the Reichs Propaganda Ministry), *Dr. Erwin Haagn*. Dittmar thought that the inflammatory articles published by *De Gil* and *Het Laatste Nieuws* would undermine the morale of the population, and of the *Wehrmacht*. Haagn, on the other hand, was convinced of its positive effect as demonstrated by the success of *De Gil*. At its peak, the popular weekly sold more than a hundred-thousand copies. The two conflicting propaganda strategies by both Dittmar and Haagn clashed together in its execution. Dittmar immediately informed *Generalkommissar für das Sicherheitswesen* (commissioner general for security) asking for Wim's arrest. Rauter submitted a formal complaint against Sternberg at General Kurt Student's army group H. The General, unsurprisingly, refused to give in to a civilian authority.

[Mertens :] *"At the time of the Von Rundstedt offensive in the Ardennes, a special courier was sent down to*

Doetinchem with the request to acquire as many copies as possible of this famous paper of which they had been hearing so much. In all haste translations were made for the benefit of the General. Some of these copies made it to the HQ of Hitler, and the result of this enquiry was that Sassen was to carry on with his work, and that Rauter and also Sonderführer E. Taubert, the Beauftrager of the Radio in Holland, and Dittmar had to cease their opposition (29-12-1944). Due to the fact, naturally, that the HQ of Hitler had shown so much interest in the matter, the attitude of the Reichskommissar turned like the wind, and promised all possible help to Sassen in the execution of his work."

Wim was not going anywhere. He was lucky yet again.

Montgomery's offensive put an end to the propaganda unit stay in Doetinchem. On 16 March 1945, the Sassen company retreated into Germany while Sassen and his staff moved westwards to *Kampfsender* (mobile radio transmitter) Hilversum. There, they were attached to the *Armee Ober Kommando* 25 (AOK), under the Command of Chief Colonel General *Johannes Albrecht Blaskowitz*. They were placed under the direct command of *Hauptmann* Otto, head of the propaganda *Einsatz Staffel* 625, who sent them to Utrecht with the orders that they were to continue as best as possible with both the paper and the radio.[67]

On 19 March, Wim moved into a private house requisitioned by the SS on the Witte 126 Vrouwensingel, in Utrecht. This house was the operational centre of the propaganda section *"Skorpion"* (West). Wim operated both from Utrecht as well as Hilversum for the German war propaganda machine.

In the building of the Feldgendarmerie at the s'Gravenlandseweg in Hilversum, Sassen became a member of a team of well known Dutch broadcaster stars and well experienced radio-propagandists like the former broadcaster of Radio Bremen *Corstiaan Tonneman* and *Cor "Willy" van den Hout*. Van den Hout took care of the content of *De Zender van het Bevrijde Zuiden* (The Voice of the Free South) and *Radio Gil Club*. Both broadcasting stations were coordinated by the *Aktivpropaganda* and appeared to carry news from the liberated zone. Besides the overtly anti-German news, the station reported on the scandalous behaviour of the Allied forces, ridiculed the authorities, and tried to discourage any assistance to the Resistance to hasten the liberation of Holland. The underlying tone was nevertheless unadulterated anti-capitalistic, anti-Semitic and anti-communistic. To make it more convincing, the radio emissions were spiced up with forbidden jazz music and radio plays. Not only Wim Sassen was active for the Hilversum radio station; his father and sister Georgette had also been previously heard on the station in radio dramas and propaganda speeches.[68]

After the war, colleague Willy van den Hout described the "Hilversum group" to which he belonged as follows: *"In that period there was a bunch of Dutch SS who were acting like playboys. They wore oversized uniforms, to which they had sewn themselves laced collars. They did not fight; the only thing they were in for was picking up girls and getting their hands on drinks. These scoundrels belonged to the disorderly army of Hauptmann Otto, and included Hakkie Holdert, the successor of De Telegraaf, and the Sassen boys, of which one, Willem (Wim) sold the memoires of Eichmann in*

Argentina to the American magazine Life. Yes they belonged to the SS, but they were easy to mess around with. I would say, for example, that I needed a truck for the Wehrmacht, and they would tell me they could fix one for me. What was it all about? A few cases of clandestine goods, I told them. No problem, they would fix it. They thought it was all about women and liquor. Everything arrived safely in to my hometown The Hague, without a problem..."[69]

These Sassen boys, Wim and his younger brother *Alfons*, as well as Van den Hout, were in contact with the underground movement. The Sassens occupied themselves with Amsterdam and Noord Holland, and Willy van den Hout with organisations in The Hague. Van den Hout confirmed after the war that he was in contact with the Resistance group *Vogel* (Bird), a subdivision of the *Geheime Dienst Nederland* (GDN: Secret Dutch Service). The question arises whether they, as masters of deception (Aktivpropaganda), were encouraged to contact the Resistance groups. In both resistance groups, former members of Arnold Meijer's *Zwart Front* (Nationaal Front) were active: Anthony Mertens and *Marinus Gageling*.

Alfons

Wim stepped in for his younger brother Alfons, from the moment he signed up for active duty with the *Waffen SS* in 1944. Alfons was the problem child of the Sassen family. His SS career was short-lived. He was even disqualified for active service. Nevertheless, Alfons aspired to become a war reporter like his older brother, and Wim came to his aid.

When Wim left for Doetinchem, he had asked his brother to join him. He could work as a speaker for the radio and help out distributing issues of *Het Laatste Nieuws*. Alfons did not really take his work very seriously. From time to time he would disappear for a day, and when asked for an explanation he would give evasive answers. Wim learned, however, that there were two men connected with his brother from whom he seemed to receive orders, namely a man called *"Onkel Richard"*, and a certain *"Lange"*, who was connected with the *Wehrmachts kommandantur* in Utrecht. From these two men, Alfons would receive bottles of cognac and petrol. To find out what his brother was up to, Wim called Lange.

The stay-behind unit NEUROP

It seemed that young Alfons was encouraged by his own father Sassen senior to lend his services to the German military contra-espionage service, *Abwehr*. He worked, under the alias *"A. Jongerijn"*, as an undercover agent and a line crosser for the *Frontaufklärungstruppe* 365 (FAT, Field Reconnaissance Troops).

Wim finally learned that his brother was connected through *Untersturmführer Herman Wilhelm Ferdinand Gottlob Lange* to espionage work and line-crossing. He was also told by Lange that the Germans had the intention of forming organizations ("werewolf cells") within the territory held by the Allies in Holland.[70]

Wim, in turn, said: "*He too had developed plans to institute some kind of organization in the event that they, as he put it, would be terrorised by the 'Bolshies'. Explaining this statement he said that with his most loyal com-*

rades they were prepared to do anything under the sun, in case volunteers for the Eastern Front would be treated by Dutch courts in the same way as miserable co-operators of the SD; asking for capital punishment just because they fought on the Eastern Front out of anti-communist ideal, and not because they were pro-Nazi. This group would commit itself to propaganda and sabotage hoping to be able to change ideas of the nation in favour of what they stood for, and continue the battle against the Bolshevists."[71]

Wim considered it quite possible that once the German *Reich* collapsed, the *Bolshevists* would use this power vacuum to gain full control over the devastated parts of Western Europe. He immediately offered himself and his propaganda colleagues up to join this organisation. This group of sworn anticommunists would, in short, focus its actions on propaganda and sabotage.

At first *Lange* wasn't quite convinced:*"I had a low opinion about their capacities. Due to their membership of the NSB and/or their reputation as collaborators, I did not think they were suitable as stay behind agents, who after a possible occupation of the province of Utrecht could be activated."*[72]

Hauptmann Bulang thought differently. He wanted to recruit them anyhow, and sent his *Sachbearbeiter Werner Schramm* to check up on the Sassen brothers. Again Lange protested: *"I repeated my already known objections to Hauptmann, arguing they were completely unsuitable for this line of work. Schramm agreed with me and even stated that the creation of a stay behind group was virtually impossible, because the war was already lost."*[73]

Wim's recruitment was however still being considered. On 7 or 8 of April, Schramm visited Wim again at his home in Utrecht. He asked whether Wim was willing to take up arms against the Allied forces. He confirmed that he would. According to Lange, Wim still believed in the miraculous resurrection of Hitler's armies in the final *Endsieg*...Werner Schramm made it clear to Wim that he was only interested in espionage (*Informationsnetz; I and R-netz*), and less in sabotage or propaganda, or the questions of who dominated the area, the Bolshevik or the Allied armies of the West.

Schramm offered to help *Hauptscharführer* Wim Sassen, if he, in turn, was willing to side with his organization. Wim agreed, but stated at the same time that he was not willing to undertake anything which he might consider to be detrimental to Holland. Wim agreed to put himself and his PK team '*Skorpion West*' at the disposal of Werner Schramm.

Its members were Wim, Alfons Sassen, *SS Kriegsberichter Hendrik Adrianus "Hans" Schild* and, as an expert in explosives, Heinrich Sternberg. Their stay behind unit was code named *NEUROP*, a fusion of *Neu Europa*, the original idea for which Wim had fought for.[74]

After the war, Lange described this group as follows: *"Up to the capitulation Schramm worked hard to establish a stay behind information service (I-netz) or a Rückbleiber (R-) netz. He had difficulty in finding suitable agents. The nucleus of this service was to have been the small self appointed Sassen sabotage group which mustered collectively very little training in either wireless or sabotage-training but a considerable amount of Nazi or anti communist zeal."*[75]

Wim Sassen headed his stay behind group which covered the Zones Utrecht, The Hague and Rotterdam. In order to perform their duties for the *Abwehr*, they were relieved of their duties within the propaganda-unit of AOK 25 as *SS Kriegsberichter*. They were also excluded from participating in the final battle, the *Endsieg* for Nazi Germany.

Werner Schramm subsequently supplied the Sassen stay behind group with all necessary materials and provisions: a wireless transmitter, Dutch BS – uniforms, civilian clothes, sabotage materials, weapons, ration cards, false papers and a few automobiles. One of these cars would be turned into a mobile transmitter unit, with a reach of a 100 kilometres, in order to send back military intelligence reports. Wim wanted to go much further. Officially the stay behind group would cease to exist once the German army had capitulated, but Wim had no intention to adhere to this plan. His battle with the Bolsheviks would not be over then.[76]

On 27 and 28 April 1945, an old friend called *Louis Kuitenbrouwer* paid a visit to Wim on the Wittevrouwensingel in Utrecht. Wim was bedridden, he suffered from inflamed kidneys. The war was nearly over. Wim told Louis that he wasn't prepared to be judged by a Dutch people's court: "*I want to explain my case to someone who can understand what I did, but I will do my utmost best to stay away from Dutch or Allied field security units. I would rather commit suicide!*"[77] The next day on Saturday 28 April, just a few days before the German capitulation, three Germans of the Waffen SS arrived from Berlin. They were to join his team, but it was too late.

On 1 May 1945, Wim heard that Adolf Hitler had died. This was a severe shock to him. He claimed that from then onwards, he no longer believed in the existence of the slightest chance of realizing a true interpretation of National Socialism. Next day the *Wehrmacht* disarmed the *Waffen SS*, and all were expected to take the oath to Hitler's successor Admiral *Karl Dönitz* on the following day. Sassen and his comrades refused to do so. The capitulation followed soon. Wim was still bedridden. The R-network in the Netherlands never really got on its feet. On 5 May, NEUROP was dissolved. Wim went into hiding. Via The Hague, Wim and brother Alfons went to Amsterdam. In the building of *De Telegraaf* they spent the night in the company of Telegraaf director Hakki Holdert. On 6 May, the *Nederlandse Binnenlandse Strijdkrachten* (NBS, Interior Dutch Forces; Homeland security) besieged their building. All staff was free to go under safe conduct. Holdert decided to stay and await his fate. Wim and Alfons got into their Opel car and left for Alkmaar. Friends were expecting them.

War over

Liberation and going into hiding
On liberation day Sassen senior surrendered himself to NBS. He was immediately taken into custody, and put under surveillance at a local school. Shortly afterwards he was sent to Fort Blauwkapel for questioning. His wife Johanna and two daughters (Maria and Johanna) were still in Hildesheim, Germany. At the end of the war, daughter Georgette worked as a Red Cross nurse in a *Kriegslazaret* (Field Hospital). There was no trace of Francisca.

According to their agreement in 1944 with Anthony Mertens, *Eddy Conijn* (brother of the executed Fritz Conijn) and KP chief Noord Holland Pierre de Bie, when Wim and Alfons met with Mertens at his fiancées house (Valentine Conijn) where they were both located in different safe houses. [Wim :]*"I promised them not to run. I was assigned a safe house in the resident of the family Boot in Alkmaar, where I was eventually arrested. This family knew nothing about my real identity. Mr Mertens and his wife did visit me there. I was interrogated by someone there too. By whom I do not know."*[78]

Anthony Mertens was, at that time, staying at the house of his parents-in-law Conijn at 9 Nassaulaan in Alkmaar, when the Sassen boys appeared: [Mertens :] *"I saw Wim Sassen with his younger brother Alfons, a grammar school pupil who I believe he also dragged to the Eastern Front, in Alkmaar, where I had been in hiding for several months. Both were in civilian clothes. Wim Sassen was seriously ill and they arrived in an Opel with Utrecht number plates. Because they carried Abwehr identity papers they were able to pass all German roadblocks. Their appearance hardly provoked any argument because the house had been a hide out for many part-time-resistance members throughout the war. The only difference was that they now arrived here as deserters (officially the war wasn't over yet), and therefore put my parents-in-law in a more precarious position. The war was not over yet! The other strange thing was that they still owned a car which at this time of the war was quite unusual because of the petrol shortage. That day we took them to a safe house and deliberated on what to do with them..."*[79]

Wim was indeed still ill and needed care. Mertens had kept his word. Wim was taken to the *Boot* family.⁸⁰ During his recovery, Mertens advised him to write a report on all his activities within the *Abwehr*. This information could, in case of a trial, have a positive effect on his sentence. Brother Alfons was temporarily housed at *De Bie's* home. His final destination would be Amsterdam, where former police officer and leader of the *Centrale Inlichtingendienst* (CID) *Wim Sanders* would take of him.

The former Resistance members of KP Holland realised that Wim Sassen's hide out would be exposed one way or another, and a solution had to be sought. As a radio propagandist, Wim was too well known. Besides, he was on a search (black) list because of his activities within the German stay behind unit. Pierre de Bie left with Alfons for Amsterdam. He wanted to discuss the Sassen case with the former leader of the (CID) Wim Sanders. Before he left, Pierre de Bie promised he would provide Wim with forged identity papers. As soon as the roadblock checks decreased, he would try to get Wim through the demarcation line between the northern and southern provinces.⁸¹

It was a lot easier to get seventeen year old Alfons through the different zones controlled by the Allies. Alfons' name did not appear on any search (black) list. De Bie thought of a cunning plan. Just before Wim's arrest, Wim Sanders and the chief of the *Politieke Opsporingsdienst* (POD: Criminal Investigation Department) in Alkmaar, Eddy Conijn, tried to report Wim as a casualty of war. If Wim Sassen was officially declared dead, his description would be withdrawn from the wanted lists, and he would be able to reach the safe haven Spain without any problems

Arrested and handed over to CIC Detention Centre Fortress Blauwkapel

Just before all plans were realized, Wim's hide out was given away by his own girlfriend Miep van der Voort. After the liberation of the Netherlands, Miep was arrested by the Field Security (FS) in Utrecht and questioned about Wim. Under pressure she revealed the location of Wim's safe house.

At 16.00 hours on 5 June 1945, a month after the liberation, Wim was arrested by the BS and FS in Alkmaar. Three days later, Wim was handed over to officials of the Canadian Field Security (CFS). On 10 and 11 June, he was interrogated, for the first time, by sergeant *M.C. Chambers* of the Civil Security Interrogation Centre (CSIC) in Fort (Fortress) Blauwkapel nearby Utrecht (GS1 CDB Corps). Wim's case was numbered 31 CSIC.[82]

Fort Blauwkapel was directed by the Canadian FS of the 1st Canadian Army. The FS was tasked to liquidate the remnants of the German intelligence services and therefore also concentrated its actions on tracking down members of stay behind groups. The FS was mainly interested in the stay behind group headed by Wim, known as NEUROP. The report Wim wrote on behalf of Mertens about this unit was handed over at the time of his arrest. Within weeks, the whole organisation of *Abwehrstelle Driebergen* with its *Friedeskommando* was run down and behind bars. Wim's report was a tremendous 'success'. The whole organisation of the West European *Bulang Abwehr* organisation had been exposed. In turn for his collaboration, Wim's detention became less restrictive. *[Mertens:] "The FS later deployed Sassen and relocated him to a safe house on the*

Maliebaan in Utrecht, where he was treated like a prince. He even became best man at a wedding of one of the FS staff members. His girlfriend Miep van der Voort was there too..." [83]

Wim had offered his full cooperation in rounding up these stay behind units (or werewolf organisations) in and outside the Netherlands. He also informed his new superiors that Ireland, South Africa, Spain and Portugal were known safe havens for wanted Nazis. The Canadians were more interested, however, in the psychological warfare of the *Skorpion West* operation: its relationship between *Aktivpropaganda* and the much feared werewolf groups, and Wim's knowledge of Russia. More specifically, his knowledge about the Russian post-war strategy: *"On request of Captain Stuart I compiled a detailed report on the economic, political and military penetration into West European countries by the Russians. I enjoyed an excellent treatment and was free to wander around the detention centre during my tasks. I wasn't even bound by word of honour, but I did feel morally committed not to abuse this freedom of movement. In the camp I set up a re-education program for political delinquents, which the appropriate authorities would develop further as to guide these detainees in their post-war world. Besides, their knowledge could be useful in case of a future Russian aggression, either a Pan-Slavic or international bolshevist revolution, towards Western Europe."* [84]

Wim's liberties were expanded to such an extent that he was even used as an investigator, wearing an Allied uniform.

In July 1945, all detainees of the FS were handed over to the *Bureau Nationale Veiligheid* (BNV, Dutch Bureau of National Security), together with the interrogation centres like the Scheveningen Grand Hotel, Fort Blauwkapel and Fort Honsdijk. At these centres, SD members and *Abwehr* specialists were grilled for information. Wim was among them, yet he maintained his special status. As explained by the FS interpreter *Otto Akkermans*: "*Wim was used by the BNV, even after the Canadians had gone, to interrogate German prisoners*". He had no problems betraying his former SS colleagues. He was also used to spying on other inmates and to extract information. Under surveillance of the BNV, Wim was even assigned his own desk to work on his special project: "*the rehabilitation plans of the so-called idealistic SS (to be put to use in the Dutch East Indies)*'. Better known as the famous document *Einsatzgruppen* Japan*: "In the meantime I had engineered a plan intended to merge all former SS volunteers, who were not guilty of treason, betrayal or extortion, into a punitive division which could be deployed in a heavily controlled area like Singapore to fight the Japanese. At the beginning of July, this plan was discussed by the minister president Schermerhorn and the archbishop Cardinal De Jong, who approved it and wanted to proceed with it. The early capitulation of Japan (15 August 1945) prevented its execution.*"[85]

In August 1945, Wim was interrogated again about the propaganda organization of the *Schutzstafflen* (Nazi Black Guards – SS), the development of the *Skorpion Action* and *Aktivpropaganda*, and a list of individuals connected with these organisations. [Mertens :] "*Sassen was a member of the Skorpion West, a section of utmost importance at that time. After his interrogation, it was recommended that he be transferred to SS Camp Otterlo.*"[86]

The good days are over
The Sassen family members never lost contact with one another. In Fort Blauwkapel, correspondence was intercepted between his sister Francisca and Wim. In it, Wim expressed his concern about the now known active role of their oldest sister *Maria* within the RSHA organisation: [Wim:] "*Maria is besmirching our good name with her international high-talk about her "important" role as an agent for the RSHA. I cannot believe she was as important as she portrays herself. Nor do I believe the alleged filthiness she was involved in. Idem with father Sassen. They also claimed he reported people to the SD.*"[87]

Wim's run of good luck ended by coincidence. It was discovered that he was secretly compiling list of several prosecutors who dared to ask for capital punishment of his former idealistic SS colleagues who had fought on the Eastern Front. The main purpose of this schedule was to liquidate these prosecutors. Wim was put under arrest and sent back to prison. He immediately decided to take measures. As a well known collaborator for the German propaganda machine he most definitely did not want to be judged by a Dutch or Allied court. Wim started to look for a way out.

Prison "breakout"?
There are many versions about Wim's breakout from prison, one story more colourful and theatrical than the other. Even in 2005, when a Dutch documentary (*Netwerk*) on Wim Sassen appeared on national television and the national press dedicated some articles about his adventurous life, the following myth was

kept alive: *"Willem Sassen was detained in Fort Blauwkapel, guarded by soldiers of the Canadian FS. He would, so he announced, give a special performance of Cyrano de Bergerac, preceded by his self-authored one-act play "The Escape" to entertain the detainees in the Forts on this cold December night. In the front row was general Charles Foulkes, the man who on 5 May 1945 signed the armistice with general Blaskowitz in Wageningen. Next to him was Sassen senior, the former NSB mayor of Veghel and father of the elocutionist. "I am going to London, daddy! The radio is calling me! I cannot stay here any longer!" Sassen junior exclaimed on the stage, wearing a Canadian army jacket over is overall. He left the stage and forced himself, through a barred window that had been prepared, while the audience was waiting for the next scene."*[88]

Wims break out was a complete set up. First of all the date is wrong. He did not escape from prison on Christmas Eve, but rather, on 15 December 1945. Secondly, General Foulkes (1st Canadian Army) returned to Canada around 23 July 1945. In the autumn of 1945, the control over Fort Blauwkapel was taken over by the BNV. Only a few CFS officials stayed behind.[89]

Second it must have been an inside job. Without help Wim would never have been able to make his grand escape. As a part of the Dutch water defence system (Hollandse waterlinie), Fort Blauwkapel is surrounded by water. To gain access to the fort, one had to cross guarded bridges. Besides, it was December. Saturday 15 December was a cold day without sun. At the utmost 4 degrees Celsius, but with a wind-chill of minus 0.9 C. After an icy spell, thaw had set in. Swimming was not an option...

According to younger brother Alfons, Wim fled together with a British detainee called *"Davis"*, who was considered a spy. Alfons stated that at the two men had been assisted by a certain *"Jansen"*, a prison guard. By nightfall on 15 December, both detainees had allegedly fled over the fence surrounding the camp. This "*Jansen*" would according to the plan report their absence the following day. This would give Wim enough time to flee. Wim first went to visit first his girlfriend Miep van der Voort in Utrecht. A few hours later he headed for The Hague. An old study colleague would provide him shelter before he moved on to Antwerp.

Miep corroborates Alfons' story: *"Wim Sassen escaped from Fort Blauwkapel on 15 December 1945. He arrived at night between 23.15 and 23.30 hours at my place. He stayed briefly. I stayed up until 03.00 am because I was expecting the police. Only on the next day, three men of the BNV dropped by to inquire whether I received any visits the night before. My house was searched. Later Wim told me he had left for The Hague, where he met up with an old study mate, an Indonesian engineer. His name I cannot recall. From there he left for Limburg and crossed the border at Maastricht to Belgium. He first went to Antwerp and lived there in remnants of houses which had suffered damage from air raids..."*[90]

Anthony Mertens, stated: "*When the FS in the autumn of 1945 handed Wim, as a dangerous spy and a possible war criminal, over to the Dutch officials, he was locked up in the special detainee centre of Fort Blauwkapel (where there was still a small FS staff remaining), a so-called 030 interrogation centre.. I only know this from hearsay, because I did not see Sassen again, though I do suspect that, when he escaped, he was helped by his friends of the FS.*"[91]

Wim took his time to prepare his escape: *"Before I planned my break out, I considered all options when I went into hiding. It was my intention to reach Spain as quickly as possible through Belgium and France. For my own safety I would evade contact with other fugitives, because one arrest might lead to another. When it was necessary to contact such safe houses I would keep it short, only to obtain what was necessary. With this course of action I arrived in Antwerp, Belgium, in December 1945. In cinemas, small cafes, etc, I would hide. I didn't dare to spend the night in hotels. After a few days I picked up enough courage to arrive at Maison de Passe (cheap hotel), around midnight, were in a feigned state of drunkenness I ordered a room for me and my Jeanneke (prostitute) who would arrive shortly..."*[92]

Mertens knew much more than he let on, and was even prepared to lie for Wim in court, as we will see later. Mertens was just making the story more theatrical. He most certainly did not reveal the whole truth.

The true details of Wim's escape were only revealed after he was arrested the second time. [Wim:] *"In December 1945 I managed to escape, after I returned from work. Like every night I was locked up in my bunker. I escaped on 15 December 1945 with two other inmates, a Hungarian and a Javanese engineer."*[93]

Mid December at the office of criminal investigators the following telex massage arrived: *"IB 262 Restricted. Following three internees escaped from CSIC Fort Blauwkapel near Utrecht night 15/16, first name Andres de Kaszo van Tesco, alias Andree van Straaten, alias Hendrik van den Berg, last address 1 Blauwkamerlaan, Marlot, The Hague. Dutch engineer. Speaks English German, Spanish and Hungarian. Age 36 height 1.70, build slight, face oval. Complexion pale, long nose, black hair, lobeless ears, Brown eyes, wears metal rimmed glasses. Operation near on stomach. Second name Willem Sassen, last address 14 dr Van Mierlostraat, Breda, Dutch journalist. Speaks French, English, German, age 27, height 184, build slim, face oval, complexion pale, wears a small moustache, eyes brown, nose straight. Lobeless ears, brown eyes, 5 cm scar right knee, bullet wound scar left arm at shoulder. Third name Johannes Lowey Ball, last address 24 Graaf Florislaan Hilversum, home address 8 Wijnhaven, Delft. Dutch engineer, speaks English, French, German, Spanish, Malaysian, Javanese, face oval, pale complexion, eyes brown, broad nose, age 31, height 174, build slim, black hair, small ears, scars on both upper arms and left wrist, circumcised, other likely address in The Netherlands passed separately to BNV who are under investigation. Report arrest to originator c/o British military Mission (Netherlands)."* [94]

Did Wim randomly pick his companions? No. Both Lowey Ball and Andre Kaszo knew how to reach the Spanish border. During the war they were members of the Resistance. They ran an escape-line via France to Spain or Portugal. At that time it was used by shot down Allied pilots, escaped POW, Jews and *Engelandvaarders* (Dutch Resistance members who managed to flee to England).

Lowey Ball was a known figure within the Resistance movement and a former colleague of the arrested *Henri Scharrer*. It was Ball and Fritz Conijn who tried to buy off Scharrer; an action for which Fritz paid a heavy price. He was arrested by the SD and together with Scharrer executed in Vught.

Kaszo was a very dodgy person, a crook, a conman and an opportunist of considerable size. During the war he pretended to be a secret agent in contact with London. This way he infiltrated resistance movements and tricked them out of information and money. Two shot down British airmen confirmed, after the war, that he was a resistance member who helped them reach Spain. It was thought, however, that he was a double agent. This adventurer managed several times to escape from Spanish or SD detention. After the war he broke out twice from Fort Blauwkapel.

How was it possible that three inmates could escape? Undoubtedly Wim got help from the inside. On top of that, the camp management was poor. By autumn 1945 the situation was so disorderly that an inquiry was made by the BNV about the administration. [Captain P. Edwardson (FS) :]"*It appeared, according to statements of the British officers working in the Fort, that the secretary miss M. and her mother were factually managing the camp. Almost every night they partied, and at night Miss M. was driven home late. This laissez-faire attitude between the captain, the chauffeur, the secretary and her mother has affected the staff completely. A lot of things were happening and appeared to be unsound but there was no proof...Nothing was done properly.*"[95]

Not only Wim enjoyed his privileges. There were more detainees who enjoyed a "special treatment" and had easy access to cigarettes, money and freedom of movement...

In 1947 Werner Schramm, the recruiting officer for the spy ring Neurop, stated as follows when asked to comment on Wim Sassen: "*Wim Sassen is due to his appearance, his education and social manners a person who can easily move around in all societies. He is a funny and charming conversationalist. Very intelligent, impulsive and quickly tempted by an idea, especially when it is within his own views. His studies, -law and social politics, his short but important period as a leader of a political daily (Telegraaf), and his experience within the German propaganda service, make him a person be reckoned with in future political upheavals.*

The transit from extreme anti communism to extreme national communism is not that far. Recent incidents after the German capitulation and the growing Paulus and Seidlitz organisations show such a drastic turn might be possible.

I really believe that as a fugitive and disappointed, betrayed by his own comrades, Wim Sassen might or would join such an organisation. He is even capable of leading such an organisation or to assume an important role within.

Wim Sassen is a very energetic person and is unbeatable in words. He has, as already mentioned, a very likeable appearance and is able during interviews to quickly adept himself to the mentality of interrogator. This happened too in Fort Blauwkapel in autumn 1945. He succeeded to charm his British interrogator which was confirmed by sergeant Collars. Sassen managed to gain far-reaching liberties whilst in custody, and therefore was able to work out his escape in detail. As long as this person is on the run in The Netherlands, Belgium, France, Spain or Germany, I consider him a constant and present danger to the security of the Dutch State.

I request my answer to your questions to be dealt in the most confidential manner, because I fear for my safety, if this information on Wim Sassen, were to end up in the wrong hands.

I am convinced that Wim Sassen is capable of cold-blooded murder in order to save his personal interests or attain his political goals." [96]

On the run

Wim disappeared to Antwerp; He arrived there on 18 or 19 December 1945. For 250 Belgium francs, he bought himself a green identity card. His new name was "*Albert Desmet*", a student from Izegem, 21 Kortrijksestraat.

The ID card came from a Dominican clergyman who helped *incivieken* (political delinquents or collaborators) and provided them with clothes, money and provisions.[97] In The Netherlands and Belgium there were many individuals and small organisations who cared for the homeless, refugees and families of known collaborators. Clergymen of all orders were no different. Out of pure charity, compassion and anti-communistic ideology they tried to shelter these displaced and hunted people. This included Wim.

During the first weeks Wim hid between the ruins of Antwerp city centre. With the earnings of translation work of brochures, articles and pamphlets he took up residence in *Maisons de Passe*. His contact with the outer world, including his girlfriend Miep van der Voort and Anthony Mertens, ran via a letterbox address of the Dominican convent (23 Ploegstraat, Antwerp).

At that time Mertens was the general editor of the conservative Roman Catholic newspaper *De Linie* (133

Rozengracht, Amsterdam). He was quite willing to help Wim out again. To let him earn some pocket money Mertens asked Wim to write some articles for *De Linie*. Despite wanting to keep a low profile, Wim got into contact with some Flemish friends in hiding. The Belgian *Securité* (Security Service) as well as the Dutch BNV were looking for him: "*On 27 April 1946, the Dutch consulate in Ghent informed the BNV headquarters in Brussels that Wim stayed in Ghent with the family Boone, 33 Gustave Gallierlaan, between 19 and 21 of January*". The Boone family was related to the wife of the well known Flemish nationalist *Edward Herreweghe*, a personal friend of Wim's father Sassen senior.[98]

Shortly afterwards Wim left for Brussels, where he and Miep were to be reunited at her the home of her uncle, a former member of the Flemish movement.

In February 1946, the BNV requested the international war crimes investigators' unit for any information pertaining to Sassen's whereabouts, and further, instructed that he be arrested if located and turned over to them.

The search description of Wim and Miep was as follows: "*Big black flambard (felt hat), navy blue sweater, navy blue winter coat, grey tweed suit with very worn down, frayed legs, long hair, possibly wearing a blue overall, and in appearance a typical artist. Specific characteristics: scar 5 cm above right knee, shot wound left upper arm, bullet exited via torso. Description of Miep van der Voort: pretty girl, blondine (coloured), 1.60 tall, well manicured, dressed well. Speaks all modern languages. Grey blue eyes, thin straight nose, good figure. Lives together with Willem in Brussels and both intend to flee to Spain.*"[99]

In Antwerp and Brussels Wim also received aid from the *Albert 'Pim" Persijn organisation*.[100] [Wim:] "*Young aides of the organisation would provide me with provisions and money. When I asked when I had to return the favour they answered it would happen in good time. Not now. Over a three month period I went every two weeks to Antwerp for supplies."* Persijn was Flemish SS and had met Wim when he was working for Radio Brussels. Until his arrest Persijn managed a productive clandestine movement which provided political delinquents with money, provisions, stamps, false identity cards and passports. More importantly, he provided safe houses for those who wanted to flee to Spain. After his arrest, his escape-line and organisation managed to operate without him.

In January 1946, Miep van der Voort found Wim a room in a Hotel in Brussels, 49 Phillippe le Bon-street (near the train station of Brussels North) via an ad in the daily *Le Soir*. According to the owner *Elisabeth Bucker*, a Dutch blondine speaking French with a Dutch accent had responded to the advert. She showed Wim's ID card and said she wanted to rent this attic-room for a friend called "Desmet" from Izegem, for 800 Belgian francs a month. To avoid any inquiries as to why he hardly left his room, Wim said he would be studying hard and would be working out his assignments on his typewriter. The next day Miep left and the owner never saw her again. There was, however, a strange coincidence. Elisabeth Bucker, married to the Belgian *Dubois* was originally from Hildesheim, Germany. The exact same place where Wim's mother and sisters were located at the time.

[Wim:] *"I started soon to make some earnings. First I did manual labour, and when possible I did some translation and advertising works. In March 1946 I met, by accident, a former study colleague J. Nijs in Ixelles (Brus-*

sels). During my studies (Political and Social Sciences) in Ghent we had been comrades, I wrote plays and he interpreted them on the stage. In 1943 when I met him in Ghent again I noticed he wasn't very pro-British or pro-German. That's why I did not mention my active service at the Eastern Front. I invited Nijs, who was in that time in financial trouble, to work for the Dutch radio. This pure literary cycle was called: "In een Hoekske met een Boekske" (In a corner with a booklet). Together with Nijs we worked on this cycle for the NIR for a while. When I met him after the war I invented some story about me working for the intelligence service to penetrate the communist movement, also to explain why I used the alias "Desmet". For some time he visited me regularly, but after some time he stopped visiting me because he felt something was not "kosher". In Antwerp, I read in the Flemish daily "'t Pallieterke" the column where they made fun of the bad translations of the advertisements of Wallonian companies. I approached these firms and told them I could improve their adverts linguistically but also commercially. I got paid well for these works and earned a decent living. No one knew of my true identity."[101]

Miep could travel freely. She wasn't wanted and could visit Belgium any time. She acted as a messenger between the Sassen family and friends. Wim's whereabouts in Belgium soon became known to former detainees. Not even a month after Wim's so-called escape from Fort Blauwkapel, Miep was asked for help by an individual by the name of *H. Kerken*, from Amsterdam. Kerken knew Wim and knew of his plans of escaping to Spain or Argentina: Kerken wrote in poor German: *"18 Januari 1946, Sehr geëhrtes Fräulein Miep. Sie erzählten mir das Sie damals nach Belgien reisen wollte. Nun bin ich in die Situation, das ich nach Antwerpen zum Argentinischen Consul muss um das Visum für Argentiniën anzufragen. Es ist so schwierig dahin zu kommen und ich kann auch nicht so lange warten bis endlich in Holland auch ein Consul kommt. Über den Belgischen Consul ist es mich nicht möglich. Wissen Sie eine Wege? Bitte Teilen Sie mir so rasch möglich mit; ob, und wie. Ich währen Ihnen sehr dankbahr wenn Sie mir irgendwie helfen könnten. Vielleicht wissen Sie auch einen Weg um an Belgischen Franken zu kommen"* [102]

It seems that Miep played an more important role within the preparations of Wim's escape line to Spain.

Wim's younger brother Alfons visited him also. Like Miep, the eighteen year old Alfons was not wanted. Even better he walked around in an Allied uniform and carried papers stating he worked for *Wim Sanders*, the chef of the BNV. In Brussels he was supposedly on mission… Alfons would supply Wim with a passport. In Alkmaar (Holland), he tried to purchase a passport from a contractor who had made a fortune working for the *Wehrmacht*. It did not work out, but former resistance member Pierre de Bie thought he could lay his hands on one. According to Alfons, Pierre de Bie was involved in all sorts of dodgy business after the war.

On his twice a month trip to Antwerp to collect money and provisions from the Persijn organisation Wim was, through this organisation, also kept informed about the escape-line southwards. With his new ID papers he also received a raw sketch of this escape route via Switzerland to Spain. Did the moment arrive? [Wim:] *"The road-map for Spain was handed to me together with the first ID. In St Jean de Port of Tar-*

dets, I had to reach a lumberyard, which was directed by a widow. There I had to pay much for three guides who would lead me through the Pyrenees... I never made use of this route. On the one hand I thought it to be too risky, and the closure of the French – Spanish border made it virtually impossible. I was warned that in Spain I would be detained and placed in the concentration camp Miranda de Ebro. This prospect was not very appealing to me. One way or another I had to reach the Spanish border on my own."[103]

The report of the Dutch Consulate in Ghent stated that Wim possessed several ID cards to be able to embark on his journey to Spain. The Belgium ID papers were of a certain *"Jef Verellen"* and Wim's French alias was *"Van Verdonck"*. The only problem was raising sufficient money for paying the safe houses and guides. The BNV, in particular the political criminal investigator in charge of the Sassen case (Wim and Alfons) *Edo Westendorp* stated the following: 14 May 1946: *"In Belgium, Wim Sassen had campaigned hard for the union of Flanders with The Netherlands. Wim, who is at the moment residing in Brussels, and living under a false identity and papers, is convinced that once he is arrested in Belgium he will be condemned to death. In The Netherlands he would get 20 years of forced labour. If he should be arrested, he would try to commit suicide. Wim Sassen is in possession of information of how to reach Spain. As soon as the border tension between France and Spain has decreased and human contraband is resumed, he will leave. He knows how to cross the Swiss frontier. It is his intention to leave in September for Switzerland or Spain and from there onwards. Wim Sassen is married, but does not maintain any relationship with his wife. He lived with a certain Miep* van der Voort. Her address is known. At the moment their relationship has ended (27 July) and they no longer see each other. It is most likely of temporarily nature because Miep is expecting his child (Saskia)."[104]

Captured again

In July 1946, when Wim was bedridden because of jaundice, the Belgium state police raided the building where he was staying. The building was frequented by *Jean le Beau*, at that time a well known Flemish gangster. The Belgian police wanted to arrest him, but coincidentally, also stumbled onto this ill man called "Desmet". Wim pretended to be a Jewish man whose family had been murdered in a *KZ-lager* (concentration camp) during the war. His disguise was too transparent...when they searched his flat, they found two different identity cards; one in the name of 'Albert Joseph Desmet', the other in the name of "*Richard Bosmans*". Realizing that his cover had been blown, Wim revealed his true identity. On 20 July 1946, he was officially charged with the infringement of article 113 and 117 B, as a member of the *Waffen SS* and *Kriegsmarine*, article 118 bis as a war correspondent and as a contributor to the spoken broadcasts of Radio Brussels.[105] He was not, as he had believed, sentenced to death.

In the courtroom, Wim sought to explain the provenance of his false papers to the investigating officer P. *van Pelt*[Wim:] *"The first false identity papers in the name of Albert Josef Desmet, born in The Hague, 16-05-1918, profession student, living at Izegem (Belgium), 21 Kortrijksestraat, I received from an unknown man from the Persijn organisation. I do not know this man called*

Persijn personally ...the second card I received from Jean Le Beau, who I met in café Au Chien Vert in Brussels. I told Le Beau that I was a black market smuggler of American luxury products. To evade problems and being searched by the Military Police, I needed a false identity. Le Beau had asked me whether I was an "inciviek", a political delinquent. I just laughed. Three days later I received an ID card in the name of Richard Kamiel Bosman, born in Hasselt (Belgium), 11-12-1918, student, living in Antwerp, 157 Grote Steenweg. I paid 750 Belgium Francs for it. Somewhere in February 1946 I took up residence in 49 Philippe de Goede straat (P. Le Bon) in Brussels, under the alias Desmet. There I rented an attic for 800 Belgian francs."[106]

Wim was put in cell number 404 of the *Prison á Forest* (Vorst, Brussels), at 52 Verbindingslaan. The Belgian authorities wanted to know more about Wims activities in Belgium during and after. Wim was asked to write his own biography, in chronological order of events. In August, he was grilled about his knowledge of the so-called *Werewolf-organisation* in West Europe and the communist infiltration of Belgium: *"End of March 1945 I was shown, by a staff officer of the OKW West colonel Damrau, an important report retrieved by their main German agent in Russia. This man was referenced with one or two words and a number, and had been one of their most successful political spies who had laid his hands on this report, dating from February 1945. It revealed the Comitern (Communist international) future plans concerning the relationship between the Allied forces in the post-war era. The well known Kriegsberichter Fernau had insisted in sharing this document with me for my own orientation. During my interrogation at Fortress*

Blauwkapel, I had already briefed captain "Stuart" on the scale of this report on the economical, political and military penetration into Western European countries by the Russians: The re-education of POWs and the set up of an underground sleeping cell network for future activities in the Western territory. It also dealt with their future in African politics, like their activities in the Congo; the instigation of and propaganda for equal rights of the native population, uniting tribes and inciting them in the strife for national independence...in short, anything to disrupt the dominance of the Western colonialist powers." [107]

It did not take long before help arrived. Mertens was doing his utmost best to have Wim released. On 28 August 1946, he wrote a letter to a "Dietse" (ideological partner of the Greater Netherlands) comrade, in which he asked for the address of Wim's lawyer in Brussels. In contradiction to his later statements made in the course of the Mertens trial, Mertens wanted to have Wim extradited to The Netherlands. He was convinced he had better contacts within the Dutch judiciary system, so as to obtain a better verdict for his troubled friend. Hadn't Wim aided the Resistance during the war? Had he not assisted in the dismantling of the former Bulang network?

Mertens approached the Public Prosecutor Den Bosch (The Netherlands), baron *F. van Voorst tot Voorst*: "*Highly esteemed Baron Van Voorst tot Voorst, I have received your letter of 4 October this year, nr. 2093, and I do want to thank you for your efforts and thoughts concerning this case. By chance I just received a message from Wim Sassen's lawyer stating the charges of the accused. Wim Sassen is strangely enough not persecuted for the crimes committed during the war in Belgium but for the illegal residence in Brussels and the possession forged identity papers. Only when additional information was received by the BNV his charges where extended. Maybe a possible solution would be a request for his extradition. Should you discuss this matter with your fellow colleague in Breda. If this colleague is Public Prosecutor Jacques Houben, he is a very good friend of mine and a former study companion in Nijmegen, so please give him my utmost regards, Tout a toi in Christo, Th. Mertens".*[108]

No effort was left unscathed, however, to go after Wim. Even the Vatican-mission was asked by family members to locate Wim Sassen. The director *Od. Schellekens* of the Dutch Vatican-mission was informed by the *Political Investigation Department* (*Politieke Recherche Afdeling,* PRA) in Breda of his whereabouts. In the ensuing correspondence it became clear that Wim was to stand trial in The Netherlands as well. This time there was no chance of escape.

In the meantime, the Dutch investigating criminal officer of the PRA who was in charge of the Sassen case, Edo Westendorp had left for Brussels. Between 21 and 23 August 1946, Westendorp was allowed, by the Belgian justice department, to interrogate Wim. On 23 August, Westendorp spoke to the court martial Public Prosecutor *Jean Nys* in Brussels. During the meeting, the possible extradition of Wim Sassen was discussed: "*The extradition of W. Sassen cannot be realised before October 1946. In September 1946 the court will treat the Radio Brussels case. During the occupation W. Sassen contributed to the emissions of Radio Brussels. If during this trial it is demonstrated that his broadcasts where not only restricted to Belgium but also to neighbouring countries, and therefore not solely against the Belgium people, I will advise that W. Sassen be extradited to the Netherlands, if the Dutch or other authorities request this".*[109]

A month later on 23 October 1946, Wim was sentenced by the Belgian criminal court in Brussels to three months of confinement and a fine of a 100 Belgian francs because of forgery of documents, false name gestation, fraudulent trading and being an illegal alien.[110]

In December 1946, Wim Sassen was handed over to the Dutch authorities. His confiscated belongings were sent to the PRA, which held its office in the Dutch consulate in Brussels, 1 Lakenwerverstraat. It contained two files, 27 phonographs and Sassens typewriter of the brand "Empire". On 4 November 1946, the military Public Prosecutor Nijs wrote to the chief commissioner of the Security of State (Veiligheid van den Staat – T.I. Dienst), stating that he agreed with the extradition of Wim Sassen to the Dutch authorities, and that he had to contact the PRA in order to fix the date and place of the handover of the subject, along with his file and personal belongings. He then explicitly asked the commissioner to take all precautions in order to prevent a possible escape of the subject.[111]

On 5 December, the Belgian police had Wim picked up at the Belgian – Dutch border nearby Essen. He was to be picked up by a Dutch army truck. In one way or another, he managed to escape yet again. Apparently, [Stan Lauryssens] he had cut the canvas of the truck with a razor blade and escaped through the hole. According to Stan Lauryssens, Wim jumped out of the truck nearby Utrecht and went on foot to Amsterdam, where he sought the help of Mertens. Whether his escape actually happened like this remains questionable. Wasn't Wim handcuffed during the transport? Wasn't there a guard or other detainees present in the cargo compartment? Hadn't the Belgian authorities already warned about the possibility of a break out?

Saving angel Mertens

On 6 December 1946, having made his second escape (as described above), Wim found his way to Mertens' house in Amsterdam. Outside it was cold, and raining. It was about 3 degrees Celsius. During the Mertens trial, Mertens stated: "*It must have been on a late night somewhere at the end of December 1946. I was home alone, my wife and baby were staying with my mother-in-law. It was late when the doorbell rang. At the door there was this unshaven drifter in a ragged coat. He said "Don't you recognize me anymore?" Then I knew who was in front of me. He said the lawyer in Brussels gave him my address. I received him in the hallway and told him how awkward and difficult it was to shelter him. He told me that he managed to escape during the exchange of prisoners between The Netherlands and Belgium at the Roosendaal train station.*"[112]

Mertens ended up taking Wim in. After several days, he found him a safe house. It was too dangerous to stay with Mertens: "*It occurred to me that the secretary Jose working at De Linie, the daughter of the Limburg press photographer W. Van der Randen, at the Leidschegracht in Amsterdam, would be able to harbour Wim. Her mother was Flemish and they were known to be a very hospitable family for friends from Belgium. Wim Sassen could easily pass for a Belgian with his accent. He even spoke with a heavy Flemish accent and had the air of a Belgian. His travel papers indicated he was the Belgian resident Albert Desmet."*[113]

Mertens asked *van der Randen* to help him out. On 10 December 1946, Wim took up quarters with this family. There, he would hide for more than six months, until 27 May 1947. For the outside world he was "Albert Desmet", a Belgian student from Kortrijk, who had worked for the German propaganda machine during the war.

Around that time, Mertens was still the chief editor of *De Linie*. The founder of *De Linie* the Jesuit *Josephys Hendrikus Cornelis Creijghton SJ* had attracted for his paper some editors and journalist who where known anticommunists. Some even were known Catholic fascists or former collaborators, including ex *Zwart Front* member Anthony Mertens.[114]

Even more striking is that the members of this rightist Catholic group already knew each other from before the war. A number worked for the Dutch known Catholic papers *De Tijd, De (Nieuwe) Gemeenschap, De Bundel* and *De Zonnewijzer*. In particular the last one is interesting. In 1938 *De Zonnewijzer*, an almanac for the Catholic family, was founded by a commission of the *Katholiek Comité* van *Actie voor God* (KA) (Catholic Committee of Action for God). Among its founders were well known Catholic fascists: *Henk Kuitenbrouwer*, his brother *Louis Kuitenbrouwer*, *Ad Sassen*, *Gabriel Smit*, *Kees Spierings*, *Karel Thole*, etc. Apparently their political beliefs formed no obstruction to the KA.

It was, therefore, to no one's surprise that Mertens introduced a member of the Sassen family under an alias to *De Linie*. The new recruit was apparently a Flemish inciviek, who called himself "Albert Desmet". Did no one recognise him? A great number of former colleagues of his uncle Ad and his father were working for this newspaper. Had Wim never previously paid a visit to the editor's house? According to the communist paper *De Waarheid*, Wim delivered his articles in person to the editors.

113 Rozengracht, nicknamed also *De Roothaanhuis*, not only accommodated the redaction of *De Linie*, but also a Roman Catholic centre for the youth and the *Roothaan club (*named after J.P Roothaan (1785-1853), the first Dutch Jesuit general). Through Mertens and Van der Randen (a member of the Roothaan club), Wim was introduced to prominent members of this society, among which the founder of the Roothaan house, the Jesuit *Cor Ligthart SJ*. There was an immediate "understanding" between the two. Ligthart SJ saw a young driven man who wanted to pursue his career as a journalist. Their relationship was strengthened by the fact that Ligthart took Wim's monthly communion. In order to save this "poor" Albert Desmet, the Jesuit gave him some reading and (translation-) work: "*He (Albert Desmet) wanted to work, to be busy, to write and he also wanted books. I gave him the Roothaan books and he became fond of them. In one night he wrote the Greatest Dutch General*!" (Roothaan SJ). A 35-page article that Wim Sassen published under the alias "Steven Wiel" in 1947.[115]

This cooperation led to another publication, this time about the Franciscan *Contardo Ferrinni*. Together with a certain *Karl Breyer*, Wim wrote a long about Russia, which Mertens placed under his own name in

De Linie. The former German Eastfront soldier Karl Breyer had just started as an intern at *De Linie*. Wim Breyer, as opposed to Wim, was not a person in hiding. During the war he had joined the Resistance. Due to his pro-Dutch resistance activities he was allowed to live and work in the Netherlands. Breyer was another person who allegedly had no knowledge of Sassen's true identity or of his past, just like Ligthart SJ. However within the walls of the Roothaan house on the 133 Rozengracht, plans were prepared to smuggle Wim out of the country. He couldn't stay there forever.

Eximorg and the Flemish ratline

Wiel van der Randen and his Flemish wife maintained strong ties with the Flemish expat community in Amsterdam. Within this group there was a certain *"Ward" Opdebeeck*, who also had the intention to leave the country. Wim knew Opdebeeck as former student in Ghent. Edward Opdebeeck was at that time the founder of the Ghent *Katholiek Vlaams Hoogstudenten Verbond* (KVHV). This association would unite all rightist Christian Flemish student movements: *Dietsch jeugdverbond,* Rex, Dinaso, VNV and *Jeugdfront*. He was also the man who during the '*Erstes europäisches Studenten- und Frontkämpfertreffen*' asked his fellow students to fight the Bolsheviks on the Eastfront. After the war, he sought refuge in Amsterdam.[116]

This group of henchmen was expanded. According to Stan Lauryssens, plans to set up a ratline for former collaborators in hiding had already been made in December 1946. The planners consisted of Edward Opdebeeck, *Leo Overvelt*, Wiel van der Randen, *Amaat*

Bockaert, *Frans Daels*, Karl Breyer, Anton Mertens and Wim Sassen.

The idea was to set up a cover firm. On 1 July 1947, the firm *Eximorg* (Export and Import) was registered at the Chamber of Commerce. The office building at the Singel in Amsterdam would be the headquarters of "relocating" their comrades in hiding: old SS and collaborators. The owner was the former *Zwart Front* financial contributor, the thirty year old Dutch man *Harry (Henricus Norbertus Josephus) van Puyenbroek* of Tourcoing (France).[117]

Puyenbroek remained in the background while Opdebeeck and Bockaert ran the firm. Officially Eximorg was a firm dealing with the in- and export of textiles, washing machines, chocolate, bicycles, carton and chemicals. Later, the former employee of *Rost van Tonningen Jan Godefroy* joined to group. Already in 1944, Wim, Mertens and Godefroy had planned to create an after-war Nazi organisation. Now these plans had materialized.

Eximorg predominantly dealt in money; money that was needed to help former Nazis to start a new life abroad. Opdebeeck and *Bockaert* used to launder considerable amounts of capital to foreign banks via branches of the company in Antwerp, Rome, Barcelona, Dublin and Buenos Aires. These subsidiaries were founded *in situ* and controlled by fugitive Nazi-friends. The end of the line, in Buenos Aires, Argentina, was operated by the leader of the former Flemish SS René Lagrou.

The Dutch operation was set in action. Wim was to open branches in Dublin (Ireland). Wim's ID papers were being prepared. Karl Breyer stole the passport of a young assistant at *De Linie*, called Jack Janssen. Breyer then handed the document over to press photographer W. Van der Randen, who altered the papers and doctored the image. From that moment onwards, the alias "Albert Desmet" was abandoned and the new one "J. Janssen" came to life. Wim was no longer a "student", but an "office clerk".

On 24 May 1947 Wim left in a taxi for the Dutch Airport Schiphol. Just before boarding, someone took a picture as evidence of this successful operation. Soon after, the KLM-plane left for Dublin, Ireland. Wim was finally a free man.

The other members of the organisation also went their way. In 1947, Amaat Bockaert left under the alias "*A. Timmermans*" in a KLM plane for Barcelona (Spain). In Barcelona he opened a branch of the Eximorg firm in the quarter of L'Hospitalet de Llobregat. There, he waited to be reunited with his family. The plan was to leave for Latin America. On 24 December 1948, he boarded the ship *Italia* together with his family as well as *Renaat van Thillo*, *Frans Schoorens* and other fugitive Flemish nationalists, with the final destination: Argentina. In 1948, Edward Opdebeeck left for Ireland.

Wim's fiancée Miep had no intentions of staying behind. She visited Wim in Dublin on several occasions. In February 1948, she and her daughter Saskia took their last flight to Ireland. The paperwork for emigrating to Argentina was had been completed.

How many collaborators and SS actually fled Europe through this ratline called *Eximorg* is unknown. The Dutch newspaper *Nieuw Israëlitisch Weekblad* (22-10-1976) mentioned also another fugitive with destination to Ireland: *"Besides Sassen, the notorious Nic Stassen also escaped via this secret escape-organisation to Ireland. Stassen was wanted for the murder of Russian miners in Limburg (The Netherlands). Stassen now lives in Dublin as "Lode van den Brande" and earns his living as representative of the Roosendaal biscuit factory LIGA."*

The Dutch communist daily *De Waarheid,* in an article published 22 July 1950, suggests that it was convinced there were many more: "*The Flemish lawyer Opdebeeck, the close friend of Mertens was one of the most active members of Eximorg. When the firm was up and running in Amsterdam, he left for a subsidiary in Dublin. Flemish lawyer Bockaert, who had been sentenced to death in absentia, went into hiding with a staff member of De Linie, and, accompanied by Puyenbroek, escaped in an American army truck to Barcelona, where another ex-SS runs the branch. Over the last three years many French, Flemish and Dutch fascists have been helped to reach safe havens abroad. The present overt preparations of war (the increasing tension between the Allied forces and Russia) and the growing measures of fascist origin for which former Nazis openly gave their support, has loosened the relation between De Linie and Eximorg. There has been a fight about the money between the employees and Opdebeeck and the last one has separated himself from Eximorg and started his own firm in Dublin. The organisation has fulfilled its purpose.*"[118]

The publication of article in the daily *De Waarheid* two years after Wim's escape was a bombshell. *Eximorg* wasn't the first illegal organisation which was exposed. In November 1948 the police raided the headquarters of the probationers (released political delinquents under supervision). The confiscated documents showed their involvement in aiding fugitive war criminals, political delinquents, former collaborators and undesirables (stateless persons) abroad. Many Flemish collaborators sought their refuge in The Netherlands because of the very mild prosecution of political delinquents. In contrast, the purge of *incivieken* was much tougher in Belgium.

Nevertheless, the redaction of *De Linie* received a heavy blow due to this article. The Roothaanhuis was branded a hotbed of Nazis. As a result of this article and the resulting police investigation, Anthony Mertens and his secretary Miss Van der Randen had to stand trial before the magistrate (22 July 1950).

Mertens sentenced

"*I gave Sassen my word of honour, my lord*" was Mertens' reply on 13 June 1951 to the magistrate *L. De Blécourt* when questioned why he had helped Sassen. Mertens was fully convinced he helped Wim Sassen in good faith. "*It was a matter of honour*". Mertens turned and twisted during the trial. His statements were in many cases contradictory. He mixed up the precise dates of events. He stated he met Wim only in the autumn of 1944, after *Dolle Dinsdag* and after the death of Fritz Conijn. While Wim Sassen himself, when interviewed by criminal investigator Westendorp, had stated: "*During the war I maintained contact with several friends... Already at the end of July 1944 my case was known to the Dutch government in exile, and I was reassured of my amnesty after the war.*" This statement was confirmed by an article in the Dutch daily *Vrij Nederland* (1976): "*Mertens maintained contact with Wim Sassen throughout the war. Sassen lived with a German aide at the Minervaplein in Amsterdam. Mertens visited him in 1944 together with Godefroy. The meeting was about the creation of a Nazi organisation after the Germans had lost the war...*" Didn't Mertens want to reveal the contact between Ed Conijn and the government in exile? Had there been a certain concession made with regard to Wim, in exchange for information? What role was Wim Sassen supposed to play after the war?

During the trial not one word was said about the former resistance group *KP Noord Holland* hiding two wanted war criminals. Mertens did reveal that he had informed Wim Sanders (former section head of BNV) when Sassen knocked on his door after his second successful escape in December 1946. [Mertens:] *"When reacquainted with Sassen after one and a half years I would never think of calling the police. It would an infringement on our deal, the promise we made during the hardship of war, in return for his aid. It was clear to me that this man was in need, and that he was to be helped in any way, a meal, clothes or bed, one way or another in order to gain enough time to think of a solution. It was purely improvised help.*"[119] It was Mertens who looked for him when Wim was arrested in Brussels. Not only did he locate Wim, but he also did his utmost best to have him extradited to the Netherlands.

Mertens denied his own efforts: *"As far as I recall I must have received a letter of Wim's lawyer in Brussels. It did not, however, mean anything more than a notification that Wim was imprisoned, and that he needed some help. Nothing more. I had more or less forgotten Sassen when he suddenly appeared at my door in Amsterdam."* Apparently Mertens forgot Wim wrote several articles for *De Linie* which he placed under his own name, or that Miep van der Voort acted as a courier between them. *"Some days after our renewed encounter in December 1946, I took up contact with Sanders, former criminal investigator chef of the BNV, and chief of police with whom I worked closely during the war, and asked him what to do with this man who suddenly appeared out of nowhere. I did not say where and how. We decided to engage F. Baron van Voorst tot Voorst, at that time a lawyer in Den Bosch..Our intention was to meet and discuss what value Wim Sassen could be for the Politieke Opsporingsdienst POD. I wasn't quite sure what would happen. But I had the impression that this Public Prosecutor from Den Bosch was a man of conscience and broad-minded. We were, of course, dealing with a wanted fugitive and we had not informed the proper authorities to hand him over. I was in a moral dilemma, between law and sentiment. That's why I sent him this letter, in order to see what might happen. In the mean time it would give me enough time to find a possible solution if there was one. This is the only reason I can think of why I offered Wim Sassen my help."*[120]

During the Mertens trial he did, however, write the prosecutor in Amsterdam saying Mertens was really troubled by this moral dilemma, and that he wasn't engaged in a criminal act.

With regards to the stolen passport, Mertens first blamed Ward Opdebeeck: *"Breyer and Wim met each other while writing the piece on Russia. Apparently Sassen had used his flair to get Breyer to steal, within days, somewhere around May 1947, an identity card from the pocket of this young apprentice. This unfortunate young man had just shown everybody his new pass. The age, eye and hair colour of this J. Janssen could match Wim Sassens, so the falsification of the pass would only mean the replacement of the picture. It could not be more simple. Breyer put the stolen pass in an envelope and gave it to my secretary. It all happened in the same week Sassen left for Ireland. I heard the whole story two or three days later, when the story went around that Wim Sassen had obtained a pass and would soon leave the country. The father of Van der Randen, a press photographer, had no trouble replacing the old picture with a new picture of Wim Sassen (now with moustache and glasses) – a job he had done many time before during his days as a resistance member. They never informed me how they came into possession of the new pass. I thought Wim Sassen had received it from our mutual Flemish acquaintance, a convicted lawyer from Ghent by the name of Opdebeeck, who lived in Amsterdam as a representative of some firm and knew the Van der Rande family well.*" Mertens finally admitted: "*My Lord, my former employee Karl Breyer had stolen it on my request and on my directions.*"[121]

Anthony Mertens was sentenced to four months of imprisonment because of his assistance in offering a safe house and helping this well known SS man and spy Wim Sassen flee to Argentina. For her part as an accomplice, his secretary Miss A.J.A. van der Randen was sentenced to a fine of 50 Dutch Guilders and a month of probation. Mertens appealed his conviction. The outcome, however, didn't change much. The verdict was reaffirmed in January 1951. The Prosecutor Baron *A. Van Dedem* emphasized that Wim Sassen was a considerable collaborator . On top of that, Mertens knew: "*Sassen was one of the most wanted and dangerous SS men who at the end of 1944 had plans to create a pro-German spy ring in order to aid fugitive fascists in hiding and to commit attacks on people involved in the prosecution of war criminals."* The Public Prosecutor W.P.Bakhoven: *"was convinced that the criminal act committed was serious enough for the verdict to be reaffirmed."* Mertens had to serve his sentence.[122]

Breyer's part

The main prosecution witness in the Mertens trial, Karl Breyer, had exposed the details of Wim Sassens escape. He sold the story to the Dutch communist newspaper *De Waarheid*. Why Breyer betrayed Mertens remains unclear. He did however explain his own part in exposing Wim Sassen's escape in the German newspaper *Politische Rundschau* of 16 December 1960: *"Der junge Breyer zeigte sich von seinem ältern Kameraden und ehemaligen Vorgesetzten stark beeindruckt und erbot sich, seinem Chef, Dr. Mertens, behilflich zu sein, um dessen unerwünschten und gefährlichen Gast* (Sassen) *wohlbehalten unter die Grenze zu schaffen. Aus der Rocktasche des Buchhalters Janssen in der Geschäfsstelle der „Linie" stibizte er* (Breyer) *dessen Pass, der von einem befreundeten Graphiker prompt für Sassen „umgearbeitet" wurde. Unbehelligt bestieg Sassen auf dem Amsterdamer Flughafen Schiphol das Linienflugzeug nach Dublin."* [123]

Twenty years later Breyer stated the following: *"I was just twenty years old. Sassen made a very sympathetic and intelligent impression. I stole a passport for him. With it he could escape from The Netherlands. I had my own arguments to do so. You have to know that I, as a German, deserted from the SS and joined the Dutch resistance. However I could not grasp why a man like Sassen was condemned to death for something he had done for Nazi*

Germany. To me that was no crime. There was, you have to understand me, a difference between a soldier, even though he was SS, and someone who was a guard at a concentration camp. That is why I helped Sassen."[124]

The Mertens trial did affect Karl Breyer. He was also charged. These charges alleged that *"Somewhere in 1946/47 in Amsterdam, he together and in alliance with other conspirators aided Willem Antonius Maria Sassen in offering a safe house, meals and a stolen identity card in order for him to leave the country unhindered, after six months in hiding.*"[125]

Karl Breyer received the same verdict as the secretary Van der Randen. But then something strange happened. On 10 January 1952, the weekly *De Waarheid* reported: "*The main witness in the Mertens case, a deserted German soldier who was a brave participant of the Dutch Resistance and after the war an employee for De Linie, did not appear at trial. During statements of the defendant this witness was extradited by the foreign police a month earlier (December 1951).*"[126]

De Linie a roman ratline?

During the Mertens trial, not one word was said about the *Eximorg* organisation. No mention was made to the *De Linie* either. The only reference of the judge to the involvement of *De Linie* was the following: "*If De Linie opens its doors to people like Albert Kuyle (Kuitenbrouwer) and Sassen in spite of their misconduct during the war against the Dutch, when it assumes an attitude of forgetfulness or forgiveness to those who collaborated, it doesn't understand the true meaning of compassion. A paper who gives access to people who have seriously misbehaved dur-*

ing the war in our country, did not object to the ideology of these men. And the forgiveness or mercy to which they refer is, in one way, charity..." [127] The judge was referring to Wim Sassen's articles which were published in *De Linie* under an alias or in Mertens' name.

Mertens took all the blame. Was it a distraction manoeuvre aimed at saving the members of the Roonthaanhuis? Most likely.

Mertens could not have been solely responsible for sheltering people like Wim. He simply could not have orchestrated it all by himself. The other employees of *De Linie* weren't unsympathetic to the National Socialistic ideology. Like Creijghton once said*: "[t]here was much good in National Socialism – it fought the same battle against modernity as the Roman Church – and was pro-Greater Netherlands."* Within the Roman Catholic Church, young clergy had welcomed a new approach to the faith. They did not embrace political criminals (war criminals) only out of Christian charity and compassion, but also for their anti communist conviction.[128]

Mertens was pardoned. After serving his sentence he was, due to the intervention of father *Van Gestel SJ*, able to return to *De Linie*. Van Gestel was a high official of the Society of Jesus, situated in Rome. He was convinced that compassion for another human being should not be punished.[129]

The Dutch newspaper *Vrij Nederland* described the activities of *De Linie* as: *"Anthony Mertens continued the war in the columns of the paper De Linie. This Jesuit newsgroup located in the Roothaanhuis, 138 Rozengracht [Amsterdam] was indeed a very striking paper. its editors pro-Franco Spain, pro-militarized Germany as a buffer against the Soviet Union, and supporters of a defensive war of aggression against the Soviet Union. Mertens as the editorial secretary used the back page to write about the Greater Netherlands movement, adventure stories, war and resistance, fascism and communism. He was one of the first (and of the few) who accused Adolf Eichmann as the main person responsible for the murder of Jews. He also asked for the compassion for those lost ideological souls who called themselves 'communists' to be embraced in God's immeasurable forgiving love."*[130]

On 5 September 1944, this forgiveness of God was officially pronounced by the Catholic Church. The clergy was notified on *"the position they were to take with regards to traitors on liberation day. It was their duty to stay true to the Christian values and to receive all men and offer them refuge. Especially now when hatred and revenge could rule, it was incumbent to prevent these actions for the love of God. Those harboured in churches must be kept safe until the proper authorities are informed."*[131]

Reunion in Ireland

Wim was received well in Ireland. The Jesuit network had a far reach. According to *Marc Lindeijer SJ*, father Ligthart SJ contacted the Jesuits in Dublin. They would harbour him and help him out. The money for the KLM ticket was earned by Wim's published works for the Roothaanhuis. The booklet on the Jesuit-general Roothaan made around 470 Dutch guilders. Ligthart handed this money to Wim just before his flight.[132]

Wim Sassen knew where to go. Opdebeeck had given him an address of a safe house in Dublin. His contact was *May Dole*. He could stay there for some days. Another contact was *Kees van Hoek*, a renowned international Catholic journalist and a friend of Wiel van der Randen. Shortly after his arrival Van Hoek introduced this "Janssen" (Wim) to the prominent leader of the Dutch expat society in the Irish capital, *Johannes Bernardus Romein*, professor of the *National College of Art*. Professor Romein gave Wim some pocket money in order to pay for his expenses.

The plans for opening a sub-office of Eximorg were never materialized. According to Stan Lauryssens, Wim spent his money and bummed around, until the Franciscan father *Senan Moynihan* intervened. Senan was the chief editor of the Catholic magazine *The Capuchin Annual*. He recruited Wim to write articles, for 5 Irish pounds each.

Despite Lauryssens' sombre view of Wim during this period, other circumstances suggest, however, that he was in rather good shape. His girlfriend Miep visited him three times, before finally settling down with him in Dublin. A remarkable detail was that Wim's daughter Saskia (8 months at the time) went by the last name of Miep's new husband in The Hague, *Nicolaas Johannes Haremaker*. Miep and Haremaker married on 16 August 1947. Two days before she married Haremaker, she visited Wim in Dublin. What role Haremaker played at this point, is only speculation. Haremaker could have be an old acquaintance of Miep, Mertens or the Sassen family. It could well be that the change of name was used as some kind of a distraction manoeuvre. The fact that Wim Sassen had fled to Ireland only became clear in 1950 Miep left her husband on 1 March 1948.[133]

It did not take long before Wim Sassen was reunited with former comrades in the Irish capital. Dublin wasn't that big a city. Willem Smekens, a former colleague from Radio Brussels, arrived in Dublin from Marseilles (France) two months after Wim, under the alias "Gabriel Vinck". Smekens started working for the firm *L. Warnants*. Another fugitive was the Belgian *Albert "Pim" Persijn*, who lived in the capital under his alias "A.P. Bonnaire". He also made it safely to Ireland after his escape from prison in 1947. His benefactor was Willem Smekens. The Flemish comrades had found safety, together.

Argentina is calling

In Dublin, Wim met the former U-boot commander captain *Schneider*. One of his twin daughters lived with Wim Sassen and Miep van der Voort. The captain owned a coastal vessel, *Der Adler* (De Adelaar/The Eagle), which carried the flag of Panama. Wim asked Schneider whether he was willing to take him and other SS men to Argentina. He would be paid handsomely. Schneider was willing to take that risk.[134]

From Ireland, Wim contacted René Lagrou. As a member of the Argentinean immigration society, *la Sociedad Argentina de Recepción Europeo* (SARE), Lagrou could supply the necessary landing permits (libre desembarco) in Argentina for those Flemish in need. It was the second time Lagrou had set up a rescue mission. The first time around, he repatriated his ideological comrades. This second time, he expatriated them to reach safety in Argentina.

"[Pierre Daye:] *Known is the hardship on the European home front, for those who have won as well as for those who have lost. There are hundred thousand people who are in extreme conditions, homeless, without any means or economic sustainability, stateless, without any form of hope of who would be able to help them out of this misery. These conditions call for a helping hand to aid these lost people. That's why we turn to Argentina to make use of our means to benefit its own economic development. It's why we founded a society under the name Sociedad Argentina de Recepción Europeos (SARE). A society, without any political or ideological motives, dedicated to help fellow countrymen to Argentina in order to let this land prosper. We hereby created a committee that received and relocates immigrants in those firms and factories accordingly to their technical or professional skills.*

We dispose of a guesthouse, Casa de Huéspedes, in the centre of Buenos Aires. It can offer residence to known refugees who have no money or contacts in this new homeland. We can offer room, feed and look for work for up to 60 people. The organisation is financed by our well known friend Rodolfo Freude."[135]

After a period of more than 17 months, the stay in the Irish capital had come to an end. All was ready. On 23 September 1948, the coastal vessel *The Eagle* left the docks. On board were captain Schneider, his wife, the twin daughters *Inge* and *Antje*, sailor *Willem Meyer*, SS man *Klaus Fabini* (engineer), Willem Smekens, *Achille Hollants* (together with wife and children), Willem Sassen, a pregnant Miep van der Voort, and their daughter Saskia Haremaker. *Leo van Overveldt*, a friend of Edward Opdebeeck, paid for the trip. *The Eagle* went along the French coast, the north of Spain, Portugal and the African West-coast in the direction of Cape Verde, the last stop before crossing the Atlantic towards Brazil. From there, the vessel followed the coastline until *Rio de la Plata*. In its estuary lay its final destination, the port of Buenos Aires.[136]

Refuge in Argentina

Bienvenido señor Quillermo Sassen

Wim expressed also his gratitude to the Argentinean president *Juan Domingo Perón* in his autobiographical essay. The man who made SARE possible and was willing to shelter these hunted refugees: "*Without asking for much this young lad had offered thousands of comrades a new existence. Not only out of common ideology, but also in defence of the right of asylum for the political soldier, who suffered defeat and who wished to escape from cheap revenge.*"[137]

On 3 November 1948, 41 days after leaving the docks in Dublin, *the Eagle* arrived in the *Dársena Norte*, the harbour of Buenos Aires. On 6 November, the Sassen family were permitted to disembark. They took up temporary residence in a suburb of Buenos Aires, *Ciudad Gardin Lomas de Palomar, calle Los Nardos 329*. Miep was about to deliver her second daughter, Hadewych (30-12-1948).[138]

Nazi publishing house Dürer Verlag

In 1948, Wim had met the former Hitler *Jugend-Landesführer Eberhard Fritsch*(also referred as Eberhard Fritzsche or Fritz), the editor of *Dürer Verlag*. Fritsch was looking for right extremist authors who wanted to propagate the old school Nazi ideology through its publication of neo-Nazi magazines for the expat communities in Argentina and neighbouring countries.[139]

Wim immediately felt at home with the publishing world of Dürer. Here the crème de la crème of all exiled *Kriegsberichter*, propaganda specialists and a great number of prominent Nazis who glorified their Nazi past were to be found: *Reinhard Kops*, *Fritz Neubert*, *Johann von Leers*, *Werner Naumann* and *Karl "Carlos" Freiherr von Merck*.

As an experienced propaganda specialist Wim was a lucky find for the editor. Their teamwork would be extremely advantageous for both parties. With the recruitment of Wim, Fritsch disposed of a very talented young author whose writing style and charisma would attract a wide audience. It also meant that Wim could pick up his old profession as a journalist, something that would not have been possible in Europe. Under the guidance of Fritsch, Wim was asked to help the German *Luftwaffe* heroes *Adolf Galland* and *Hans Ulrich Rudel* ("*Juan Ulrico Rudel*") with their memoires. Within three years (1949-1952), 3 autobiographical works of Rudel appeared: *Trotzdem, Mein Dank an Argentinien* and *Es geht um das Reich.* They all became instant bestsellers. This collaboration and friendship with Rudel would open many doors to Wim.[140] Rudel's works were published at Dürer Verlag (Buenos Aires) between 1949-1952. Wim Sassens (Willem Sluyse) published at this editor own work 'Die Jünger und die Dirnen' in 1954.

Wim became a popular member of the Flemish and German expat communities. In 1950, he ran into his old colleague from the ministry of propaganda *Wilfred von Oven*. The former secretary of Josef Goebbels lived at the suburb of Bellavista, Buenos Aires. Like Wim, von Oven was a former *Kriegsberichter* and still maintained strong ties with the German press. Under the alias *Willy Oehm*, he had continued his profession as a journalist for the Frankfurter *Allgemeine Zeitung* and had maintained contact with *Der Spiegel* editor *Rudolf Augstein*. Two years later, von Oven became editor-in-chief of *Die Freie Presse* (1952) and *La Plata Ruf* (1967), to which Wim also contributed.

Wim Sassen was doing well. After four years of his arrival in Argentina, he could afford a luxurious wedding abroad. On 16 May 1952, he married in the Mexican state Civil de Tlaquiltenango, Morelos with Miep van der Voort. Five years earlier, on 9 January 1947, (Maastricht, The Netherlands) he officially divorced Paula Fisette. Miep had, in the meantime, divorced Haremaker.[141]

In September 1952, Wim approached the Dutch embassy in Argentina for the first time. He wanted to know whether he could still apply for a Dutch passport. When the embassy verified his whereabouts in the province of Córdoba they discovered that Sassen was known to the local police as a certain "*señor Hendriks*". The request was denied, he was still a wanted war criminal, but no extradition treaty existed between the Netherlands and Argentina concerning political delinquents.[142]

On 25 August 1954, Wim finally received his Argentinean residence permit. His *cedula de identidad* (identity paper) was issued by the police in Córdoba under no: 384917: *Guillermo Antonio Maria Sassen*, married to *Maria Juana Gerharda van der Voort de Sas-*

sen. By profession director of theatre, living at *Manuela Pedraza 2390, Nuñez*, a suburb of Buenos Aires.[143]

Next to his work for the German publisher Dürer Wim performed all sorts of jobs, between 1950 - 1955. The German investigative journalist *Gaby Weber* stated in *La Conexión Alemana*, that Wim also acted as a chauffeur for his friend, the Siemens- and Mercedes representative Hans Ulrich Rudel. The German paper *Die Zeit* claimed that former sabotage expert Otto Skorzeny and Wim acted as advisors for the Argentinean president *Juan Domingo Perón* and his wife *Evita*. Stan Lauryssens described him as a translator and a ghost-writer, the owner of an export and import company, representative in Argentina of the Austrian factory of agricultural machines *Büssing SA*, and salesman of renovated refrigerators and washing machines.[144]

When the Dutch *Prince Bernhard zur Lippe Biesterfeld* paid a visit to Argentina in 1951, Wim acted as press officer for Evita Perón. Coincidentally (or not?) Wim became the official translator and guide during Prince Bernhard's visit, which formed part of the Latin American tour, the so-called *Good Will* mission. It was a business tour in which the Prince, as ambassador *extraordinaire et plénipotentiaire*, represented Dutch firms that wanted to do business with this emerging Latin American power. All was set upon fixing contracts for *Philips SA*, *Werkspoor NV* (Railways) and *Fokker*. The path was lubricated with bribes, titles and honours. Business wise the trip was a great success.[145]

Prince Bernhard's interest also went out to the exhibition of Argentina's first jetfighter *Pulqui II*. Not only the prince was a keen pilot but also had taken along his best friend the Fokker test pilot *Gerben Sondermann* on this business trip. When he was introduced to the principal inventor of the *Argentinean Instituto Aerotecnico Córdoba*, he saw a familiar face. It was the former and famous German technical director of the *Focke Wulf Flugzeugbau Kurt W. Tank*, who managed with a great number of technicians and WWII Aces to build this super jet. When Bernhard asked for a demonstration of the plane, Kurt Tank apparently said: "*Yo no hago demostración delante de Alemanes traidores*", I do not perform any demonstration to German traitors. In his eyes the Prince as a former member of the *Reiter SS*, had betrayed Nazi Germany by joining the Allied forces during the war.[146]

A more seedy side of this tour concerned the discussion of weapon supply with Evita Peron. In *The return of Evita Perón* (1980), the author *V.S. Naipaul* revealed: "*[i]ndeed, through mediation of Prince Bernhard of the Netherlands, she bought 5.000 automatic pistols and 1.500 machineguns... which were distributed to the police...*"

Was this the beginning of Wim's career in arms, or just a coincidence?

Wim resumes his journalistic career

Wim was a journalist to the core. Despite being prohibited from performing his profession in the Netherlands, he was free to do so in his new home country. Up to 1953 Wim ran a one-man press agency by the name of *Prometheus*. He took care of the photography himself and published a number of articles under several aliases (*Steven Wiel, Estéban Rueda, Juan del Rio and Guillermo Sassen*). "*Willy*", as he was known to friends, wrote about life in the Nazi colony in Argentina and passed these articles on to *Latin*, the Latin American correspondent of *Reuters*. In his free time he performed on the stage of the *Deutsche Theatre* of Ludwig Ney (*Ney Bühne*). Wim enjoyed his reputation as a journalist, ghost-writer and actor.

Prometheus was located at 374 Avenida Córdoba, Buenos Aires. The same building offered offices to *Compania Argentina para Proyectos y Realizaciones Industriales* (CAPRI) for which Wim Sassen worked before. Former *SS Hauptsturmführer Horst Fuldner*, the founder of CAPRI in 1950, recruited only well known Nazis as his employees like the former *Reichskommissar für die Preisbildung Hans Fischböck*, the former chef of Hitlers bodyguards *Wilhelm Möhnke* and *Adolf Eichmann*. The rent of Wim Sassens office was paid by CAPRI SA, until the company went bankrupt in 1953.[147]

The following year, Wim published his first autobiographical essay *Die Jünger und die Dirnen* under his alias "Willem Sluysse", at Dürer Verlag. His work was well received within the Nazi community. In 1955, he lived in the suburb Florida, 2755 calle Libertad. At this address, his third daughter *Francisca* (30-05-1955) was born. That year his ultimate wish to become a renowned international journalist came true.

On 16 September 1955, a putsch took place to dispose of Juan Perón. The *Revolución Libertadora* was taking place. One of the participants of the putsch was Wim's acquaintance from Córdoba, General *Eduardo Lonardi*. with whom Wim was acquaintances. The General was involved in the coup of the commander of the Argentinean forces *José Domingo Molina Gómez* against the presiding president. During this revolution, Wim managed to interview both Perón and his adversary Gómez. Perón ended up capitulating and fled with the help of Ludwig Freude to neighbouring Paraguay. Wim sold the interviews to the American magazine *Time-Life;* his articles made it to the international headlines. From that moment onwards, Wim Sassen became the correspondent for *Time-Life* from Buenos Aires.

Adolf Eichmann

It did not take long before Wim met Adolf Eichmann in the German clubs of Buenos Aires. Wim was introduced to Eichmann by Eberhard Fritsch. Eichmann liked the idea to become famous like Rudel as a prominent member of the Nazi party. He most definitely had a story to tell the world. A horrifying account.

Contrary to what has been claimed in many publications on the subject, the whereabouts of Eichmann were well known within the German expat community. Across clubs in the capital, he would regularly meet with other Nazis like Rudel, Skorzeny and *Holocaust* colleague *Erich Rajakowitsch.* Around this time, Eichmann lived in the quarter of Olivos, BA. Like Wim, Eichmann supported himself financially through all sorts of jobs. He worked for CAPRI, in a laundry and textile shop, as logistic manager of a plumbing business, and through Josef Mengele's friend *Robert Mertig,* as a heating specialist at the company *Geisers Orbis* (1957).[148]

Since 1952, the German Secret Service (*Bundesnachrichtendienst* :BND) was fully aware of Eichmann's stay in Argentina. The Service was alerted to it by Informant no. 35, who reported it to the main quarters at Pullach (Munich), the head office of *Reinhard Gehlen*. According to the Informant's briefing, Eichmann lived there under the alias of "Ricardo Klement".[149] The BND was also keeping an eye on Wim Sassen, whose exact address in BA was known to them. German dispatches of the embassy in Buenos Aires revealed that Wim was being investigated because of his refusal to pay his alimony fees. He apparently fathered a child with a woman in the German city of Oldenburg. According to the author *Bettina Stangneth,* Wim was close friends with the German ambassador *Werner Junker.* Junker was fully aware of the safe haven Argentina offered to alleged war criminals. As a matter of fact, Junker maintained close contact with neo-Nazi circles in the capital.[150]

Every Sunday between 1956 and 1957, Eichmann and Wim would meet at Wim's residence in the suburb of Florida, 2755 Calle Libertad, Buenos Aires. Adolf Eichmann would sit down. The audio-recorder was switched on, and Eichmann would talk about his role as the logistical organiser of the Final Solution.

Both Wim as Eichmann started to collect additional information on the *Endlösung*: the Holocaust of the Jews. The plan was to record Eichmann's experience on audio-tape. The recordings were to be supplemented with Eichmann's notes, reference work and interviews of former SS involved in the *Endlösung*. Through this, an authentic account was reconstructed by someone who played a central role within the *Final Solution*. It was to be a bestseller. This account would definitely stir things up and make them instantly famous. In an interview with the Dutch paper *De Volkskrant (17 10*

1960), Wim was asked about Eichmann: "*When I discovered his true identity, his case started to interest me. And I tried to find out whether he wanted to clear his conscience or whether there were other motives. I considered it my duty as a professional reporter to clarify this shocking and bloody history of the murder of Jews during the war. I thought that through Eichmann's detailed accounts of the events, I had to shed light on this dark and horrifying part of history. The Germans, as well as the Jews, and indeed mankind, were entitled to this clarification.*"

Friends and members of the Nazi expat community wanted to hear in person the horrors of the Holocaust and would sit in at these sessions. Over the years many attended, among which the twin daughters of Captain Schneider; a friend and business partner of the Dutch war criminal *Abraham Kipp*; the former Luftwaffe pilot *Dieter Menge;* and the South America representative of the chemical concern *Bayer*, a certain *Löns*. Eichmanns stay in Argentina was most definitely no secret.[151]

Interest for the Eichmann recordings was even sparked from the Netherlands, from no other than Wim Sassen's loyal friend Anthony Mertens. The contact between Wim and Mertens was never lost. Whether Wim had informed Mertens of his collaboration with Eichmann is unknown. Mertens declared later that he was informed of Eichmann's whereabouts in Argentina at the beginning of 1956. This information came from the former *Sicherheits* officer *SS Sturmbahnführer Dr. Wilhelm Höttl* in Alt Aussee, Austria.

Mertens soon came up with a cunning and daring plan. Höttl joined him in *Operation Hitchcock*. Mertens and

Höttl approached the famous suspense film director *Alfred Hitchcock* and suggested a new theme for a movie to him; "The hunt for Adolf Eichmann". With the revenues, they would finance the true hunt of Eichmann and once caught bring him to justice. Hitchcock declined the offer.

That same year Wim contacted the correspondent of *Time-Life Phil Payne* in Buenos Aires to talk about an important manuscript. Wim revealed little about the story but did let him know it would be a most unique story. Payne wasn't interested. He did however inform the CIA that Eichmann was in Argentina.[152]

It did not stop there. According to journalist Gaby Weber, Eberhard Fritsch contacted the BND in 1956, and showed the BND copies of the Wim's manuscript. His intention was to sell the very controversial testimony of the Holocaust to the highest bidder.

From 1957 Adolf Eichmann was working for *Mercedes Benz*. Together with Wim, Eichmann wanted to import old Mercedes cars into Argentina, *where* they would fix them up in the Mercedes factory and sell them on with a big profit.

On his European tour in 1959 and 1960, Wim had tried to become a correspondent for a number of Flemish dailies. The year before (1958) he had helped out the Flemish reporter *Louis De Lentdecker* with arranging an interview with the Argentinean president *Arturo Frondizi*. De Lentdecker wrote an article for the Belgian Daily *De Standaard* on the Flemish who had emigrated to Argentina. He had met this 42 year old Wim Sassen while interviewing former Flemish fascists and nationalists for his column "Argentijns prentenboek voor Vlaanderen" (Argentina picture book for Flanders): *"Sassen claimed to be more Flemish than Dutch. I thought of him a typical public announcer. Everywhere were people gathered he held speeches. He always had the last word, was very jovial and clever, a certified actor and an intelligent man, but nevertheless a wee bit of a dreamer."*[153]

Nevertheless De Lentdecker was full of praise for this Dutch-Flemish man: *"I have to tell you about Wim Sassen, although he is Dutch – It wasn't his fault - he belonged to the Flemish community in Buenos Aires. During the war as we know he worked in Belgium. When I tell you he had fought on the Eastern Front and worked for Radio Brussels we already know that he was, as a war correspondent, on the wrong side. One can write what one wants but Wim must be regarded as one of the good guys. So Wim went to prison, to his own indignation as a Jew from Amsterdam. This was why he escaped from prison and fled to the Argentina, where he translated Shakespeare and other important works into Spanish, and even performed them on stage. He has learned the Argentineans big spectator theatre and open air theatre…Wim had been one of the best war correspondents during the war. Of course he isn't allowed to continue his career in The Netherlands and Belgium. However Sassen is now a well paid editor of Time-Life . He was the first to interview both Perón as Frondizi with accompanying pictures. Using an alias, he even managed to make a documentary for a Dutch broadcaster. Sassen used his Flemish accent and nobody in the Netherlands ever found out."*[154]

Both Anthony Mertens and Louis de Lentdecker put in a good word for Wim with the Flemish dailies. Wim Sassen even used his recommendation letter of the chef de bureau of Time-Life when he was recommended for his excellent documentary of the *Revolución Libertadora*. The editors of the Flemish daily *De Standaard*, however, turned Wim down. In Belgium they still remembered him for his pro-German activities during the war. Louis de Lentdecker then tried a recently created new daily called *Zondagmorgen*. In two of his articles, he tried to put in a good word for Wim Sassen, stating he wasn't such a bad collaborator after all.[155]

In 1959, Wim went to West-Germany (Federal Republic of Germany) for two reasons. First of all, his mother *Johanna Sassen van Bavel* had passed away on 28 April 1959 in Munich. Secondly, he wanted to see whether the import business would be viable. He stayed with his sister Francisca in Munich, and her new husband. Sister "Franzl", as she was known, had done well. After the war she married *Graf von Tauffkirchen*.

On his European tour, Wim travelled as "Sassen van Elsloo", a reporter for several international newspaper agencies, among which the German Newspaper *Der Stern* and *Bildzeitung*. Wim knew *Henri Nannen*, the founder of the German paper *Der Stern,* personally. *Nannen*, like Wim, had been a *Kriegsberichte*r, and like Wim he was an active member of the *Aktivpropaganda*. Wim had been a member of *Skorpion West*, and Nannen of *Skorpion Süd* (Italy). Wim had never abandoned his faith in the National Socialist ideology. He still wrote articles for European neo-Nazi magazines like *Reichsruf* and *Nation Europa*. On top of that, Nannen worked under his cover name *"Nebel"* for the German BND. An intelligence service for which Wim would offer his services too.[156]

Working for Secret Services

Wim's visit to his family in West Germany, Munich, was controversial. The headquarters of the BND Pullach was nearby Munich. It is well known that its chef Reinhard Gehlen (and his successor) recruited former SS, SD and other prominent Nazi party members. Rudel and Klaus Barbie belonged to the group of agents and informants who were recruited and stationed abroad. It was through this old school Nazi network that Eichmann's whereabouts had been "discovered". The question is, had Wim Sassen also been recruited by then?

Investigative journalist Gaby Weber seriously questioned this case in a radio documentary on Deutschlandfunk (4 March 2011): *The Abduction Legend or how Eichmann came to Jerusalem*: "*Sassen is thought to be playing both sides of the fence. He is suspected of working both for "Gehlen" and for the Americans. Up to this time he has no official passport. He claims that he is working for a German organization about which he could say nothing. It is led by a prominent German General whose name begins with G(ehlen). He has recently (1959) been in East Germany. In contrast to an earlier period Sassen has ample funds. Although the Netherlands only took his name off the wanted list 1969, Sassen received a West German passport in January 1959. Why? - the Foreign Office later wanted to clarify this. But the BND would not give out this information, only replying laconically: We have no knowledge here on the question of the nationality of Sassen.*" To this day, Weber is trying find out what part Wim Sassen had within the BND and CIA. The answer so far is a wall of silence.[157]

It is a fact, however, that Wim Sassen received German citizenship. It is common knowledge that many foreign volunteers like Wim lost their Dutch citizenship after joining the SS in 1941. His passport was issued on 4 July 1960, in Grosse Kreisstadt Konstanz (Baden Württemberg) in the name of "Willem Antonius Mario Sassen van Elsloo", no.: NB 3404153, by profession reporter-photographer, residing in Munich.[158]

Eichmann "abducted" by the Mossad?

A year later, to be more precise, on 11 May 1960, Adolf Eichmann was abducted by the Israeli Secret Service *Mossad* and taken to Israel. Some days after, Wim appeared in the agency of *Time-Life* in Buenos Aires and asked to speak to the new correspondent *Piero Saporiti*. Wim Sassen claimed for the second time (first time with Phil Payne) to be the spokesman of the Eichmann family. They were desperate to find out where Adolf was. Wim offered to sell the manuscript at the highest price. With this money, his possible kidnappers could be paid off. The events, however, took their own course.

[De Volkskrant, 17-12-1960] "Saporiti telegraphed New York and some hours later two chief editors of Time-Life headed for Buenos Aires. They arrived on 5 June, and were received by Sassen and Saporiti. They immediately went to Sassen's home, where Vera Eichmann, who had gone into hiding (with her three sons) would join them. She soon arrived with her oldest son Klaus. When Saporiti entered the hallway, he tripped over a big leather bag in which the manuscript was hidden. They all came to an agreement and the manuscript was put safely in a bank in the capital. It took a week to copy all the documents.

The copies were sent to New York, and the original stayed in the bank. How much they paid for it? The money was paid to the family, which in their turn gave Sassen his share. Subsequently, Sassen left for a short visit to West Germany. [159]

The official story is that the Mossad abducted Eichmann, although investigative journalist Gaby Weber disputes this account in her documentary on Adolf Eichmann called *Disinformation – The wanted historical lie of Mossad*: "*At the time of his arrest, Adolf Eichmann had Israeli citizenship and there was no "heroic kidnapping" by the Mossad, but a legal extradition by Argentinean officials in May 1960.*" Nevertheless Eichmann stood trial. In the proceedings that followed, Eichmann's handwritten comments were used as evidence: "*Eichmann made use of a number of notes that had been recorded and pieced together by Wim Sassen; it remains unclear how the prosecutor came in the possession of these and other notes, it was all accepted by the criminal court, although Sassen's statement was not. The interview first appeared in a shortened version in Der Stern in July 1960, then as a series on 28 November and 2 December in Time-Life. But Sassen had already offered the story, apparently with approval of Eichmann, some four years before to a Time-Life correspondent in Buenos Aires, and even if it was true that the name of Eichmann wasn't revealed, the contents of the manuscript would however indicate it was a first-hand (eyewitness) testimony.*"[160]

In June 1960 Wim was in Hamburg,[161] where he visited his old friend Henri Nannen. In his bag he carried a scoop. The courtage received by *Time-Life* magazine wasn't enough. Wim once again offered the Eichmann memoires to *Der Spiegel* and *Stern*. Nannen ended up buying them for 30.000 *Deutschmark*. On 4 July 1960, two months after Eichmann's disappearance, a docu of Eichmann's life in the Argentina appeared in *Der Stern*. The author was a certain "Van Elsloo", Latin American correspondent; none other than Wim Sassen himself. Eichmann's lawyer *Dr. Robert Servatius* wanted Wim to testify. Servatius was convinced that some statements recorded on tape were made under the influence of strong liquor and in answer to provoking questions: "*I can prove that Sassen turned these conversations to his own hand in order to make it a more marketable book. He called for two witnesses to confirm this: Sassen himself who lived in the Argentina, and a witness whose name was Fritsch/ Fritz, his first name unknown, who lived in Austria.*"[162]

Wim was never made to testify. Strangely enough, however, the Sassen tapes were admitted as evidence. Servatius "*Sassen was our key witness, he knew everything. And the strange thing was that Eichmann never wanted to talk to me about Sassen. Every time I spoke of him he just waived it away. Very strange. According to me it went like this: They sat down at the table. Sassen lured Eichmann with the prospects of making a fortune out of the sales of his memoires. Then under the influence of alcohol he let him speak. Sassen seemed, I got that impression when I met him in Salzburg, a very unreliable person. A man who lived off international espionage and political intrigues.*"[163]

The editors of the Dutch daily *Het Vrije Volk* contacted Wim in November 1960. On the phone Wim told them: "*They took my Dutch citizenship. I was a stateless person. At this moment I have the German nationality. In my heart I am still a Dutch man.*" The editor asked whether Wim had any contact with Adolf

Eichmann after his arrest. Wim confirmed and ended the interview with: *"I wrote about Eichmann. I cannot tell you more"*. In November 1960, he sent a telex to *Het Vrije Volk* asking for a rectification. He was never an SS agent: *"Absolute nonsense. I was a volunteer and a war correspondent at the Eastern Front; never a member of the Dutch SS or party. I am too much of a non-conformist, please some objectivity."*

Was Wim recruited by the Mossad?
Isser Harel, the Eichmann specialist of the Israeli Secret Service, took his residence in the Claridge Hotel on the Calle Tucumán, Buenos Aires. In this hotel (according to eye-witness accounts collected by Stan Lauryssens) they had met on a daily basis before 11 May 1960. The "hunt" for Eichmann had entered its last phase. [164]

Wim Sassen kept a very low profile after the Eichmann publication in *Time-Life*. The story and Eichmann's trial negatively impacted upon Wim. Within the German community rumours went round. His possible involvement in the disappearance of Eichmann had cost him his credibility. Did he rat on Eichmann?

Some newspapers implied his involvement: *"Sassen would benefit financially with the conviction of Eichmann. This is why he betrayed the exact location of Eichmann to the Israeli Secret Service."*[165]

According to *Ian Black* and *Benny Morris*, Sassen was recruited by the Mossad in early spring 1962: *"'Zvi Aharoni was given authorization to hunt for Josef Mengele. He set up headquarters in Paris, where he stayed until*

1964. In the spring of 1962, after several visits to Paraguay, Aharoni believed he was finally on Mengele's tail. The breakthrough came from an informer, a former SS officer called Willem Sassen, who had interviewed Eichmann before his abduction, and Sassen became convinced that everything the Jews said about the holocaust was true and that German Honour had been sullied. Sassen was approached in Uruguay Aharoni paid him 5.000 Dollar a month for his intelligence. Sassen led the Mossad agent to a farm outside Sao Paolo."[166]

Wim's role as an informer was corroborated by *Gerald L. Posner* and *John War* in *The Complete Story*. They submit that Willem Sassen had indeed been approached by the *Mossad* in the year his father died, to track down *Josef Mengele*. The authors opined it wasn't the first time that they had met. Sassen had always been the man behind the scenes. He must have known about the Israeli intention to get Eichmann to Jerusalem.[167]

Within his own circles, Wim was considered to be playing on both sides. In the extreme right French magazine *Notre Europe* Wim Sassen was claimed to be a secret agent of the "enemy", whose goal it was to cause division within the neo-National Socialist movement in the Argentina. Even in the expat Flemish nationalist circles there was a deep distrust. In correspondence between Flemish nationalist *Roeland Raes* and former Belgian collaborator *Leo Poppe*, the latter stood up for Wim. Poppe stated that Wim was a family friend of the Eichmann's. Wim Sassen, apparently, had not sold all the tapes to *Time-Life*. With the proceedings of the other tapes, the Eichmann family would pay for the legal fees of the court case. In the year 1963 when Wim's daughter *Godelieve* became Miss Holland, things would change for good.¹⁶⁸

In the Service of Merex
In 1963 the former SS and then BND agent *Gerhard Georg Mertins* and Otto Skorzeny founded the weapon distribution firm *Merex AG/ Deutsche Merex Gesellschaft mbH* in Heisterbacherrott (Königswinter) nearby Bonn, Germany. *Merex* was a widespread organisation with auxiliary branches in Spain, Switzerland and the rest of the world. It focussed its business on international arms trade. Better said: Merex used covers (import and export firms) to trade with those countries that were under a UN weapon embargo. Under guidance of the BND, Merex was used in specialized illegal transactions of surplus *Bundeswehr* (German Army) military hardware that were then distributed to conflict areas.¹⁶⁹

Skorzeny operated from Madrid. His international "construction firm" delivered weaponry to African warzones (Biafra war). Latin America was another very lucrative continent to do business. Several auxiliary firms under the name *Estrella* (Star) were established. Estrella's main office was situated in La Paz, Bolivia. It was run by Klaus Barbie.

From Germany, the organisation was supported by Hans Ulrich Rudel. In 1953, he had returned to West Germany. He immediately set of to organize a strong political influential network that was heavily supported by the German industry. His contacts in Latin America opened many doors. As a man of reputation, he represented in a great number of German companies in Latin

America, among which *Siemens*. Rudel did not forget his ghost writer Wim Sassen. According to former Leo Poppe, Wim Sassen represented Rudel's business in the Argentina. A number of major German firms took part in the hydroelectric works, petro chemical business, and electronic development of the Argentina. The most famous was the construction of the hydro-electric power plant Yacyretá by the German firm *Lahmeyer International* in collaboration with Carlos Fuldner (CAPRI). One of their Latin American business-partners was dr. Josef Mengele. Rudel and Mengele represented the Bayern firm *Mengele*, which exported agricultural machines to Latin America.[170]

Arms trade

From his German homefront, Rudel maintained secret close contact with international neo-Nazi organisations and the German Secret Service. It was Rudel who pointed out Wim Sassen to BND agent Mertins for his outstanding qualities and loyalty. Not soon after, Wim was recruited as Merex-representative for the Argentina. This is confirmed by the released documents on Wim Sassen under the *Nazi War crimes Disclosure Act* (2000-2006). A report of 12 January 1967 (Fritz Schwend 0146) revealed: "*Hans Ulrich Rudel has developed numerous contacts in the local military communities during his foreign residence. Rudel was instrumental in introducing former WWII Staff colonel Walter Drück to a variety of governments and military officials during Drück's Latin American tour (July-August 1966). He also led Drück to other expatriate Germans who have been living in Latin America since WWII, individuals who have developed contacts and who might be able to assist Merex in its scheme to push the sale of surplus military hardware there.* According to the report of the USA Field Support Group dated 6th of January 1967: "*Schwend maintained close contacts with the Intelligence Services of both Peru and Bolivia. As a cover for his intelligence activities, Fritz (Frederico) Schwend reportedly operated a Volkswagen repair facility in Lima. The two offers (Drück and Schwend) claimed to have excellent connections not only to the Peruvian military procurement authorities but also to the military establishments of Argentina and Chile. During December 1966, Rudel undertook a trip through various Latin American countries on behalf of Merex. In Argentina, Rudel introduced Drück to Sassen van Elsloo. Merex has also been in contact with Otto Skorzeny, another famous WWII figure, for the past several years regarding the arms business. Skorzeny resides in Madrid but claims to have excellent contacts in the general staff of Peru. It has also been revealed that Skorzeny has been involved with Rudel in the scheme to exploit sulphur deposits in a remote area of Bolivia.(see Alfons Sassen too). Walter Drück was debriefed by officials of the BND headquarters upon his return from Latin America. the BND officials were very interested in Drück's contact with Rudel and other expatriate Germans presently residing in Latin America.*"[171]

Together with Friedrich Schwend, Wim represented the Merex concern in Latin America: "*On 16 January 1967. The activities of Friedrich Schwend in Latin America and his reported affiliation with the intelligence services of Peru and Bolivia, and his involvement with Merex AG (owner Gerhard Georg Mertins), representatives in dealings in West German surplus munitions, was discussed."* In that same report a certain Wim Sassen van Elsloo was mentioned as a former German SS officer who had then been living in Argentina for some 18 years and who had become partner in the firm *Technicum, S.A.,* 383 Piedras, Buenos Aires, a firm appointed by Merex, where he represented their (Merex) interest in Argentina.[172]

Their meeting point is Madrid. In the Spanish capital. all Merex representatives gather: Wim for the Argentina, Klaus Barbie for Bolivia, Friedrich Schwend for Peru and Walter Rauff for Chile. They were the Latin American branch. Wim's younger brother Alfons soon joined the organisation, for Ecuador. BND chef Reinhard Gehlen would also (secretly) attend these encounters in the Madrilenian restaurant *Edelweiss.* [173]

Madrid was the operational base of Otto Skorzeny. From there, he coordinated his contacts with neo-fascist organisations and cover businesses. It was the centre where like-minded Nazi diehards had formed themselves into an international fanatic anti-communist brigade. On 29 May 1951, the *Times* correspondent *C.L. Sulzberger* already pointed out the existence of a group known as the *Fascist International:* *"They revived the Fascist International, and were functioning in various countries stretching from Malmö (Sweden) to Tanger (Morocco), and from Rome (Italy) to Buenos Aires (Argentina)."* On 6 May 1956, the Washington Post identified its members: *"Observers in Bonn saw an increasing activity of former Nazis who travel between Germany and the main centre of the Fascist International: Spain, Sweden, Switzerland, Egypt and the Argentina. In many cases they work for import and export firms, agencies and for German car manufacturers. Members include Johann von Leers, Otto Skorzeny, Hans Ulrich Rudel. Skorzeny and Rudel are assisted by SS colonel Eugen Dollmann, in running a smoothly operating underground organisation aiding war criminals to flee to Spain, Egypt and Argentina. Stille Hilfe, Helfende Hände, HIAG of the SS, the Stahlhelm, the union of German soldiers, Kameradenhilfe in Spain, and similar groups in Latin America were all under direction of colonel Hans Ulrich Rudel.*"[174]

All were known actors in Wim's play. Whether Wim already participated in these international groups in the 50s is unknown. He maintained a low profile about ten years after the Eichmann trial before he changed careers.

Leaving Argentina
The Eichmann affair placed a heavy burden on the Sassen family. It was so bad that Wim's daughter Saskia decided to leave the home at the age of sixteen. In an interview, she stated she wasn't happy at home in the suburb Florida, 2755 calle Libertad. She wasn't the only one. Her mother Miep wanted to return to Europe with her children. She contacted the Dutch embassy in 1961, asking for a Dutch passport. This was denied. Due to her marriage to Wim she also lost her Dutch citizenship. This, however, did not stop Saskia. She boarded a liner and after 23 days she arrived in Hamburg, Germany. From there she continued to The Netherlands.[175]

The Sassen family left the Argentina after the Eichmann trial. According to daughter Saskia, this was around 1963. Wim's activities during the nine years up until this point are difficult to reconstruct. He left for Paraguay and Uruguay. He rendered his services to Paraguayan dictator *Stroessner*, the CIA and Mossad, just like Skorzeny and Walter Rauff. Accordingly to Stan Lauryssens, Wim ended in Rome, Italy, where he ran a travel agency in the Via Falmina under the name Sassen van Elsloo. It could also very well be that Wim represented Merex in Rome.[176] When Wim decided to return to the Argentina in the 70s, Miep stayed behind. It is unknown for how long they were separated. In 1971, she filed for a divorce. By that time she had moved to the German city of Hamburg, 17 Hansastrasse.[177]

Back in Buenos Aires
On the basis of interviews with Wim Sassen by several different reporters, it can be concluded that he returned to Argentina in 1972. At that stage, Wim no longer feared sanctions from the German and Flemish expat community…though in Italy he claimed to have survived two assaults on his life (Stan Lauryssens).

Upon his return to Argentina, Wim put an end his journalistic career. The Argentinean journalist *Jorge Camarasa* stated Wim started a business relation with the Argentinean secret agent of the SIDE (*Secretaría de Informaciones del Estado*), *Antonio Domingo Mingolla*. He returned to his international arms trading profession on Latin American soil. According to the

German *Stern* journalist *Kai Hermann*, Wim was working for an Austrian firm: *"The office in the calle Córdoba 475 did not reveal anything to the public. The sign at the entrance mentioned something of import and export. Sassen was specialized in the area of import business. He imported weapons and is representative of the Austrian business chain Steyr Daimler Puch for Latin America."*[178]

Wim had a German passport with which he travelled to Spain, Germany and The Netherlands for business transactions and family visits. Wim could visit Europe unhindered. He had no reason to fear extradition to The Netherlands or Belgium. His crime was too old to prosecute. In 1972, he was interviewed by the Belgian journalist and television producer *Maurice de Wilde* together with the Flemish illustrator and caricaturist *André Delbaere*, while sipping a cocktail and wearing his swimming trunks. The subject of conversation was the return of Juan Domingo Perón into politics. Wim stated that the only option for the Argentina at the moment was Perón. During the interview, he emphasised that the balance between right and left was seriously endangered if Perón was not elected.[179]

The influence of Castro-ism and communism in Latin America was a real threat. A year after Perón's successful re-election he died. Evita II took over the reins for a short while, but then the country plummeted into a severe dictatorship under *Jorge Videla*. The *Dirty War* (1976-1983) had started. In 1975, the countries of the *Cono Sur* joined forces and *Operation Condor* was effected. The war on Marxists, exiled dissidents and other "leftist thugs" was opened. All of this meant business. Things could only get better for Wim.[180]

On his business tours in Europe, Wim would visit his sister Georgette and her partner *Louis Peeters* in Bruges, Belgium. A family friend who was present at one of these meetings described Wim as follows: "*Sassen is still a full-blown Nazi, a real Hitler-fanatic. This is the impression I got when I spoke him. While Peeters condemned Hitler's actions, Wim would shout at the top of his voice about the greatness of the Germans. His sister was quite amused. For them Sassen was first and foremost an artist, a great personality. They only knew him as a charmer.*"[181]

Wim's friend Anthony Mertens also lived in Bruges. According to Peeters: "*In the 60's and 70's, when he lived in Antwerp, Mertens led an agency that advocated the Apartheid regime in South Africa, which was financed by the South African regime! He travelled (to South Africa) many times accompanied by Leo Delwalde, who lived next door. Mertens used to be a member of the fascist movement Zwart Front, like him.*" Mertens was accordingly to Peeters had always remained loyal to his extreme right ideology. [182]

Valentine Mertens-Conijn, the wife of Anthony Mertens, never liked Wim's visits. She always believed that he had been implicated with the death of her brother Fritz, the executed resistance leader of Alkmaar. Officially, Mertens and wife Valentine had broken with Wim Sassen. In 1960, Valentine stated to the press that they had never seen him again: "*His wife (of Mertens) told us this morning: "We only saw Sassen in 1947 for three days. After his escape to Argentina we lost contact.*" According to Peeters, this was complete nonsense. "*Wim always contacted Mertens and his wife when he visited Belgium, and the telephone conversations were quite jovial.*" Peeters knew this because it happened many times in his presence!"[183]

In 1973, the 55 year old Wim married again in Buenos Aires. His new partner *Elsje Delbaere* came from the Flemish exile community. She was the daughter of the known Flemish illustrator André Delbaere.

Interactions with (former) Gestapo chef Klaus Barbie
Wim's encounter with Klaus Altmann Barbie was a result of their common representation of the Merex group and the Austrian arms manufacturer Steyr Daimler Puch. In 1966, Barbie was recruited by BND department 934 as an agent. Soon after, he was assigned assignment as representative of Steyr in Bolivia. When exactly the two met each other is unknown. Once they met, however, they became instant friends. Shortly afterwards Wim introduced Barbie to his younger brother Alfons and Barbie operated in the same field of expertise in Bolivia and Ecuador. As experts in counter espionage and domestic security they became advisors for local military juntas and police, their main task being the containment of leftist (communist/ pro-Castroist) movements and supporting the junta.[184]

In Buenos Aires, Wim worked with Antonio Domingo Mingolla. Mingolla had close ties with the Argentinean army, and through his contacts, had access to Argentinean defence material. Their business was to sell clandestinely surplus defence stocks to foreign countries via intermediaries or ghost firms. Through these cover firms the Bolivian colonels under *Luis García Meza* were provided with Steyr AUG machine guns. These guns were needed for the coming putsch against the democratically elected president *Lidia Gueiler* and her successor *Hernán Siles Zuazo*. The duo did not only sell handguns but also delivered armoured cars to the Bolivian juntas as well as to the private army of drugs baron Roberto Suárez, "el rey de la cocaína".[185]

In 1983, the quiet life of the Sassen brothers was abruptly disturbed when the arrest of Klaus Barbie made it to the international headlines. A year later German reporter Kai Hermann wrote a sequel of articles (6) for *Der Stern* magazine on Klaus Barbie, called "*Eine Killer Karriere*". Through these articles, Klaus Barbie's Latin American connection was exposed, and in particular his contacts with exiled Nazis, Secret Services, fascist mercenaries and even more importantly with the Sassen brothers. For the first time Wim Sassen's participation within the organised neo-Nazi groups, the international intelligence world and the illegal arms trade was brought to light. This time Wim was not only known for his role as Eichmann's ghost writer, but also as a man of intrigue who maintained close contact with a network of rightwing extremists and dictators. For his younger brother Alfons, the news came as a complete bombshell. Their family history was suddenly splashed out on the front pages of the international press: their collaboration during WWII, their escape to Latin America, their present profession in the cloak an dagger world of the illegal arms trade, and their role as military advisors to rightwing juntas, was completely exposed.

The revelations of Kai Hermann in *Der Stern* were confirmed by the declassified CIA documents dated 6

November 1987 (*Nazi War Crimes Disclosure Act*): "*J.) Djethart Jan Hendrik Cyriel Sassen, alias Willem Sassen, gave 200 FAL rifles, each worth USD 450, to Roberto Suarez Gomez, king of the cocaine trade traffickers in Beni Bolivia. These arms were used during the 17 July 1980 coup d'etat in which (Arce) Gomez and Luis (Garcia) Meza overthrew the civilian government of Herman (Siles) Suazo...*

L.) Djethart Sassen is in contact with the following persons: Frederico Schwend, *alias Wesceslao (Turi), counterfeiter (US Dollars and Pound Sterling); Ecuadorian army lieutenant Herbs (Chiribogas) in Quito; and (Mingolla) an official of the Argentina State Intelligence Secretariat in Buenos Aires...*"[186]

The Klaus Barbie trial and the articles of Kai Hermann sparked a renewed interest into the affairs of Sassen, even triggering an investigation into his person by the U.S. On 23 March 1984, the American ambassador in the Netherlands contacted the Dutch Ministry of Justice. The Americans did not understand why the Dutch authorities were not interested in prosecuting Wim Sassen as a war criminal. The Dutch answer was that the crimes committed were too old. According to the Dutch national prosecutor *De Beaufort*, the opportunity to try Wim for criminal offenses had expired in 1976.

Wim Sassen in peace

Wim Sassen made it to the headlines until the end of the century. The allegations of his war crimes and activities within international consortiums of dubious character pursued him. Even when he thought of retiring, his past once again caught up with him. His cousin *Roberto Sassen*, son of Alfons, was involved in an enormous corruption and arms deal scandal at the time of the *Cenepa War* (1995) between Peru and Ecuador. As Roberto Sassen's uncle, Wim was mentioned in connection with the international arms trade. Wim disappeared for the last time. He wanted to spend his remaining time quietly at his daughter's home in Santiago de Chile. In 2001 or 2002, (the exact date is still unknown) Wim passed away after a turbulent life, at the age of 84.

When interviewed, the well known sociologist and daughter of Wim's second marriage Saskia Koop Sassen van Elsloo, reveals little about her father. She referred to him as an adventurer with whom she was able to get along when she got older. In an interview with the Spanish daily *El País*, she described him in a romantic way, stating that within the Goebbels propaganda machine, Wim Sassen and fellow war reporters were just a loose band of uncontrolled young men. When she referred to her grandfather, Jan Sassen, she was equally imaginative, claiming he was a descendent of a mine-owning family. According to Saskia Jan became the mayor of the wonderful grand city of 's-Hertogenbosch...During the German invasion he personally prevented the town being bombarded. In exchange for his full cooperation the city was saved. She also stated that while granddad was mayor no Jew in his city was sent off to the extermination camps... After the war, however, her grandfather was sentenced to ten years in prison and her father Wim was sentenced in absentia by a Dutch court.[187] When Saskia is asked for more information on her father or family she remains silent. She never spoke of her father's role as a arms dealer, or of her uncle Alfons or other family members who fled to Latin America after the war.[188] According to the last interviews she gave, her father's past was a huge burden, and she considered herself a victim too. Francisca Sassen, the other daughter, when interviewed by *Bettina Stangneth* for her work *Eichmann in Argentina*, never revealed the date of Wim's death, and even though Saskia and Francisca helped Stangneth out with her research, little was in fact revealed on Wim Sassen.[189]

Even after his death, Wim remained in the picture. In 2005, a Dutch television documentary on *Willem Sassen: The biographer of Adolf Eichmann* by *Roelf van Tilt* was made. In 2010 *Raymond Ley* produced his theatre play *Eichmann's end, Love, Betrayal, Death*, in which the part of Willem Sassen was played by *Ulrich Tukur*. Both documentary and play represented a highly romantic and unverified story on Wim Sassen.

In March 2013 questions were raised in the German *Bundestag* about the relationship between the government, the BND and Adolf Eichmann. Apparently, since 1952, the German authorities knew of Eichmann's whereabouts in Argentina. The German political party *Fraktion Bündnis 90/ Grünen* asked to be informed about the contacts the German embassy in Buenos Aires had with former Nazis like Adolf Eichmann and Wim Sassen, and why Wim Sassen had become a German citizen while he was still an internationally wanted man. In 2014, Gaby Weber questioned the truth behind Eichmann's abduction by the Israeli in "*Disinformation, The wanted lie of the Mossad*". She investigated the early days of Zionism in Germany,

Eichmann´s role in that movement and the nature of his citizenship. Her conclusion is as follows at the time of his arrest, he had the Israeli citizenship and there was no "heroic kidnapping" by the Mossad, but a legal expulsion by Argentinean officials in May 1960. There is still much to be verified and investigated...[190]

Family picture of the Sassen family. Left to Right: Alfons, Maria, Wim, mother Johanna, father Jan, Francisca, Georgette, Johanna. Source: Historical Archive Brabant (Holland) BHIC: BHC001055063, id.: VEG1557, Sassen family, Veghel.

Picture of the Sassen's shop in Geertruidenberg up to 1940. (provided by journalist Paul De Schipper)

Wim Sassen as a Kriegsberichter (war reporter). Dutch National Archive: NL-HaNA, Justitie/CABR, 2.09.09, inv.nr: 87844.

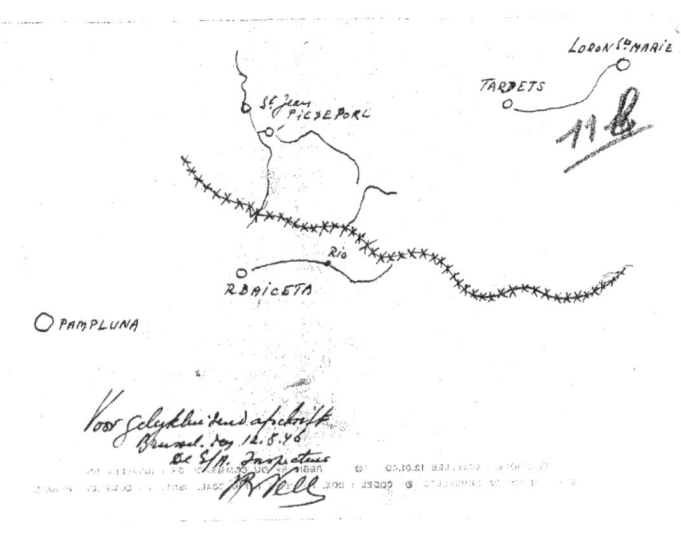

Escape route to Spain.

Kölnische Rundschau, 16 December 1960, Karl Breyer, part 1.

Kölnische Rundschau, 16 December 1960, Karl Breyer, part 2.

Wim Sassen in 1960. Dutch National Archive: NL-HaNA, Justitie/CABR, 2.09.09, inv.nr: 31614.

La Razón, 9 December 1960, Wim Sassen in an interview with Argentinean General Leonardi.

THE EDITORS OF  Vol. 30, No. 1 January 9, 1961

PRESENT A MAJOR HISTORICAL DOCUMENT

EICHMANN TELLS HIS OWN DAMNING STORY

On the following pages LIFE begins its publication of the confession of Adolf Eichmann, the Nazi who engineered the murder of millions of Jews—and who now awaits trial for his crime in Israel.

In this document, Eichmann convicts himself as one of the major Nazi war criminals. Yet he set it down in the belief that his version of the truth would go far to "explain" his actions and even to exonerate him. Several years ago in Argentina, where he had fled after eluding Allied agents and lived under a false name, he began telling the story to a German journalist, talking into a tape recorder for hours at a time. He had finished the account by last May when, in a dramatic cloak and dagger operation, Israeli intelligence agents found him, captured him and carried him off to Israel.

A month later, LIFE came into the possession of the huge transcript of Eichmann's words. After six months of translation, editing and research which confirmed the absolute authenticity of the document, LIFE is now able to present, in two instalments, Eichmann's own story of his work.

"I was merely a little cog in the machinery," Eichmann argues. Engaged in an effort that dwarfed the exterminations of Genghis Khan or Tamerlane, he preserved the mentality of a competent bookkeeper, eager to please his superiors. He tells how he himself worked out the timetables for the obliteration of Europe's Jewish population and how his men rounded up Jews and put them on the trains that led to the deathly sidings at Auschwitz and Maidanek or to the lime pits in Poland.

The question may be asked: why publish this account?

LIFE does not publish it simply as a reminder of the terrible slaughter of European Jewry. The self-told story of Adolf Eichmann is a major contribution to the history of a horrifyingly brutal era, and it has a bitter relevance in our own time. Eichmann gave over his conscience to a totalitarian state out of perverted patriotism and in return for the supposed solidarity and security that the state promised him. His deeds, of course, make him an extreme example. But among the Nazis, the Communists and other totalitarians, past and present, he could find a great deal of company: men who totally abdicate their individual sense of morality in favor of a set of instructions and directives.

The Eichmann story reveals how evil can be rationalized because it has been codified. It is not pleasant reading, but it stands as a warning to every member of the human family.

ADOLF EICHMANN

This man, now a prisoner in Israel, was head of the Gestapo's notorious office for "Jewish affairs." Given the job of rounding up the Jews whom Hitler had sworn to exterminate, Adolf Eichmann became a power in Nazi Germany and was the man more responsible perhaps than any other for carrying out the greatest, cruelest mass murder in history.

Time Life, Vol 30, no.1, January 9, 1961.

147

NAZI war criminal Willem Sassen, sentenced to death in Belgium after WWII for war crimes, being interviewed by a Buenos Aires television station.

Two more Nazi criminals discovered in Argentina

BUENOS AIRES: Two unrepentant Nazi war criminals were exposed by Argentine television yesterday, three weeks after the unmasking of a former SS officer involved in Italy's worst World War II massacre.

The two former Nazis sentenced to death for crimes during the German occupation of the Netherlands were tracked down by the Buenos Aires private television channel Telefe.

In a preview of the programme, correspondents were shown footage of the channel's interviews with former Dutch policeman Abraham Kipp and with Willem Sassen, a Belgian who ran a newspaper and a radio for the Nazis in the Netherlands.

The two were found about the time the US television network ABC unmasked Erich Priebke, a former SS captain who was living in the southern Andean resort of Bariloche and faces extradition to Italy on murder charges.

Priebke lived quietly in Argentina for decades before acknowledging publicly he had taken part in the Ardeatine Caves killing, in which 335 Italians were shot in retaliation for a bomb that killed 33 German soldiers in Rome in 1944.

Jewish groups say Kipp, 77, escaped from a Dutch prison after the war and made it to Argentina in 1949, the same year an Amsterdam court sentenced him to death in absentia on 23 counts of murder.

Telefe found the bespectacled, white-haired Kipp in a Buenos Aires suburb and interviewed him briefly while he stood behind a wrought-iron door.

"I don't want to talk about the past. It's all over," said the former Gestapo officer.

Sassen, on the other hand, was happy to talk to Telefe.

The programme's producer Lucia Suarez said the 76-year-old former propaganda officer had been sentenced to death in Belgium after the war but his extradition was apparently never requested.

Picture of interview by television reporter (Telefe) Lucia Suarez with Wim Sassen in 1994 published in *Brisbane Gazette* (Australia, June 1994, archive Stan Lauryssens).

DEPARTMENT OF THE ARMY Mr. Schnackenberg/mck/56159
OFFICE OF THE ASSISTANT CHIEF OF STAFF FOR INTELLIGENCE
WASHINGTON, D.C. 20310

ACSI-DFIRP

18 Feb 1967

MEMORANDUM FOR: DIRECTOR OF CENTRAL INTELLIGENCE
DEPUTY DIRECTOR, PLANS

ATTN: [ ]

SUBJECT: Klaus ALTMANN (U)

1. (S) Subject, whose true name is Klaus BARBIE, aka BECKER, BEHRENS, MERTENS, SPIER, HOLZER, BEHRENDIS, KREITZ, and MAYER, was born in Germany on 25 October 1913. Subject was a source of the 970th CIC Detachment and later the 66th CIC Detachment in Germany during the period 1946 until early 1951. During this period, he was considered to be a valuable source of information.

2. (S) In 1951, because of the French and German efforts to apprehend Subject, the 66th CIC Detachment resettled him in South America. Subject was documented in the name of Klaus ALTMANN and routed through Austria and Italy to Bolivia. Since that time, the Army has had no contact with Subject.

3. (S) In December 1966, a source of USAFSG reported that an individual named Klaus ALTMANN of the firm Standard Industrial (Bolivia), La Paz, was being used as a contact man in Bolivia by Merex A. G. ALTMANN is a close friend of Hans U. RUDEL, a former Luftwaffe ace. ALTMANN allegedly has a close relationship with a number of high-ranking Bolivian officers. The latest information from the USAFSG source indicates that ALTMANN is now representing Merex A. G. in Bolivia and that he is the owner of the firm Standard Industrial (Bolivia). An Alfonso Fernandez de Luis G. (sic) is reported to be a part owner of Subject's firm. Alfonso is a former Lieutenant colonel of the Bolivian Army and is an occasional instructor at the Bolivian Military Academy.

4. (C) It is requested that [ ] be queried for any available information on Subject. For purpose of identification, inclosed are photographs of Subject and his wife. The photographs are sixteen years old, but they were excellent likenesses at the time they were taken.

DECLASSIFIED AND RELEASED BY
CENTRAL INTELLIGENCE AGENCY
SOURCES METHODS EXEMPTION 3B2B
NAZI WAR CRIMES DISCLOSURE ACT
DATE 2000 2006

SECRET — EXCLUDED FROM AUTOMATIC REGRADING
DOD DIR 5200.10 DOES NOT APPLY

FOR COORDINATED WITH ___DOD___

Freedom of Information Act (Foia): Declassified Nazi War Crimes Disclosure Act (CIA files) on Barbie, Klaus, Vol 1_0033 ; Barbie, Rudel and Merex operations in Latin America.

DISPATCH	CLASSIFICATION SECRET	PROCESSING ACTION MARKED FOR INDEXING
TO: Chief		NO INDEXING REQUIRED
INFO: Chief		ONLY QUALIFIED DESK CAN JUDGE INDEXING
FROM: Chief, European Division		MICROFILM
SUBJECT: CATUSK UJVAULT - Headquarters Trace Reply		

Action: ☐ - See paragraphs 2 and 3
COS - See paragraph 2

Reference: EGMA-72853, 14 July 1969

1. There are no WOMACE or WOHIVE traces on Willem SASSEN van ELSLOO. FYI: CENTREG files indicate that one Wilhelm Antonius Maria SASSEN, aka Willy DE FONTEIJN, aka fnu BRUIN, aka fnu SKORPION, born 16 April 1918 in Geertruidenberg, was the subject of an interrogation in August 1945 at which time he furnished information about the propaganda organization of the Schutzstaffel (Nazi Black Guards - SS), the development of the Skopion (sic) Action and Aktif Propaganda, and a list of individuals connected with these organizations. SASSEN was a member of the Waffen SS, and in 1944, became a member of the Skorpion West, a section of SS Standarte Kurt Eggers which was the propaganda organ of most importance at that time. He attained the status of SS Oberscharfuehrer. After his interrogation, it was recommended that he be transferred to SS Camp Otterloo. In February 1946 the Netherlands Security Service requested any information pertaining to SASSEN's whereabouts, and further, instructed that he be arrested if located and turned over to them. CENTREG files show that he was last known to be in the custody of the British. Available records disclose no further information. This information is dated 14 October 1960; it is a trace reply to the AMCONGEN Stuttgart. We find no connection between SASSEN van ELSLOO and Frederico SCHWEND other than that noted in paragraph 4 of Reference.

2. FYI: The most recent information on SCHWEND is correspondence originating with CALLIKAK, but provided to RVROCK by LNERGO concerning a letter written by SCHWEND to Julius MADER. Pertinent to this exchange are other letters written to MADER, dated 1969, which may be the reason for CATUSK's renewed interest in SCHWEND's activities. The 1969 letters are discussed in EGBA-22333, 20 June 1969, et al. We believe that there may be a connection between the letter written by SCHWEND in 1966 and those recently acquired, written in 1969, and will discuss this possible

CROSS REFERENCE TO: DISPATCH SYMBOL AND NUMBER: EGMW-16386 DATE: 29 August 1969
CLASSIFICATION: SECRET   HQS FILE NUMBER: 32W-5-25/7

BEST AVAILABLE COPY

DECLASSIFIED AND RELEASED BY
CENTRAL INTELLIGENCE AGENCY
SOURCES METHODS EXEMPTION 3B2B
NAZI WAR CRIMES DISCLOSURE ACT
DATE 2001 2006

EXEMPTIONS Section 3(b)
(2)(A) Privacy ☐
(2)(B) Methods/Sources ☐
(2)(G) Foreign Relations ☐

COORDINATED WITH FBI, ARMY

NAZI WAR CRIMES DISCLOSURE ACT

Freedom of Information Act (Foia): Declassified Nazi War Crimes Disclosure Act (CIA files) on Schwend, Fritz_0116; Sassen and Friedrich Schwend.

```
                                        CL BY: [    ]
                                        CL REASON: 1.5(c)
                                        DECL ON: X1
                                        DRV FROM: HUM 4-82

++SECRET++RYBAT
WNINTEL RYBAT C   35710[  ]    89826      ASR    87-7157959              MI
D COMET  871211       [  ]89826C1287  156        7           UPID
    / /                       SECRET                FRP: , , , , , , ,
                                                     STAFF

ACTION: C/LA/APUB (881) INFO: DEFAULTI, DOMDS, LADORECORD, ODPD-D, RF,
FILE, C/EUR/ACS, C/EUR/BNL-3, C/EUR/CI, C/LA/CPB-2, C/LA/RB, C/LA/VCEP,
DC/LA/RB, C/EPO, C/INT/RR, C/LA/SO, C/SAS/CNG-5, (20/W)
---------------------------------------------------------------------
87 7157959    ASR           PAGE 001         IN 7157959
                        TOR: 111701Z DEC 87     [   ]9826
---------------------------------------------------------------------
S E C R E T 111622Z DEC 87 STAFF

CITE [       ] 89826

TO:  DIRECTOR INFO [       ]

WNINTEL RYBAT XLWAY VNDAGGER FGI TRACE

SUBJECT: ADDITIONAL INFORMATION ON AN ARMS MERCHANT IN
         [       ]

REFS: A.  DIRECTOR 743582
      B.  DIRECTOR 740616
      C.  [    ] 57754
      D.           88991
      E.           71935
      F.           88892

  1.  ACTION REQUESTED:  SEE PARA FOUR BELOW.

  2.  REFS PROVIDED INFORMATION ON WILLEM ((SASSEN)),
AN ARMS MERCHANT IN BUENOS AIRES OF INTEREST TO VNDAGGER
LIAISON, AND ON HIS BROTHER, ALPHONSO ((SASSEN)) WHO LIVES
IN QUITO.

  3.  [     ] PASSED THE [   ] THE FOLLOWING ADDITIONAL
INFO 6 NOVEMBER 1987 ON THE SASSEN BROTHERS:

    A.  WILLEM SASSEN HAS BEEN IDENTIFIED AS DJETHART JAN HENDRIK
CYRIEL ((SASSEN)), ALIAS JACK ((JENSEN)).  HE HAS ARGENTINE
IDENTITY DOCUMENT NUMBER 92437859 AND LIVES AT ALMIRANTE BETBEDER
1231, BOULONGE, PROVINCE OF BUENOS AIRES, ARGENTINA, TELEPHONE
NUMBER 747-0994.

    B.  SASSEN IS A DUTCH NATIONAL, PRESUMABLY BORN IN
MASSTRICHT, AND ALTHOUGH HE NEVER LIVED IN WEST GERMANY,
IT IS PROBABLE THAT HE HAS IN HIS POSSESSION A WEST GERMAN
DIPLOMATIC PASSPORT.

    C.  DURING THE SECOND WORLD WAR, SASSEN WAS AN SS OFFICER
IN THE NETHERLANDS AND WAS SENTENCED TO 20 YEARS IN PRISON
IN 1945.  IN THAT YEAR, HE ESCAPED FROM PRISON.

    D.  ON 24 MAY 1947, SASSEN TRAVELLED TO DUBLIN WITH A
PASSPORT PROVIDED BY PNWORLD IN THE NAME OF JACK ((JENSEN)).
```

**DECLASSIFIED AND RELEASED BY
CENTRAL INTELLIGENCE AGENCY
SOURCES METHODS EXEMPTION 3B2B
NAZI WAR CRIMES DISCLOSURE ACT
DATE 2001 2006**

EXEMPTIONS Section 3(b)
(2)(A) Privacy
(2)(B) Methods/Sources
(2)(G) Foreign Relations

Declassified and Approved for Release
by the Central Intelligence Agency
Date: 2001

NAZI WAR CRIMES DISCLOSURE ACT
SECRET

Freedom of Information Act (Foia): Declassified Nazi War Crimes Disclosure Act (CIA files) on Schwend, Fritz_0128; Wim Sassen, Alfons Sassen, F.Schwend in arms deals.

SECRET

E. ON 23 SEPTEMBER 1948, HE LEFT (EUROPE) ON THE SHIP "DE AELAAR" ACCOMPANIED BY HIS DUTCH WIFE, MIEPJE.

F. IN 1951, HE SERVED IN BUENOS AIRES AS AN INTERPRETER FOR THE THEN PRESIDENT OF ARGENTINA, JUAN DOMINGO ((PERON)) WHEN PERON MET WITH PRINCE BERNHARD OF THE NETHERLANDS DURING THE LATTER'S VISIT TO ARGENTINA.

G. SASSEN IS CURRENTLY MARRIED TO HIS SECOND WIFE WHO IS A BELGIAN NATIONAL AND THE COUPLE HAS A SMALL SON.

H. HE CURRENTLY IMPORTS ARMS THROUGH HIS COMPANY, "BUSY S.A." LOCATED AT AVENIDA CORDOBA 475, FIRST FLOOR, BUENOS AIRES, TELEPHONE NUMBER 311-7094 AND 311-2573, TELEX NUMBER "23648 SETBL". THE FIRM HAS THREE EMPLOYEES. SASSEN IS THE LEGAL REPRESENTATIVE FOR THE SOUTHERN CONE OF SOUTH AMERICA FOR THE AUSTRIAN ARMS MANUFACTURING COMPANY "STEYR-DAIMLER-PUCH."

I. HIS BROTHER, ALFONSO SASSEN, ALIAS "VAN AALST", HAS AN OFFICE LOCATED AT CALLE 9 DE OCTUBRE 520, QUITO, ECUADOR.

J. DJETHART JAN HENDRIK CYRIEL SASSEN, ALIAS WILLELM SASSEN, GAVE 200 FAL RIFLES, EACH WORTH USD 450, TO ROBERTO ((SUAREZ)) GOMEZ, KING OF THE COCAINE TRAFFICKERS IN BENI, BOLIVIA. THESE ARMS WERE USED DURING THE 17 JULY 1980 COUP D'ETAT IN WHICH COLONELS LUIS ((ARCE)) GOMEZ AND LUIS ((GARCIA)) MEZA OVERTHEW THE CIVILIAN GOVERNMENT OF HERNAN ((SILES)) SUAZAO.

K. SASSEN HAS A MERCEDES 300 SEC COUPE WITH CD (DIPLOMATIC CORPS) LICENSE PLATE 1857. ▢ ▢ COMMENT: THE ▢ ▢ REPORT DID NOT IDENTIFY THE EMBASSY TO WHICH THIS LICENSE PLATE IS ASSIGNED.

L. DJETHART SASSEN IS IN CONTACT WITH THE FOLLOWING PERSONS: FEDERICO ((SCHWIND)), ALIAS WENCESLAO ((TURI)), COUNTERFEITER (US DOLLARS AND POUND STERLING) WHO HAS TELEPHONE NUMBER 352-356 IN LIMA, PERU; ECUADOREAN ARMY LIEUTENANT HERBAS ((CHIRIBOGAS)) IN QUITO; AND (FNU) ((MINGOLLA)), AN OFFICIAL OF THE ARGENTINE STATE INTELLIGENCE SECRETARIAT (SIDE) IN BUENOS AIRES). (NO ▢ ▢ TRACES ON THESE PERSONS.)

4. PLS ADVISE IF SASSEN'S 201 FILE CONTAINS ANY INFORMATION CONCERNING THE ALLEGATION IN PARA THREE (D) ABOVE. ALSO REQUEST HQS TRACES ON THE PERSONS MENTIONED IN PARA THREE (L) ABOVE.

5. FILE: ▢ ▢ 004-005-025. DECL OADR DRV HUM 4-82. ALL SECRET. END OF MESSAGE   SECRET

SECRET

```
                                SECRET
                                                              CIDORECORD
   //                                         FRP:  ,2, . . . . .    INCOMING
                              PRIORITY        STAFF

ACTION: CI/CLFL (981) INFO: ODPD-D, RF, FILE, CIDORECORD, QA/FILE,
C/LA/RB, DC/LA/RB, LA/APUB-4, LA/OPS, NE/ISR-4, C/CI, CI/LA-2, DCNE/10,
EPO/LA, SA/ODDO,  (21/W)
------------------------------------------------------------------------
85 7551615   ASP              PAGE 001         IN 7551615
                          TOR: 112123Z JUN 85     29975
------------------------------------------------------------------------

S E C R E T 111841Z JUN 85 STAFF
CITE[    ]29975
TO:  PRIORITY DIRECTOR,[     ] INFO[     ]
WNINTEL TAZZA LWCATCH
SUBJECT:  REQUEST FOR INFORMATION ON POSSIBLE EX-S.S.
          OFFICER IN BUENOS AIRES

    1.  ACTION REQUESTED:  SEE PARAGRAPH THREE.

    2.  ON 11 JUNE, U.S. MARSHALL WHO IS IN SAO PAULO IN
CONNECTION WITH THE INVESTIGATION/EXAMINATION OF THE
ALLEGED REMAINS OF NAZI WAR CRIMINAL JOSEF MENGELE,
REPORTED THE FOLLOWING TO[    ] U.S. DEPARTMENT OF JUSTICE
OFFICIAL NEAL SHER, ALSO IN SAO PAULO, HAS BEEN ADVISING,
VIA TELEPHONE, THE ISRAELI PROSECUTOR (NFI, PRESUMABLY
THE ATTORNEY GENERAL) IN ISRAEL ON THE STATUS OF THE
INVESTIGATION.  THE ISRAELI PROSECUTOR, WITHOUT SOURCING
HIS INFORMATION, TOLD THE JUSTICE OFFICIAL THAT AN ALLEGED
EX-S.S. OFFICER CURRENTLY LIVING IN BUENOS AIRES WAS AT ONE
TIME IN CONTACT WITH WOLFGANG GERHARD, THE INDIVIDUAL WHOSE
IDENTITY MENGELE IS REPORTED TO HAVE ASSUMED SHORTLY BEFORE
HIS (MENGELE'S) DEATH.  IT IS NOT CLEAR WHETHER THIS EX-S.S.
OFFICER WAS IN CONTACT WITH GERHARD/MENGELE OR THE ACTUAL
GERHARD, WHO REPORTEDLY TRAVELLED TO GERMANY IN THE SEVENTIES
AND DIED THERE IN 1978.

    3.  ACTION REQUESTED:  THE U.S. MARSHALL HAS REQUESTED
TRACES ON THE ALLEGED EX-S.S. OFFICIAL:  WILLIAM (SASSEN))
(SPELLING PHONETIC), ADDRESS:  LOMAS DE SAN ISIDRO, LAS
LOMAS 563, BUENOS AIRES;  TELEPHONE:  747-0994 RPT 747-0994.
PER THE ISRAELI PROSECUTOR, SASSEN WAS CONVICTED IN
ABSENTIA IN THE NETHERLANDS AND WAS SOMEHOW INVOLVED WITH
THE ADOLF EICHMANN TRIAL.  REQUEST DIRECTOR AND[
    ]TRACES.  LIAISON MAY BE QUERIED.  IF POSSIBLE,
A CHECK OF THE [               ] WOULD BE
APPRECIATED.
    4.  FILE:  DEFER.  DECL OADR DRV HUM 4-82.  ALL SECRET.
END OF MESSAGE                  SECRET

                          DECLASSIFIED AND RELEASED BY
                          CENTRAL INTELLIGENCE AGENCY
FOR COORDINATION WITH  USMS   SOURCES METHODS EXEMPTION 3B2B
                          NAZI WAR CRIMES DISCLOSURE ACT
                          DATE  2000  2006

        RECORD COPY
                                                  11 Jun 85
                                                  201-994286
                                SECRET
```

Freedom of Information Act (Foia): Declassified Nazi War Crimes Disclosure Act (CIA files) on Mengele, Josef_0069; Josef Mengele, W. Sassen and the Mossad.

Eine Killer-Karriere

Klaus Barbie: Folterer für Hitler und Militärdiktatoren. Massenmörder in Lyon und La Paz. Agent von SS, CIA und BND

Eine Serie von Kai Hermann

Es war ein sonniger, kühler Vormittag im Juni 1982 – wie jeder Junivormittag in La Paz. Die Herren kamen gegen elf Uhr, wie immer. Ein Kellner rückte ihnen wie jedesmal die Stühle zurecht, im Ecktisch hinten rechts im Café La Paz. Ein kleiner, alter Mann wies den anderen mit sehr bestimmten Handbewegungen die Plätze zu. Er setzte sich so, daß er den Eingang im Blick behielt. Das runde, faltige Gesicht hatte von vorn beinahe etwas Gütig-Großväterliches. Im Profil wirkte es dann plötzlich ungeheuer brutal. Die Augen grünlich, immer irgendeinen Punkt angestrengt fixierend.

Der alte Mann war Klaus Barbie, der sich in Bolivien Klaus Altmann Hansen nannte. Neben ihm – ebenso klein, bucklig, Mestizengesicht, Nadelstreifenanzug – Barbies langjähriger Sekretär und Leibwächter Alvaro de Castro.

Dann noch am Tisch Dr. Emilio Carbone, mit affektierten Bewegungen und näselnder Stimme, wie immer nach Bonmots ringend – der Ideologe der italienischen und bolivianischen neofaschistischen Terroristen.

Und als Gast am Stammtisch ein Besucher aus Deutschland, ein Waffenhändler offenbar.

Klaus Barbie hatte einen »Spiegel« mitgebracht. Der 68jährige bekam jede Woche »Spiegel« und »Nationalzeitung« aus der Bundesrepublik. Im »Spiegel« stand etwas über Herpes. Man witzelte über eine Blase an Carbones Oberlippe. Barbie meinte, diese Krankheiten kämen von den Hippie-Mädchen: »Wenn ich diese verkommene Jugend in Deutschland sehe, wird mir immer ganz anders. Die haben überhaupt so viel Scheiße da in Deutschland und meinen noch, anderen Ländern Ratschläge geben zu müssen. Milliarden-Defizite. Die Deutschen sind blöd, daß sie sich das gefallen lassen. Der Strauß ist gut, das ist unser Mann. 80 Prozent der Bevölkerung sind anständig und wollen Arbeit. Aber die holen die immer mehr Türken...«

Der Ober brachte Koka-Tee. Ein älterer Mann ging durch das Café und grüßte auf deutsch hinüber. Barbie wartete, bis er außer Hörweite war, und sagte: »Ein Jude, ein guter. Der hat mir mal gesagt, wenn er kein Jude wäre, wäre er SS-Mann geworden.«

Der Mann war ein Geschäftsfreund. Barbie hatte einige geschäftliche Kontakte zu Juden. Er sagte: »Es gibt ordentliche Juden. Unter den israelischen Militärs. Das sind rassisch wahrscheinlich gar keine echten Juden. Manche hätten wirklich in unseren Haufen gepaßt.«

Dr. Carbone, den sich Barbie an seinem Stammtisch als eine Art Hofnarr hielt, sang: »Es war einmal ein schönes Judenmädchen...«

Ein anderer Italiener kam, grüßte herablassend. Pierluigi Pagliai, der sich Mario Bunomi nannte. Er war nach übereinstimmender Meinung seiner Freunde der härteste Killer und Folterer unter Barbies Mitarbeitern. Er gilt in Italien als der Hauptverantwortliche für das Bombenattentat von Bologna, bei dem vor vier Jahren 85 Menschen starben.

Barbie stand auf und sprach leise mit Pagliai. Der Italiener ging bald wieder. Barbie kam zum Tisch zurück. Man unterhielt sich über Freimaurer. Eigentlich redete nur Barbie. Er duldete allerdings Carbones verworrene Witzeleien. Barbies Geschichten wiederholten sich endlos. Er sprach an diesem Vormittag meist deutsch mit dem Deutschen. Dr. Carbone versteht deutsch.

Barbie: »Stalin war ein Freimaurer und Churchill auch. Die Freimaurer sind immer noch enorm gefährlich. Das einzige, was man machen kann, ist, sie lächerlich machen. In Berlin hab' ich mal in einer Loge ein Skelett gefunden. Dem hab' ich eine Trillerpfeife in den Mund gesteckt. Als die Freimaurer dann reinkamen, hab' ich selber auf meiner Pfeife ganz laut gepfiffen. Die haben sich vielleicht erschrocken.«

Der Stern, 10 May 1984, 'Barbie Eine Killer Karriere', by Kai Hermann.

Textdokumentation

P1L 341B5   Klaus Barbie

STE Stern   14. Juni 1984   # 25
Quelle   Datum   14.6.84

A685E06   B18†☩

Das Netz der „Spinne"

> Barbie -- Eine Killer-Karriere (6)

Eine Serie von Kai Hermann

Unter den Augen von US-Geheimdiensten gründeten ehemalige SS-Führer eine Faschistische Internationale und stiegen ins Waffengeschäft ein

Alfons Sassen zählt sich zu den engsten Freunden von Klaus Barbie. Er hat vieles gemeinsam mit dem ehemaligen Gestapo-Chef von Lyon und Oberstleutnant des bolivianischen Militär-Geheimdienstes. Auch beruflich. Sassen, bis 1945 holländischer SS- und „Abwehr"-Agent, wurde später Offizier des militärischen Geheimdienstes – in Ecuador. Sassen: „Ich habe den höchsten militärischen Rang, den man als eingebürgerter Ausländer erreichen kann."

Der 58jährige Holländer hält sich ohnehin für einen der wichtigsten Männer in Ecuador: „Schon unter der ersten Militärregierung war ich Berater des Präsidenten für innere und äußere Sicherheit. Und dann bei jeder anderen Regierung, bis auf eine – ob das nun Militärs waren oder Zivilisten."

Sassen hat nach eigenen Angaben in Ecuador unter anderem „ein Bataillon maßgeschneidert" – nach dem Vorbild der SS-„Bandenbekämpfungseinheiten" und „mit etwas neuer Technologie". Er hält es für sein Verdienst, daß Ecuador als einziges Land Lateinamerikas nie eine Guerilla gehabt habe. „Es ist bei uns nämlich sehr ungesund, Guerillero werden zu wollen."

Alfons Sassen hat da seine eigenen Vorstellungen. Er meint, Ecuadors Bevölkerung sei noch auf einem sehr niedrigen Entwicklungsstand und müsse hart angefaßt werden: „Wenn man gerade vom Tier kommt, dann kann man doch gar nicht von Menschenrechten reden. Die sind ja ganz hysterisch in Europa. Das ist so lächerlich."

Er sagt, er mache seine Arbeit in Ecuador, weil er „großes Mitleid mit diesem Land" habe. Bald trete da wieder „dieser versoffene Verein, das Parlament zusammen". Da sei jetzt einer drin, ein Alkoholiker und Analphabet: „Der kommt bei der Masse natürlich an. Das ist einer, der ganz physisch weg. Den muß man betrunken machen. Dann muß er halt unter einen Wagen kommen."

Sassen reist als jemand, der auf seinem „Gebiet überall anerkannt" ist, viel in der Welt herum. Dieses Gespräch wurde am 26. September vergangenen Jahres im Münchner Hotel „Vier Jahreszeiten" geführt. Sassen ist regelmäßig in München. Er erzählte, daß er gerade einen Trip nach Saudi-Arabien vorbereite und dann als Berater in Sachen „Bandenbekämpfung" eine Rundreise durch Lateinamerika.

Der ausgebürgerte Holländer hat einen bundesdeutschen Paß, obwohl er offiziell nie in der Bundesrepublik gelebt hat.

Auf die Frage, ob er bei seinen weltweiten Aktivitäten auch mit bestimmten Nachrichtendiensten zusammenarbeite, zum Beispiel mit den Deutschen, tut Alfons Sassen empört: „Für diese Verräter?"

Aber der Klaus Barbie habe es doch gemacht? Um ihn herum seien doch immer CIA- und BND-Leute gewesen.

Sassen: „Dem Klaus blieb doch nichts anderes übrig. Nur so hat er doch überleben können. Man hat ihn ja gerade in letzter Zeit gebraucht."

Wer hat ihn gebraucht?

Sassen antwortet ausweichend, rechtfertigt noch einmal die Zusammenarbeit von Barbie mit CIA und BND: „Klaus ist doch noch an dem Tag, an dem er in Bolivien ankam, zum bolivianischen Geheimdienst gegangen und hat denen gesagt: Dies ist mein Curriculum vitae. Leute. Mir bleibt nichts anderes übrig, als für die Deutschen und die Amerikaner zu arbeiten. Aber ich werde euch immer informieren. Klaus war also eine Art Doppelagent. Aber mehr auf der Seite der Bolivianer."

Freunde Barbies wußten von dessen vielseitiger Agententätigkeit. Einige hatten schließlich dieselben Verbindungen. Sie diskutierten nach Barbies Verhaftung, ob man die westlichen Dienste nicht noch einmal für den Freund mobilisieren könne. Notfalls mit der Drohung, etwas über Barbies nachrichtendienstliche Beziehungen zu veröffentlichen. Barbies CIA- und BND-Verbindungen waren auch Thema eines Treffens am 6. Oktober 1983 in Kufstein. Teilnehmer der Zusammenkunft: Barbies Sekretär Alvaro de Castro, Mike Barrientos, Neffe des ehemaligen bolivianischen Diktators Barrientos, Barbies Tochter Ute Messner und deren Ehemann.

Man spricht über den „Mann mit dem Vogelnamen", gemeint ist der BND-Pensionär Herbert Kukuk vom „Freundeskreis" Barbie. Ute Messner berichtet: „Die haben sich gemeldet. Aber das ist alles sehr diskret. Denn soviel wissen wir inzwischen – die sind heillos zerstritten da im BND. Da ist eine Gruppe, die helfen möchte. Wie in Amerika auch." Ute Messner lacht: „Das ist so geheim. Auch daß er noch '81 in Deutschland war, das ist ja so geheim. Die haben doch furchtbare Angst. Ja – daß da mal was an Tageslicht kommt. Das wäre unangenehm. Nicht für meinen Vater – für Deutschland. Denn seine Linie ist der Kampf gegen den Kommunismus. Und da ist es ganz egal, mit wem man das macht."

Barbies Linie ist auch Sassens Linie. Die beiden SS-Kameraden haben beinahe identische Karrieren, und sie haben auch eng zusammengearbeitet. Als Barbie 1980 den Putsch in Bolivien vorbereitete (STERN Nr. 24/1984), schickte Sassen ihm einen seiner Männer, den Leutnant Pablo Hérbas Chiribogas. Sassen hatte den Kollegen auch schon früher unterstützt. Zur Jagd auf den Guerilla-Führer Che Guevara kam er nach Bolivien und arbeitete mit Barbie zusammen.

Alfons Sassen begann seine Agentenlaufbahn in jungen Jahren. Mit 17 ging er 1944 in Holland zur SS, mit 18 war er schon „Abwehr"-Spezialist, beauftragt mit der Infiltration des kommunistischen Widerstands. Als er nach Kriegsende, am 8. Juli 1945, von Angehörigen des US-Armee-Geheimdienstes in Maastricht verhaftet wurde, da hatte er schon den Ausweis eines anderen amerikanischen Dienstes mit dazugehörigen falschen Personalpapieren auf den Namen van Aalst in der Tasche. Sassen war gerade damit beschäftigt gewesen – nun für die

Gemäß § 1 Abschn. 3 des Bundesdatenschutzgesetzes vom 27. 1. 1977 werden personenbezogene Daten ausschließlich für publizistische Zwecke gespeichert und herausgegeben

'Das Netz der Spinne' *Stern* serie by Kai Hermann, 14-06-1984.

National Archives NL-HaNa, Justitie/ABR, 2.09.09, inv.nr: 87844. Alfons Sassen in front of a Peugeot 202 with Antwerp (Belgium) numberplates. Picture taken after 1945.

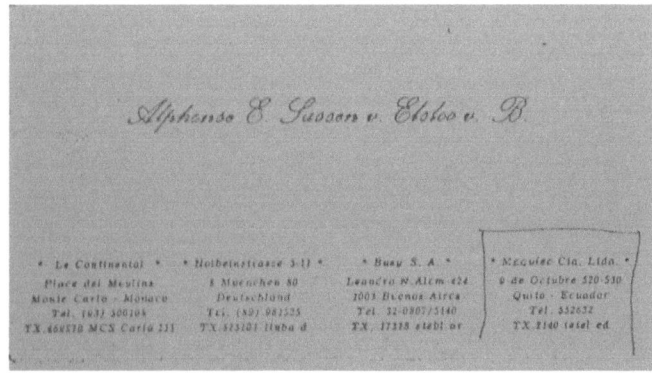

Businesscard Alfons Sassen van Elsloo van Bavel. (Otero)

```
                              DIRECCION GENERAL DE REGISTRO CIVIL, IDENTIFI
C
ACION Y CEDULACION                          CONSULTA ALFABETICA DE CEDULA
D
OS


 CEDULA.: 170307326  0   NOMBRE: SASSEN VAN BAVEL MARIA JOHANA JACQUELINE


 FECHA DE NACIMIENTO:   1   12   1912   LUGAR DE NACIMIENTO: PAISES BAJOS***
*
                    PAGINA:    99   ACTA: 66357   LUGAR INSCRIPCION: PICHINCHA**
***              1951   NACIONALIDAD: HOLANDES**********    UTILIZADO POR MA
G
VA:               SECUNDARIA  PROFESION/OCUPACION: COMERCIANTE


 ESTADO CIVIL: VIUDO        CONYUGE: ROLF BURK
                          ***************


 PADRE: JAN WILLEM SASSEN                            NACIONALIDAD: HOLAN
)
ES**********                                         NACIONALIDAD: HOLAN
)
ES**********
 DOMICILIO: PICHINCHA****** QUITO*************** SAN BLAS          CALL


 INSCRIPCION DE DEFUNCION: FECHA:   0    0     0  TOMO:   0  CLASE:   PAGINA:
)                           ***************
                        0    0     0  LUGAR DE FALLECIMIENTO: ***************


 OBSERVACIONES: DDF_T8_P341_A4705_1996_QUITO    ETNICO:     RESERV3:
```

Registro Civil issued by Embassy of Ecuador.

DIRECCION GENERAL DE REGISTRO CIVIL, IDENTIFICACION Y CEDULACION
CONSULTA ALFABETICA DE CEDULADOS

CEDULA.: 170014878 4 NOMBRE: SASSEN VAN ELSLOO VAN BAVEL ALPHONSE

FECHA DE NACIMIENTO: 28 12 1926 LUGAR DE NACIMIENTO: PAISES BAJOS***

PAGINA: 83 ACTA: 31 LUGAR INSCRIPCION: PICHINCHA*****

1965 NACIONALIDAD: ECUATORIANA******* UTILIZADO POR MAJVA:

SUPERIOR PROFESION/OCUPACION: ASESOR

ESTADO CIVIL: CASADO CONYUGE: ANA ESMERALDA CHALEN LASSO

PICHINCHA****** QUITO*************** GONZALEZ SUAREZ**

PADRE: JAN C SASSEN VAN ELSLOO NACIONALIDAD: HOLANDES**********
  NACIONALIDAD: HOLANDES**********

DOMICILIO: PICHINCHA****** QUITO*************** COTOCOLLAO CALLE

INSCRIPCION DE DEFUNCION: FECHA: 22 9 2008 TOMO: 2 CLASE: D PAGINA:

PICHINCHA****** QUITO*************** LA MAGDALIA
21 9 2008 LUGAR DE FALLECIMIENTO: PICHINCHA****** QUITO***************

OBSERVACIONES: ETNICO: RESERV3:

Georgette Sassen published *Ponchos, Zhanzas y bananas* (ed. Fray Jodoco Ricke, 1960, Ecuador), describing life in Ecuador.

Hace pocas semanas un capitán era condecorado en el salón "Los Arupos" del Hotel Alameda Real. Nuestra redacción se enteró, de fuentes bien informadas, que entre sus actividades está la de dictar conferencias en los comités de damas del Frente de Reconstrucción Nacional. Según la revista alemana STERN, se trata de un ex agente de las SS. Holandés de nacimiento y portador de un pasaporte alemán, se llama Alfons Sassen...

Denuncia la revista alemana STERN:

Alfons Sassen

Un nazi en el Ecuador

"Tengo el más alto rango militar que puede poseer un extranjero inmigrante en el Ecuador", confesó Alfons Sassen a la revista alemana STERN, en una entrevista aparecida en la edición del 14 de junio pasado.

Las declaraciones forman parte de un amplio reportaje sobre las actividades de una llamada "Internacional Negra", organización fascista creada en la post guerra y apoyada por el servicio secreto norteamericano para infiltrar y espiar a los gobiernos latinoamericanos.

Bajo el título *"La tela de la araña"*, el periodista alemán Kai Hermann reproduce las declaraciones exclusivas del holandés con pasaporte alemán (nunca ha vivido en Alemania) Alfons Sassen, 58, ex agente de las SS en Holanda, capturado y deportado a Francia en 1945 y más tarde enviado al Ecuador, donde se emplea como oficial del servicio secreto ecuatoriano, según explica STERN.

La denuncia abarca la presencia de ex naxis en por lo menos siete países latinoamericanos en los que utilizan diversas fachadas, siendo la más importante la de representantes del mayor consorcio austriaco de venta de armas de guerra: la *Steyr-Daimler-Puch*.

Sassen, quien se considera según STERN *"uno de los hombres más importantes del Ecuador"*, afirma haber servido *"desde el primer gobierno militar (?) como consejero de presidentes para seguridad interna y externa y, después, para todos los otros gobiernos, sin importar si eran civiles o militares"*.

Afirma, igualmente, haber colaborado estrechamente con los militares en Bolivia en la captura del Comandante Ernesto "Ché" Guevara y señala que *"gracias a él y sus labores, el Ecuador es uno de los países de América Latina que nunca ha tenido guerrilla"*.

Ecuadorian magazine *Nueva*, October 1984, page 18-22.

Julio Prado Vallejo

"De confirmarse la denuncia, Sassen debería ser expulsado"

NUEVA conversó con el doctor Julio Prado Vallejo –Presidente de la Comisión Nacional de Derechos Humanos y miembro por el Ecuador de la Comisión Andina de Juristas– sobre la denuncia aparecida en la revista alemana *STERN*. A continuación la entrevista.

–Doctor Prado Vallejo, la revista *STERN* denunció recientemente que un ex agente de las SS holandesas, cuyo nombre es Alfons Sassen, vive en nuestro país desde hace algunos años a donde llegó a desempeñarse como asesor del ejército. El mismo sostiene, en una entrevista concedida en Munich, tener "el más alto rango militar que puede poseer un extranjero inmigrante en el Ecuador". ¿Qué opinión le merece a usted esta situación?

"De confirmarse esa denuncia, yo diría que dicha situación es absolutamente inaceptable. No solamente dada la filosofía del nazismo, sino la propia situación personal del señor Sassen. En tanto que ex guardia nazi, es un delincuente que ha cometido delitos contra la humanidad, si es que perteneció, como dice la denuncia, a las SS, que tantos crímenes cometieron".

DELITOS IMPRESCRIPTIBLES

"De acuerdo con la legislación internacional, el Ecuador está comprometido a dos cosas: primero, a considerar que los delitos contra la humanidad cometidos por los nazis antes y durante la Segunda Guerra son delitos imprescriptibles; es decir que pase el tiempo que pase, no prescriben. Hay convenciones de Naciones Unidas y declaraciones que el Ecuador ha suscrito por las cuales se sostiene, como política interna e internacional de nuestros países, que esos delitos son imprescriptibles y que deben ser sancionados una vez que se toma presos a quienes fueron responsables de dichas masacres en Europa.

"En segundo lugar, hay otro principio establecido también en la legislación internacional: el de la cooperación para la administración de la justicia en el mundo. El Ecuador está obligado a proceder de conformidad con ese criterio, cooperando en la entrega de este tipo de delincuentes para que sean juzgados en sus respectivos países y de acuerdo con las normas que el derecho internacional y tiene establecidas.

"En ese contexto, mi reacción es la de considerar inaceptables, si es que es cierto, que este señor sea asesor del ejército. Yo no puedo creer que en el momento actual así lo sea. Quizás vino en aquellas épocas en que no solamente se introducían aquí asesores nazis sino asesores peronistas que llegaron al país cuando el auge de Perón. Se habían ubicado en Venezuela y yo mismo denuncié que habían constituido, también con algún europeo, un grupo de pesquisa para investigar e interferir las comunicaciones. Se introducieron en la Policía Nacional para tales tareas.

"Si el señor Sassen llegó entonces, no me llamaría la atención que hubiera podido desempeñar algún tipo de asesoría en la Policía. Pero si dicha asesoría continúa de algún modo, yo pienso que hay que hacer todo lo posible porque este señor deje de prestarla".

–En efecto, la misma revista denuncia que el hermano del señor Sassen llegó incluso a ser traductor de Perón y que continuaría asesorando a las fuerzas armadas argentinas. En todo caso, Alfons Sassen asevera en la entrevista concedida, en 1983 a *STERN* haber sido el asesor de todos los últimos gobiernos en materia de seguridad interna y externa. De otro lado, al referirse al Parlamento de la época, lo califica de "grupo de simples borrachos". Usted, en tanto que parlamentario de entonces, ¿qué piensa sobre tal aseveración?

"No me cabe sino repudiar el hecho de que pueda permitirse un extranjero hacer esas declaraciones. Sería importante conocer si el señor Sassen se ha naturalizado en el Ecuador...

–... la denuncia afirma que el señor Sassen, al igual que su hermano, tiene un pasaporte alemán a pesar de nunca haber vivido en Alemania y él se refiere a sí mismo como "extranjero inmigrante"...

"... entonces seguramente no está naturalizado. Y que un extranjero intervenga en política interna es razón suficiente para expulsarlo. Yo, de autoridad ecuatoriana, lo primero que haría es expulsar al señor Sassen, porque no tiene derecho, como extranjero, a intervenir en nuestra política interna.

"Considero de suma necesidad seguir investigando esta situación. Yo desearía, a nombre de la Comisión Nacional de Derechos Humanos, saber si el señor Sassen, con pasaporte alemán, extranjero, está actuando en política interna para pedir su expulsión".

SASSEN Y LOS "DERECHOS HUMANOS"

–A propósito de Derechos Humanos... Preguntado el señor Sassen sobre el pueblo ecuatoriano, manifiesta que este "tiene aún un nivel muy subdesarrollado de vida" y añade que "cuando se viene recién del animal, no se puede hablar tan fácilmente sobre derechos humanos"...

"Es que para él, si la denuncia de que fue nazi se confirma, los derechos humanos no deben existir. Para un ex agente de las SS, seguramente son una cosa absurda. De tal manera que no debe sorprendernos. Lo que sí no se puede aceptar es que viva en el Ecuador un hombre con esa mentalidad y menos aún, como se afirma en la denuncia, desempeñando determinadas labores.

"Todo lo que se dice en la denuncia nos obliga a nosotros, como ecuatorianos, a investigar a fondo los antecedentes de este señor. Y yo quisiera participar personalmente en cualquier investigación que se haga al respecto para exigir al Ministerio de Relaciones Exteriores que si se confirma la veracidad de dicha denuncia, el señor Sassen sea expulsado del país. Le haríamos un positivo servicio al país y a los Derechos Humanos".

Ecuadorian magazine *Nueva*, October 1984, page 18-22.

Ex espía nazi en Ecuador

QUITO, 2.- Un ex espía del Servicio Secreto alemán vive en Ecuador desde hace varios años y habría sido asesor de diferentes gobiernos de este país sudamericano en "seguridad interna y externa", trascendió hoy en Quito.

La denuncia es recogida por la revista ecuatoriana Nueva, de próxima aparición y a la que tuvo acceso IPS. La publicación cita como fuente un reportaje de la revista de Alemania Federal Stern a Alfonso Sassen, el ex espía.

Según Nueva, Sassen dijo que "tengo el más alto rango militar que puede poseer un extranjero inmigrante en Ecuador".

Refiriéndose a sus actividades en este país, el ex espía nazi afirma que "desde el primer gobierno militar", se ha desempeñado como "consejero de presidentes", en materia de seguridad, sin importar el carácter del gobierno.

Al hacer un recuento de la vida de Sassen, se aseguró que nació en Holanda, e ingresó en 1944, a los 17 años, como miembro del Servicio Secreto alemán (SS). A los 18 años "era yo un especialista del servicio", afirmó Sassen.

Al finalizar la guerra, el 8 de julio de 1945, fue capturado por los norteamericanos e ingresó al servicio secreto de Estados Unidos, donde recibió documentación falsa a nombre de Van Aslat.

Posteriormente se trasladó a España y se puso en contacto con miembros del servicio secreto del régimen del general Francisco Franco.

En España se decidió ampliar la red de espionaje a América Latina –agregó– siempre al servicio de Estados Unidos.

En América Latina se dividieron por países y a Sassen le correspondió Ecuador, a Klaus Barbie Bolivia, a Wim Sassen (hermano de Alfonso) Argentina, a Walter Rauff Chile, a Friederich Swend Perú y a Joseph Menguele Paraguay.

Alfonso Sassen, quien tiene pasaporte de la República Federal de Alemania, pese a que nunca pisó suelo de ese país tras la guerra, afirma Nueva, representa en Ecuador a la firma Export-Import que se dedica a la exportación de armas desde Austria.

Roberto Sassen, hijo de Alfonso, dijo a Stern que la familia Sassen tiene mucha confianza en un oficial del ejército ecuatoriano: el teniente coronel Fausto Banderas.

Sobre el militar Banderas, Sassen hijo dijo que se trata del "filósofo tras el militar", y que una de sus tesis es que mientras un gobierno electo mantenga contentos a los militares puede "permanecer en el poder".

Alfonso Sassen relató a la revista alemana que efectivamente actúa como "consejero de seguridad" para el gobierno ecuatoriano, trabajo que realiza "porque comparte el gran dolor de este país (Ecuador)".

(IPS)

Ecuadorian Daily *Hoy*, 3 October 1984.

Ecuatoriano-holandés responde a afirmaciones de revista alemana Stern

"Nuca he sido espía", dice

Por Vicente Olmedo

Revela que está a punto de ganar un juicio de imprenta a la revista alemana Stern

Ya nos habíamos encontrado en alguna ocasión pasada, por motivos periodísticos. Lucía igual que entonces: sereno, cordial y de buen humor. Se trataba de Alfonso Sassen, a quien hace algunos años se lo acusó de ser un criminal de guerra nazi, ante una versión que se originó en Francia, cuestión que fue aclarada por el señor Sassen en una entrevista exclusiva que logró por aquellos días HOY. Ahora pesa sobre él otra acusación: "Alfonso Sassen es un ex espía nazi en América Latina", de acuerdo a una publicación aparecida en la revista alemana Stern.

Lo ubicamos en un hotel de la capital, acompañado de varios amigos ecuatorianos. En esta ocasión, Sassen hizo importantes revelaciones como aquella de que tampoco fue un espía nazi, ni miembro del servicio secreto de país alguno, sino voluntario, cuando tenía la edad de 16 años, de las tropas de asalto (SS) de Alemania, durante la segunda guerra mundial. Sassen atribuyó esta serie de imputaciones a una campaña internacional orquestada por la mafia y el terrorismo de extrema izquierda.

Confiesa que ya tiene miedo formular declaraciones a los medios de comunicación, por que casi siempre le tergiversan lo que dice, como el caso "de la sensacionalista revista alemana Stern, a la cual estoy a punto de ganar un juicio de

Alfonso Sassen

de hombres, dentro de los cuales figuraban 55 mil voluntarios holandeses que pelearon contra el comunismo.

—¿Es usted holandés o alemán?
—Soy de origen holandés y muy naturalizado ecuatoriano. Yo nunca he sido alemán, aunque podía haber sido alemán, por haber pertenecido a las Fuerzas Armadas alemanas. Esto me hubiera dado el derecho de tener la ciudadanía alemana.

—¿Porqué se nacionalizó ecuatoriano?
—Me naturalicé en el momento en que me establecí en el Ecuador, a partir de 1961. Formé mi familia, mis hijos han nacido en este país, mis nietos son ecuatorianos. Era entonces lógico naturalizarme en este país. Vivo y quiero morir en este país.

—Ud. niega no sólo haber sido espía nazi, pero asisten también versiones en el sentido

comunicación que se ponen al servicio de estos narcotraficantes: otra cosa ya no se puede decir. Yo he planteado un juicio de imprenta que ya estoy ganando a la revista sensacionalista Stern con el mejor abogado alemán. Ojalá que, esto lo tome muy en cuenta la prensa ecuatoriana –dice en son de broma. De cualquier manera, el periodista le advierte que esto no lo pone nervioso.

—¿Cómo es que esta revista consiguió fotos y otros datos reservados de su vida?
—Pues, de alguna fuente en Holanda.

—¿En qué año estuvo Ud. en Bolivia? ¿Es verdad que Ud. participó en la muerte del líder guerrillero Che Guevara?
—Yo nunca estuve en Bolivia, ni siquiera de paso, jamás he estado allí. Es totalmente falso que yo haya participado en la muerte del Guevara. Se trata de un invento de alguna persona interesada para que algún sicópata que se crea de este cuento atente contra mi vida.

—¿Por qué ha planteado juicio a la revista alemana?
—Estoy siguiendo el juicio por calumnia, porque Stern trata de desacreditarme. Esta es una táctica utilizada por el Krelim para poder fongear a una persona, esto quiere decir ni los amigos, ni los enemigos le miren a uno. Creo que el Ecuador, mi familia y mis amigos se merecen conocer la verdad. Yo no he sido espía ni aquí, ni en ninguna parte, y creo que no serviría para esto. Me han pedido que retire el juicio y me han ofrecido 1/2 millón de marcos, pero no lo voy hacer. Voy a ir hasta el final.

Además, debo decir que la Stern nunca me hizo una entrevista, lo que pasa es que

Ecuadorian Daily *Hoy*, 7 October 1984, part 1.

Alfonso Sassen

"Lo que se dice en las noticias es una desinformación organizada por la mafia de las drogas, porque con el trabajo que estoy realizando se sienten muy afectados, especialmente una parte de es_ mafia que es incluso alemana. Es una consigna de los traficantes de drogas y la extrema izquierda, en especial del terrorismo internacio_. Y existen medios de comunicación que se ponen al servicio de estos narcotraficantes; otra cosa ya no se puede decir. Yo he planteado un juicio de imprenta que ya estoy ganando a la revista sensacionalista Stern, con el mejor abogado _mán", dijo en entrevista concedida a HOY el acusado de ser espía nazi en el Ecuador. Se trata de un tema de nunca acabar

rich Swend y Joseph Mengele?
—La descarto totalmente. No existe ninguna vinculación política internacional, o de inteligencia internacional. El único trabajo que estoy haciendo es contra el tráfico de drogas que es una especie de crimen.

—¿Es verdad que representa en el Ecuador a la firma Export Import que se dedica a la exportación de armas desde Austria?
—Mire, mi hijo ecuatoriano de nacimiento tiene la representación de esta empresa. Yo jamás he vendido un arma, ni la venderé. A mí no me gusta vivir del armamento, pero mi hijo tiene perfecto derecho para ser representante de una casa con otros ecuatorianos, incluso ex militares, que son representantes de casas de armamentos. Yo personalmente no he vendido ni una tuerca al ejército. Están hablando tonterías.

—¿Ud. logró documentación falsa a nombre de Van Aslat, cuando al finalizar _ _ _ _ de 1945, fue consejero de presidentes de la república, ¿es verdad eso?
—Jamás he sido consejero de ningún presidente, ni se lo he manifestado a la revista Stern, porque nunca me ha entrevistado.

—¿Puede hablarnos de sus actividades en la Dinactie, organismo que combate al narcotráfico?
—No, porque puedo poner en riesgo varios operativos en marcha.

—Por último, sería importante que nos vuelva a relatar sobre su participación en el Ejército Alemán, durante la segunda guerra mundial.
—Bueno yo pertenecí a la SS, como voluntario cuando tenía 16 años. La SS eran comandos o unidades de asalto, no tiene nada que ver con la Gestapo o servicio secreto. Teníamos uniformes como soldados de primera línea y en su mayoría éramos voluntarios extranjeros.

Poco antes de finalizar la entrevista, al contestarme una curiosidad, me cuenta que una cruz que la exibe en su leva es

Ecuadorian Daily *Hoy*, 37 October 1984, part 2.

Ecuadorian Daily *Hoy*, 9 September 1984.

UNCLASSIFIED

NAZI WAR CRIMES DISCLOSURE ACT
2000

```
DOCUMENT_ID: 54686936
INQNO:         GSCAN1D 00463540
DOCNO:
PRODUCER:
SOURCE:    STATE
DOCTYPE:
DOR:       19841004
TOR:       16560000
DOCPREC:   R
ORIGDATE:  198410041656
DOCCLASS:  U

HEADER
OO RUEAIIB
 ZNR UUUUU ZOC STATE ZZH
 STU6956
 OO RUEHC
 DE RUESQI #9032 2781530
 ZNR UUUUU ZZH
 O R 041514Z OCT 84
 FM AMEMBASSY QUITO
 TO RUEHIA/USIA WASHDC IMMEDIATE 2605
 RUFHOL/AMEMBASSY BONN IMMEDIATE 0157
 INFO RUESGY/AMCONSUL GUAYAQUIL 9342
 RUEHC/SECSTATE WASHDC 4713
 BT
 EZ1:

CONTROLS
SR2

  \?NCLAS QUITO 9032\
  EZ2:

TEXT
   SR3

USIS
USIA FOR P/G; AR; USIS BONN FOR CAO;
SECSTATE FOR ARA/RONDON
E.O. 12356: N/A
SUBJECT: REQUEST FOR INFORMATION AND FAST GUIDANCE ON LOCALLY-
PUBLISHED STORY ALLEGING THAT THE U.S. USED WELL-KNOWN NAZI
WAR CRIMINALS TO FORM AN "ESPIONAGE NET" IN LATIN
AMERICA AFTER WW II
1. OCTOBER 3 EDITION OF QUITO DAILY "HOY" CARRIED A
STORY BASED ON AN IPS DISPATCH ALLEGING THAT AN
EX-NAZI SS MEMBER BY THE NAME OF ALFONSO SASSEN NOW
LIVING IN ECUADOR FLED GERMANY AFTER WW II, JOINED
THE U.S. "SECRET SERVICE," AND SUBSEQUENTLY CAME TO
ECUADOR IN ORDER TO PARTICIPATE IN AN EFFORT TO
"BROADEN THE U.S. ESPIONAGE NET TO INCLUDE LATIN
AMERICA."
2. THE "HOY" STORY, WHICH STATES THAT THE SOURCE OF THE
IPS DISPATCH IS A REPORT PUBLISHED IN "STERN," MAKES
THE FOLLOWING ASSERTIONS:
```

CIA HAS NO OBJECTION TO
DECLASSIFICATION AND/OR
RELEASE OF CIA INFORMATION
IN THIS DOCUMENT

DECLASSIFIED AND RELEASED BY
CENTRAL INTELLIGENCE AGENCY
SOURCESMETHODSEXEMPTION3B2B
NAZI WAR CRIMES DISCLOSURE ACT
DATE 2001 2007

FOR COORDINATED WITH   State

UNCLASSIFIED

Freedom of Information Act (Foia): Declassified Nazi War Crimes Disclosure Act (CIA files) on Barbie, Klaus, Vol 1_0097; Alfons Sassen.

UNCLASSIFIED

A) SASSEN WAS CAPTURED BY U.S. FORCES IN GERMANY AT THE END OF THE WAR, WHEN BE ENTERED THE "U.S. SECRET SERVICE" AND WAS GIVEN A FALSE IDENTITY.
B) SUBSEQUENTLY, HE WENT TO SPAIN WHERE HE ENTERED INTO CONTACT WITH THE "SECRET SERVICE" OF THE FRANCO REGIME.
C) "IN SPAIN, IT WAS DECIDED TO BROADEN THE ESPIONAGE NET TO INCLUDE LATIN AMERICA ...-- ADDED (SASSEN) -- STILL AT THE SERVICE OF THE U.S. (SECRET SERVICE). LATIN AMERICA WAS PARCELLED OUT (AMONG VARIOUS AGENTS), AND SASSEN WAS ASSIGNED ECUADOR, **KLAUS BARBIE** (WAS ASSIGNED) BOLIVIA, WINN SASSEN (THE BROTHER OF ALFONSO) (WAS ASSIGNED) ARGENTINA, WALTER RAUFF CHILE, FREDERICK SWEND PERU AND JOSEPH MENGUELE PARAGUAY."
D) ALFONSO SASSEN IS NOW LIVING IN ECUADOR, WHERE HE REPRESENTS A COMPANY CALLED "EXPORT-IMPORT" WHICH IMPORTS ARMS FROM AUSTRIA, AND WHERE HE HAS ADVISED SUCCESSIVE ECUADOREAN GOVERNMENTS ON "INTERNAL AND EXTERNAL SECURITY."
E) "HOY" STORY QUOTES SASSEN AS SAYING THAT HE HOLDS THE HIGHEST ECUADOREAN MILITARY RANK THAT A FOREIGN IMMIGRANT TO ECUADOR CAN ATTAIN.
F) SASSEN'S SON ROBERTO IS QUOTED AS SAYING THAT THE SASSEN FAMILY HAS CLOSE RELATIONS WITH A LT. COL. FAUSTO BANDERAS OF THE ECUADOREAN ARMY.
3. FOR P/G: SINCE THIS STORY IS LIKELY TO CAUSE CONTROVERSY HERE, POST WOULD APPRECIATE AN ASSESSMENT OF THE ORIGIN AND VERACITY OF THE STERN STORY AND ANY POLICY GUIDANCE ON THE ACCUSATIONS THEREIN.
4. FOR USIS BONN: WOULD APPRECIATE ANY INFORMATION YOU CAN PROVIDE ON "STERN" STORY.
DIETERICH
 NNNN
NNDD

GESPRÄCHSPROTOKOLL

Goltz (G)
Alfons Sassen (AS)

München, 26.9.83

G: Bleiben Sie länger hier?

AS.: Ich bin schon länger hier, ich habe verschiedene Aufträge für meine Regierung und deswegen habe ich noch verschiedene Sachen zu tun. Ich war jetzt in Wien,

G.: Sie arbeiten in der Chemie, habe ich das richtig verstanden?

AS.: Ich habe eine chemische Fabrik gehabt. Schwefelsäureanlage, Sulfonationsanlage und viele so Hilfsmittel für die Textilindustrie, Bauindustrie usw.

G.: Ich bin jetzt gerade am Umziehen und weiß noch nicht, ob ich mich in Bolivien oder Ecuador niederlassen soll.

AS.: Wie kennen Sie den Duarte?

G.: Ich kenn ihn überhaupt nicht, er ist mir nur empfohlen worden von einem Mann namens Gelver, der im Vorstand der Bank von Kuwait sitzt und für den ich da drüben also Kontakte aufnehmen soll. Und in Ecuador hat er eben nur diesen Duarte. Ich hab nicht mal seinen vollen Namen, ist das eigentlich ein Oberst oder ein General?

AS.: Er ist Coronel.

G.: Angel Duarte?

AS.: Ja, ich habe gestern noch gefragt, aber er ist ade. Ich kenne ihn, aber ich kannte ihn als Capitan. Dann habe ich noch den Oberst Banderas gefragt, der war ja mit mir in Wien zusammen jetzt bei Steyer.

G.: Ach, Sie arbeiten jetzt auch ...

AS.: Nein, nein, ich habe mit Steyer nichts zu tun, ich werde immer verwechselt. Was gut ist von Steyer das sag ich, ich bin Berater von der Armee. Hauptsächlich für Sicherheitsangelegenheiten. Und für Waffen, weil ich da genügend Ahnung habe.

Unpublished interview M. von der Goltz (G) and Alfons Sassen (AS), 26 September 1983 in Munich, West Germany.

Und z.B. die Pistole von Steyer, die nichts taugt; die nichts taugt ..., die so auf dem 3. Platz steht nach der Baretta. Diebeste Pistole ist auch eine Österreichische, da sind sie natürlich wütend drüber, das ist die Glock. Das ist was großartiges. Ich kann ja der Bruder von meinem Bruder sein, ich liebe meinen Bruder über alles, aber wenn etwas nicht in Ordnung ist, dann muß ich es sagen.

G.: Aber der Panzer ist doch gut.

AS.: Der ist gut für unsere Zwecke. Der 105er ist also gut für den Einsatz wie wir ihn brauchen.

Zusammenfassung:

Es wird über Panzer geredet.

AS.: Ich hasse Panzer, schon seit dem Krieg.

G.: Wie alt waren Sie denn im letzten Krieg, haben Sie den noch miterlebt?

AS.: Ich war bei der Waffen-SS.

G.: Ach, Sie waren auch bei der Waffen-SS. Wie alt waren Sie denn da?

AS.: Ich war 16, freiwillig gemeldet, da war noch 2 Jahre Krieg. In Arnheim, im Balkan und in den Ardennen hab ich noch mitgemacht.

G.: Aber nicht mit Ihrem Bruder.

AS.: Nein.

G.: Haben Sie noch mehr Brüder? Oder nur den Wim?

AS.: Nur Wim.

G.: Nur Wim und Ihre Schwester...

AS.: Ich bin jetzt eingeladen worden vom Verteidigungsminister, das ist der Halbbruder vom Fahd. Da ich so viel Erfolg gehabt habe mit den Guerillas, die

...

	Vermeidung einer eventuellen Guerilla in Ecuador, das ist das einzige Land, das keine Guerillas hat .. bei uns scheint es sehr ungesund zu sein, Guerilla zu werden. Da hab ich schon seit mehr als 20 Jahren ... um den Erfolg von den Guerillas zu vermeiden.
G.:	Das haben Sie auf rein militärischem Sektor gemacht oder wie die Amerikaner auch mit Civic Action?
AS.:	Nein, das ist ein Bataillon maßgeschneidert für Ecuador mit Ideen von der Bandenbekämpfungsmethode die wir gehabt haben, etwas von der neuesten Technologie und mit sehr gutem Erfolg.
G.:	Und Sie sind als Berater tätig gewesen?
AS.:	Nein, ich bin in der Armee in G2.
G.:	G2, was ist das?
AS.:	G2 ist die Abwehr.
G.:	G2, die ecuadorianische Abwehr?
AS.:	Alles, was Military Intelligans ist.
G.:	Ah, Gott sei dank, da bin ich ja am richtigen Mann ... aber kann man das denn als Ausländer überhaupt sein, Armeeangehöriger?
AS.:	Ich bin überhaupt kein Ausländer.
G.:	Ach so, Sie sind Ecuadorianer.
AS.:	Durch die erste Militärregierung bin ich nationalisiert worden und da wurde ich direkt Berater des Präsidenten was innere und äußere Sicherheit des Landes angeht. Und so bei jeder anderen Regierung, ob das nun Militärs waren oder Zivilisten, wegen meiner Erfolge. Nur eine Regierung, die hat mich mal weggeschickt nur ein sogenanntes freiwilliges Exil, aber dann als Polizeiattaché und zur gleichen Zeit war ich Konsul von Ecuador.
G.:	Das geht also noch ganz zivilisiert zu.
AS.:	Ich bemühe mich darum, nicht intern politisch wirksam zu sein ...
G.:	Laßt mein Notizbuch stehen und bringt keinen Zucker.

...

AS.: Pen Decho! ...

G.: Das mit der Chemie haben Sie dann also aufgegeben in Ecuador? Was war denn dann die Hauptsache?

AS.: Ich bin 1951 aus Spanien, ich war 3 Jahre in Spanien, 48-51, in Spanien war ich Ausbilder, ich war Protege von General Moskardon, den die Alliierten wollten mich immer ausgeliefert haben, denn ich habe einem Sonderkommando angehört und da wurden wir beschuldigt, das wir amerikanische Kriegsgefangene erschossen hätten. Und als diesen Quatsch, womit wir nichts zu tun gehabt haben.

G.: Sie als 18jähriger?

AS.: 16jähriger. Was glauben Sie, was da passiert ist, 17 jährigen wurde beim Verhör die Kinnlade kaputtgeschlagen.

G.: Und haben Sie dann noch lange Schwierigkeiten gehabt?

AS.: Nein, denn der Moskardon hat gesagt, nur über meine Leiche. Und der hat mir dann einen speziellen Pass gegeben, damit ich abhauen konnte, dann kam ich in Ecuador an und wurde gleich Ausbilder bei der Militärschule. Und der Polizeischule in San Vicente. Bis es dann mit der Chemie losging.
Und Sie sind der erste deutsche Torrero?

G.: Wahrscheinlich auch der letzte. Jetzt möchte ich aber etwas anderes anfangen, ich war im letzten Jahr in Bolivien und Ecuador und hatte da sehr gute Verbindungen, die jetzt aber leider abgebrochen sind. Das wollen die Araber, daß ich diese Verbindungen jetzt wieder aufbaue für Sachen so wie Entjuser Certificate. Und in diesem Zusammenhang bin ich glaube ich auf den Duarte hingewiesen worden.

AS.: Nein , das ist sehr schwer in Ecuador. Was ich aber tun würde, das ist folgendes: ... als Consul von Bilbao hatte ich natürlich die besten Gelegenheiten ... auf so etwas hatten die natürlich gewartet. Das war während des Krieges von Biafra, da hätt ich 10 Dollar pro Gewehr bekommen, 50 000 Gewehre. Aber ich habe natürlich nein gesagt.

G.: Das wäre natürlich ein gefundenes Fressen für die gewesen.

AS.: Das hab ich mir natürlich verflucht gut überlegt ... was ich aber tun werde, denn im November tret ich ein Reise an, erst geh ich nach Saudi Arabien, da komm ich mit dem Halbbruder vom König zusammen wegen dieser Beratung wegen eventueller Guerilla vom

...

S.:   Daran liegt es ja vielleicht. Meine Leute wollen ja
        nicht mit den Amerikanern zusammenarbeiten und
        vielleicht wollen sie eben wissen wer die BND-Leute
        sind um nicht an die falschen zugeraten.

AS.:   Die Amerikaner kontrollieren doch den BND, als ob
        das ihr eigenes Büro sei. Wenn Sie da an die fal-
        schen Leute geraten, dann müssen Sie Fehlinforma-
        tionen geben. Tun Sie so, als ob Sie mit ihr zusam-
        menarbeiten würden, wenn möglich nehmen Sie die Ge-
        spräche auf, aber auf alle Fälle informieren Sie
        gleich Ihre Leute.

S.:   Als ich damals anfing mit Altmann Geschäfte in
        Bolivien zu machen, das war ja mit Leuten, die in
        der Botschaft ein- und ausgehen.

AS.:   Ich hab in Bolivien nur einmal länger zu tun gehabt
        und das war, als die Jagd nach dem Che Guevara los-
        ging. Die Niederlage vom Che Guevara war 100 % die
        Leistung der Bolivianer, oder wenigstens der Südame-
        rikaner.

S.:   Das ist natürlich schade, daß Sie nicht dieselben
        Verbindungen in Bolivien haben wie in Ecuador.
        Denn ich möchte mir da natürlich nicht die Finger
        verbrennen. Und um den Claus rum waren das jaalles
        CIA- und BND-Leute. Aber Sie sagen ja, wenn man
        in diesem Geschäft an diese Leute gerät, dann bricht
        es einem das Genick.

AS.:   Ich wäre ja der erste, der etwas für Deutschland tun
        würde, wenn das nur eine rechte Regierung hätte
        oder wenigstens zentrumrechts. Aber doch nicht für
        diese Verräterbande.

S.:   Aber wieso hat denn dann der Claus das gemacht?

AS.:   Dem blieb nichts anderes übrig, so hat er wenigstens
        leben können. Mein Bruder hat ihm ja gesagt, geh zu
        meinem Bruder, da bist du sicher. Der (unverständlicher
        Name) das war ja der Kommandant der Polizei, der hat
        ihm seine eigene Hazienda angeboten.

S.:   Als der Siles Zuazo drankam. Aber der hatte ja keine
        Lust mehr. Das zeigt mal wieder, was für eine Verrä-
        terbande das ist. Der war ja si hier, das hätte er
        ja ohne die gar nicht tun können, da war er ja schon
        viel zu bekannt. Und jetzt lassen sie ihn einfach
        hängen.

AS.:   Wie ist er denn damals gereist?

S.:   Das weiß ich nicht, was das für ein Paß war.

AS.:   Na ja, das ist möglich, denn man hat ihn ja in letzter
        Zeit gebraucht.

                                                        ...

> Bevor wir eine Arbeiterklasse bilden können ...
> Wenn man gerade vom Tier kommt, dann kann man
> doch noch gar nicht von Menschenrechten reden,
> die sind da ganz hysterisch in Europa... Das ist
> so lächerlich.

Zusammenfassung:

Sassen entwickelt weiter seine extrem rechte Ideologie.

AS.: Am 10. August tritt wieder dieser versoffene Verein zusammen, das Parlament. Da sind auch zwei Analphabeten dabei, da geht's ja los, da war noch nie so eine schlechte Koalität, sogar zwei Analphabeten. Ich habe ja solches Mitleid mit dem Land. So'n Mann, der kommt bei der Masse natürlich so an, da ist einer, der gehört physisch weg, der wird ausgerottet, weil der bei der Masse so ankommt ... troublemaker... die haben ja alle das gleiche Problem, die trinken, da muß er halt unter einen Wagen kommen. Den muß man betrunken machen.

Zusammenfassung:

Es wird noch über die ecuadorianische Verfassung gesprochen, den Bergbau und das Rauschgiftproblem (Kokain).

Chapter II
Alfons Sassen

On 26 October 1948, *Alphonse Cornelis Eduard Maria Sassen* was released after three years of preventive custody. During his probation time, he fled. Little was known about his war crimes. In 1984, he declared to *Stern* reporter Kai Hermann that he had joined the Resistance during the war. When the German police arrested him for an ordinary robbery, however, they found *Abwehr* (German counter espionage) papers in his possession. After research in the Dutch National Archives it became clear that due to his father's involvement for the German counter espionage service Alfons ended up working for *Abwehr*-specialist Richard Protze as a "*line crosser*"*,* tasked to collect intelligence and to pass on disinformation to the *Binnenlandse strijdkrachten* (BS: Dutch volunteer army commanded by Dutch Prince Bernhard zur Lippe-Biesterfeld). In reality, however, he was never an intelligence specialist. The young man was just eighteen years old when the war was over. His adventure was just about to begin.

Youth
Young Alfons, aka "Fons", was born on 28 December 1926 in Geertruidenberg. He was the last child his mother Johanna van Bavel would give birth to. Alfons led a happy life in Geertruidenberg until the war broke out. *"On 10 May 1940 I had reached the age of 13 years, Germany had suddenly invaded The Netherlands. My fa-*

ther was gone for business in Belgium, my brother left this day to Zeeland where he had to fulfil his duties as a Dutch soldier. In the beginning I was anti-German, just like my brother and father. Though slowly I became under the influence of the German propaganda war cry: If we didn't come the British would have. My father and my brother became members of Zwart Front and I was dressed up like an Indian carrying a German eagle. I felt it was my duty to follow in the footsteps of my father. I was personally convinced that I, if I was older, would have fulfilled my duty as a good patriot, though at this age one doesn't understand much of duty.

Our family consisted of six children. When the Germans invaded my father initially did not agree with their politics, but he changed his opinion. Whatever happened, Catholic they never abandoned their Catholic faith. He thought that the Germans had some good views on the improved social position of the common workman, an objective my father had always fought for. As a Catholic boy, I heard stories at school and read in history books about Bolsheviks, which led to my opinion that Bolshevism was a threat, not only for Catholicism but also to European culture, and therefore also The Netherlands. When I read more about Russia and saw the horrifying pictures of the Katyn and Wenissa mass graves, I understood that Bolshevism was not only a threat to Germany but for Europe as a whole, and therefore also The Netherlands. Germany fought the "red" Bolshevik menace and as a Dutch Catholic, it was my war too." [191]

The war wasn't easy for young Alfons. Everybody in the village knew his family was pro- German. The move to Breda (in 1941) did not improve the conditions for Alfons. At the gymnasium he was bullied for being a Nazi, a "*moffen jong*", which was not entirely correct. Alfons never became a member of the *Hitlerjugend* or the Dutch equivalent *Jeugdstorm*, like so many children of collaborating NSB-families had become. Father Sassen senior tried to help the unfortunate son: *"When my father realized I was bullied he (I was 15) put me in a National Socialist gymnasium: the Nederlands Instituut voor Volksopvoeding (NIVO) at Schaarsbergen (Arnhem). There I wore a school uniform: a pair of blue pants, a blue windbreaker and a "kwartiermuts" a hat with a red, white and blue cockade. I also carried a dagger. This NIVO (Nationale Politische Erziehungs Anstalt) later changed into a Reichsschule. After only one year (1942-1943) my father took me away because I became too liberal."*[192]

In hiding

In 1943, Alfons was old enough to work: *"Father wanted me to join the "Nederlandse Arbeidersdienst" (the Dutch labour force). He already had a son serving at the front, and besides, all my older sisters served the German cause by working for the Red Cross or the Dutch radio. Soon I was called for Arbeidsdienst (labour service). Father said it would be better for me to respond, so he did not have to financially support me any longer. I pretended to be ill, and tried to prevent from having to serve. I wanted to hide and ended up in Breda where I met a certain Petrus Antonius Lambertus Marie de Jong (21 Hyacintplein, Breda). He offered me a hideout. After some days I left for Alkmaar."*[193]

After the war, Alfons declared: *"[t]he hiding was no success, it became clear I came from a pro-German family and nobody wanted to shelter me.*"[194] In later statements, he withdrew this comment. Was it a slip of the tongue? More about it later.

Alfons did not stay in Alkmaar for long. The exact duration of Alfons' stay in Alkmaar is unknown. Alfons stayed with friends and family members until he finally ended up in Maastricht. There he worked in the garage of Fisette (family of his sister in law), until he heard that Wim was in Brussels.

In the footsteps of Wim
Eidesformel in SS Ausbildungslager 1944 Sennheim: "Ich schwore Dir, Adolf Hitler, als Führer des Grossdeutschen Reiches und aller Germanen, Treue und Tapferkeit. Ich globe Dir und den von Dir bestimmten Vorgesetzten Gehorsam bis in den Tod, so war got helfe."

"In December 1943, my brother told me there was a rally in Antwerp held by the Catholic priest Cyriel Verschaeve. By that time, my brother had served in the Waffen SS. During this rally, I was inspired by the fascinating speech by Cyriel Verschaeve. This Cyriel compared the war on Bolshevism with the old crusades, which impressed me immensely. Directly after the rally I enlisted for the Waffen SS in Breda. My enlistment as a soldier would contribute to the Dutch cause in the battle against this menace. Like so many Flemish and Dutch Catholic youngsters, I considered the war as a true crusade." [195]

Alfons wanted to join his brother in the war on Bolshevism. Father tried to stop him, but without succes. Alfons was determined. On 15 January 1944, he signed up for the *Waffen SS* in Breda. On 7 February 1944, mother Johanna wrote to a friend: *"On 31 January Al-*

fons left to become a Waffen SS volunteer. Father took him to The Hague. He had signed up without us knowing and of course he had to go. You must understand what it meant to us. He was far too young and should have first finished his school. Besides, he was our youngest, who stayed at our fathers. We miss him terribly, even more now because Wim is most likely leaving for the Eastern Front. Now literally our whole family is engaged in the victory for Germany. Father's job as a mayor is also very dangerous. In the surroundings of Veghel there have been many robberies and it is fortunate that father is fearless. Hopefully nothing will happen to him." [196]

Alfons left The Hague by train. His destiny was *Ausbildungslager* Sennheim, where he would be trained as an infantry soldier. His stay became one big deception. He immediately had arguments with his superiors about his Catholic upbringing: *"My idealism took some serious blows. When I enlisted on 31 January 1944 and left for Sennheim, our rosaries of both Flemish and Dutch volunteers were confiscated. We were forbidden to perform our religious duties. When I protested and attended mass on Sunday, I was put under close house-arrest."* [197]

His older brother Wim helped him out by using his contacts within the ministry of propaganda. He succeeded in getting Alfons to Berlin. There, he was able to enlist himself for the "wireless transmitters school", K.B.A. (*Kriegsberichter Abteilung), Abteilung Gruppe Funk*. Then misfortune struck. During his training he broke his foot, following which he got pneumonia and was admitted to hospital. As off 25 February 1944, he spent a month and a half in the sanatorium Ferch on the Schwielowsee, nearby Potsdam. His sister Marie wrote: *"Dear Fons, father and mother are still devastated because you left. You never should have enlisted without their approval* "Nevertheless, Maria had supported his decision. She was a firm believer in the German cause and tried to encourage her younger brother: "*The training will be in the end much easier.*"[198]

Alfons was allowed to spend the last two weeks of his recovery (*Erholungsurlaub*), in Breda. At the beginning of May 1944, Alfons returned to Berlin. There, he yet again suffered some more bad luck. This time he suffered from pleuritis, and was bed-ridden for at least three weeks. Alfons was not physically fit enough for active service. At a re-examination, he was declared "Dienstunfähig", disqualified. No glory to be gained at the *Waffen SS*. What now? Alfons returned home, disillusioned. He couldn't stay with his mother, as she was hospitalised in Breda. All her life she suffered from poor health. So he joined his father who had just become mayor of Veghel.[199]

To safety in Hildesheim

After D-Day things moved rapidly. Within three months the Allied forces reached Antwerp. When British paratroops of the 2nd Army landed nearby Veghel, his father instructed Alfons to pick up mother and his two sisters in Breda by car and drive them to safety in Germany. Then he fled on his own account. They would be reunited in Hildesheim. Alfons drove via Cologne to Bad Mergentheim (south of Germany). From there mother and sister continued their voyage to Hildesheim.

5 September 1944, *Dolle Dinsdag,* meant the exodus of all Nazi collaborators to Germany. Father fled with the retreating German army up north. Up to Enschede

and then on to Hildesheim, where he would find his wife and two of his daughters at 4 Karthäusserstrasse. Mother Johanna, Francisca (Sassen-Weidenbach) and Maria were for the moment safe. In Hildesheim father met former NSB mayor of the Dutch town of Cuijck, *Chr. J.H.W. Stakenborg* and together they planned to return to North Brabant. After receiving permission by the local authorities they left by car: "*After a very difficult voyage because of the lack of petrol we arrived in Enschede. There we should shelter in a hotel. There we discussed our plans with the owner and he advised us to contact the chief of police of Enschede Antony Berends.*" Berends on his part introduced them Richard Protze.[200]

Line crosser

The operational centre of *Abwehr* specialist Richard Traugott Andreas Protze was just moved from Berg en Dal (Nijmegen) to 'Holterhof' in Enschede because Montgomery's rapid advance. Protze's operational unit formed part of the command under *A. Von Feldmann* (*Frontaufklärungstruppe*; FAT 365) which main task was the recruitment of line-crossers. These were needed to gather intelligence on allied movements and to pass disinformation to Allied forces. Protze had approached Berends to look out for civilians who were willing to pass enemy lines. Father and Stakenborg seemed willing recruits. Protze promised to help them to Brabant but only if they offered their services as a line-crosser. While passing through enemy lines they had to keep their eyes and ears open. According to the secretary of Protze, Helene Skrodzki, Sassen senior was: "*Instructed to seek contact with the liberated part of The Netherlands. Once there he had to establish the whereabouts of the British and Dutch intelligence offices, military quarters, headquarter of Montgomery and the oil-pipelines. He should also report on the morale of the liberated south and the damage the German V-bombs cause to the Allied advance."*[201]

[Sassen senior:]"*At that time when I exchanged intelligence for provisions in order to stay alive. (Times were hard, the occupied part of The Netherlands was completely cut off and shortage of began to take its toll on the Dutch population). As mayor of Oudenrijn*[202] *I frequently met with retreating German soldiers who informed me on the Allied advance. Due to these contacts I was able to pass information about the effect the V1 bombardment on Antwerp and that British ships weren't able to unload in Antwerp but in the sea-lanes in Zeeland. The rest of the information I received from my oldest son Wim... The main reason to contact Protze was because I wanted to return to the freed part of Brabant. I had realised that German interest in The Netherlands was to only exploit it at the fullest for the war effort. Therefore I did my utmost best to get myself to the freed part of The Netherlands, by handing in reports that would not damage the Dutch nor help the German war-machine.*"[203]

In Utrecht their contact man was *Untersturmführer* Herman Wilhelm Ferdinand Gottlob Lange. His cover was a desk at the local military police office, the *Ortskommandantur*, in Utrecht and a local bar. Lange was no police officer but an intelligence officer who worked for the military section of the German contra espionage service Abwehr, section 306 *Frontaufklärungskommando* (FAK), based in Driebergen. At his office in Utrecht he received his undercover agents and informants. All valuable information was sent to Protze.

Instead of going directly to Utrecht both father as Stakenborg first decided to go to Amsterdam. Sassen senior knew that his oldest son Wim was chief editor of Dutch newspaper *De Telegraaf.*

Propaganda

Alfons had to report at the Flemish editorial staff of *Radio Stuttgart* to work as an operator. This was his first working experience as a broadcaster. A month later he was transferred to the *Vlaamse Vrijheidszender* (Flemish radio freedom) in Herkenrath (Wipperfürth), Bergisch Gladbach. There the mobile transmitter *Kampfsender* "Radio Vlaanderen Vrij" operated under direction of *Jef Desseyn*: *"Wim was working for the Deutsche Europa Sender (DES) in Cologne. Radio Brussels was evacuated and was called now the Vlaamse Vrijheidszender. This radio broadcasting station had to make the impression that it was located in the liberated Belgian territory. Messages were sent about a certain Geert de rebel". It story was as follows: "This Geert the rebel had fought the Germans together with an underground movement, though he continued this battle with the invading Allied forces because he became completely disillusioned with the liberating armies, because they did not keep their promise. I was assigned to compile an American Jazz music program and to announce these over the radio. I have done this from October 1944 till the end of November 1944."* [204]

Joining the resistance?

On 20 September 1944 Alfons was back in The Netherlands. The precise date can be reconstructed by an incident at *De Telegraaf* building in Amsterdam. The state police recorded at 00.30 hours, in the night of 20 to 21 September 1944 the following incident: "*The police officers K and V. reported that around 00.30 hours am, the automatic rifle of the SS man Alphons Sassen, age 17 years old, current address unknown, in the porters loge of the building Dagblad de Telegraaf, 225 Nieuwerzijds Voorburgwal, lying the on top of the heating through unknown causes fell on the ground, which subsequently went off, and wounded J.P. ten Have, typographer, in his right shoulder.*" There were no witnesses present at the incident.[205]

It is unclear whether Alfons was on leave or he returned definitely. This period was a turning point for Alfons. According to his own statements he got disillusioned with the war. His father had joined the Abwehr and his brother Wim was banned from Festung Holland. What to do? "*In October 1944 I wanted to leave the SS officially and go to the liberated south of Holland, where I lived. I joined the Waffen SS because I wanted to fight Russia. When this became impossible because SS divisions were deployed on the Western front, the reasons for my voluntary enlistment got lost.*"[206]

In Amsterdam he requested an interview with his PK commander *Obersturmführer* Beisel. In it he asked for his release from the SS. Beisel answered that the only way he could get out of the SS was to join the German counter espionage service, *Abwehr*. Alfons doubted but followed Beisel advice and met up with Abwehrspecialist Protze in Enschede. There he was informed to become a line crosser. Alfons had to cross the frontline and gather military intelligence in Limburg and Brabant. He considered the mission too dangerous and wanted to have some time to think about it. In the mean time Wim's section was moved to Doetinchem. Not that far from Protze's operation centre: the estate Holterhof at Enschede Glanerburg. Alfons was indecisive and decided to join his brother in Doetinchem.

Alfons dealt with the printing and spreading of the so called illegal paper *Het Laatste Nieuws*. At this station Alfons met a friend, Hans Schild, who worked in Doetinchem as *Bildberichter* (cameraman and photographer) for *Het Laatste Nieuws*. Alfons had met Schild for the first time when they were both trained at the *Waffen SS* as *Kriegsberichter*. Alfons wasn't really actively involved in this process of distributing this paper. According to his own statements he was in a moral dilemma and therefore he had contacted the Resistance. He had lost his enthusiast for the German cause*: "The publication of "Het Laatste Nieuws" was several times forbidden by the German censorship. At this paper I was instructed by my brother as a future reporter. Because I became more aware I was on the wrong side, I got into conflict with my brother. It was even that bad that I asked my company commander to discharge me as SS soldier. I wasn't fit for active service on the front anyway and I thought that possibility existed. Though without result, only on the condition that I would serve as a "Frontläufer" (line-crosser) for the Abwehr, which I of course denied. Around this time (October 1944) I met a friend of my brother, Mertens, who soon noticed in our conversations that I reluctantly served the German army. Half December he even introduced me to members of the Resistance group (KP) in Alkmaar. Especially with the chef, a certain Pierre (de Bie), who asked me to join the Abwehr in order to* retrieve as much information as possible about this intelligence service, and especially about its Dutch recruits."[207]

Did Alfons offer his services to the Resistance or did he follow Sassen senior footsteps by joining the Abwehr on his instigation? *Untersturmführer* H. W. F. G. Lange (FAT 306) confirmed the latter: *"[Lange:] In the fall of 1944 I met in my department the former mayor of Veghel, Sassen senior. I was working as a non commissioned officer at the military police at the Ortskommandantur in Utrecht. There I ran the Kommando 306 Frontaufklärungskommando (FAK), which was a Dienststelle (branch) of the military Abwehr section. My part was to receive letters of informants in civilian clothes and filter information accordingly to their importance. Usually these people were Dutch men. Sassen senior was one of them. Through Sassen senior I was introduced to his son Alfons. The father wanted to see his son transferred from the SS Dienststelle to Kommando 306."*[208]

Sassen senior had offered his services to *Abwehr* specialist Protze. The debriefing did happen in Utrecht. According to Lange Sassen senior wanted to keep his son nearby. The members of the propaganda group in Enschede and Hilversum had a bad influence on his young son. Besides Sassen senior found himself too old for espionage work in hostile areas. He had a better idea. He wanted to put forward his youngest son, Alfons, to be used for line-crossing activities. Protze approved it. He did recruit Alfons under the alias "Jongerijn", his father was "Oudenrijn" Alfons started as a line crosser. Both father as his son, Alfons, selected within their circle of friends volunteers for line crossing work in enemy territory. Gabriel Smit and Hans Schild were at least two friends recruited by the Sassens.

According to the secretary of Protze, Helene Skrodzki, Alfons made an *"enthusiast impression, while he also showed signs of intelligence and insight."*[209]

At the same time Alfons had contacted Mertens, who in his turn tried to convince young Alfons into collecting intelligence on the Abwehr. To convince him, Alfons was taken to Amsterdam where he on 21 December 1944 met the other resistance members Pierre "Colaris" (de Bie), Eddy Conijn *(brother of Fritz Conijn), and* W. Sanders*, alias Hiemstra.* *"After this meeting I briefed Conijn every two weeks."* [210]

A week later on 28 December 1944 Alfons started as an undercover agent for Protze. His mission was: *"to seek contact with the Dutch Resistance movements, and through it locate the secret telephone line running to the liberated South. When this line was discovered, I had to pass disinformation (given by Protze) to the south. Protze also gave me an Ausweis (ID card) which I case of emergency I could identify me. The Ausweis stated I was in the service of the German defence."*[211]

The activities as line crossers wasn't enough for Sassen senior and junior, they wanted to serve the German cause better. In January 1945 father, in company of former NSB mayor of Berghem, *Th. M. Wagemans*, and Alfons paid a visit to the *Ortskommandantur* in Utrecht. They wanted to speak to Lange. At his office they unfolded the plan of setting up a training school for under cover counterintelligence agents: *"It was their intention to recruit agents within the Landwacht (auxiliary police force, rural guards) and Jeugdstorm (NSB youth movement) for their agent school. According to them there would be enough volunteers."* [212]

This idea did not come unexpectedly. The oldest daughter Maria, aka Gilly, had been trained at a secret agent school, *A-Schule-West*, in The Hague. Most likely Sassen senior thought of his son as a possible intelligence officer or secret agent. Protze too proposed to Alfons to join an underground cell in Noord Holland which had to become active after the Allied occupation. This *Wehrwolf* unit had to engage in sabotage and assaults in the Allied controlled areas. Alfons declined.

Wim also was aware of his contacts with the Resistance: *"I was very suspicious about the activities of my younger brother. Because he was too young to be a convinced Nazi, but against the will of my parents though for his happiness I engaged him in January 1944. He was then 16.5 years old. But I never had the facts, I only knew that he was a very disappointed boy due to his experience as a young recruit for the Eastern Front. Afterwards I learned that he was doing dangerous work for the underground or otherwise. I talked with him about it but he denied all. I told him that if it was his conviction to fight for the other side he had to do it openly. He denied it again. I expressed my fears to my father, who reproached me for having him dragged into the Waffen SS."* [213]

Did Alfons fool everybody including his own father? Did father not know that his son had approached the Resistance? Whatever it may be, Sassen senior stepped down, while his son continued the fieldwork. Sassen senior wanted to get out because he was afraid to be unmasked as a fraud. As an informant he had spiced his intelligence reports together with a mix of fantasy, history books and old news in return for scarce products and provisions. A tactic that Alfons would soon copy in the nearby future.

Due to the unforeseen Allied advance the *Dienststelle* Protze was relocated to a villa in Hengelo. *"Captain Protze told me if I could not reach him at Enschede, I had to report at Hauptmann Bulang in Driebergen (Abwehrstelle III; villa Beukenstein). Schild joined me and was also prepared to perform his duties for the Abwehrstelle Driebergen. Our mission was to infiltrate the Resistance."*[214]

Schild was unaware of Alfons contacts with the Resistance: *"[Alfons :] I still reported to Sanders. In order not to be too conspicuous, Sanders advised me to inform my German superiors that I followed the trail of an Allied secret agent who wore a German uniform. A week before liberation day I was assigned to go to The Hague to collect all data on this possible intelligence man."*[215]

Alfons did leave for The Hague and approached: *"some people (J. Coolens and Dries Daniels) who were known heavy criminals to the police. They committed robberies and had nothing to do with the Resistance or any foreign intelligence group"*.[216]

Robberies

Alfons used his status as penetration agent to cover his true activities in The Hague. In reality he joined a gang of robbers. Hans Schild also participated. From time to time they stayed over at little boarding houses and small hotels in The Hague. From these "operation centres" they selected their victims. Over a period of three to four months they carried out 14 assaults. Alfons used during these raids his service pistol, a revolver, a Tommy gun and his *Abwehr* papers in the name of "Smit". This "Smit" was supposedly a student from Amsterdam. The gang raided shops and individuals. To mislead his victims Alfons presented himself as an investigative SD officer. Once let in, Alfons showed his gun and opened the door to his fellow gang members. They were looking for money, gold, jewels, coffee, alcohol and other scarce commodities. Alfons even dared to say after the war that these raids were carried out to in accordance with the Resistance. Schild did correct him: "*The raids were so called illegal stunts and meant for our own benefit.*"[217]

When Wim started to work for Radio Hilversum (March 1945) Alfons joined him, According to colleague Willy van den Hout the two brothers led an undisciplined life. The end of the war was near and the "take it now and all before it is too late" reigned. Nights were spent in bars and clubs, with women and the illegal trade. During day time the continued their work for *Sender Hilversum* and *Het Laatste Nieuws*. Alfons and Schild disappeared so now and then for so-called "special assignments" for The Hague.

Miep van der Voort declared after the war that Alfons acted as a member of the armed Resistance (knokploeg). In her eyes he and his mates looked more like a bunch of thugs. She was absolutely right.

His sister Maria (Mies) still believed one hundred percent in the German cause. On 8 November 1944 she wrote from Berlin to Alfons: *"Have you heard that the Japanese and the Indian (Subas Chandra Bose, Indian National Army) have started their offensive. Hopefully it will be successful enough to relieve the pressure her on the Western Front. If only those Indian troops will push ahead and those Arabs will get more determined it still could turn into a real mess. What's left is only that awful Russian front, that is still a heavy burden. The day after tomorrow I am leaving for Antwerp and will stay there for a week,. Cheers and a big kiss of Mies.*" [218] If Maria was still positive what about the rest of the family?

Wim did not want to be kept in the dark about Alfons' activities. When he asked what he had been up to Wim was told that he (Alfons) was working for a certain Hermann Lange. He wanted to size up the situation [Wim :] "*I am the oldest son of the mayor of Veghel, my name is Wim Sassen and my younger brother is Alfons Sassen. Not only as his brother but also as his superior I feel responsible for his actions. He is often absent from service, and in return he speaks of special missions of confidential nature and when questioned did want to reveal anything. I would like to know what is going on.*"[219]

In the interview with Lange one thing led to another. It seemed that Alfons was working for the *Abwehr*. On top of that his superior, commander Bulang, was setting up a stay-behind network in The Netherlands. A set up that also occurred to Wim. Wim wanted to be in. He offered himself and his whole team to join this stay-behind network. Time was pressing so Bulang agreed. Then things went quickly. The entire team was relieved from any PK activities. The next face was to get the NEUROP unit ready for it subversive actions after Allied occupation. In the midst of their preparations Alfons got arrested during one of his robberies. The *Sicherheitspolizei* had kept a close eye on the gang-members and this time they were caught in the act. There were no severe consequences. Werner Schramm of FAT 365 (Driebergen) came to rescue him. Both Alfons and Schild were released. Schramm made up some story that the two boys were in the midst of an *Abwehr* penetration mission of a resistance group. The raids were part of their undercover operation. This time Alfons was lucky.

A week before liberation day Alfons got arrested for the second time in The Hague. This time he, just by coincidence, became the victim of a *razzia* (police raid). He was arrested in the *Acacia Bar* (147 Wagenstraat). When searched the SD officers found a revolver and several identity papers: a *Grüne Ausweis* issued by the *Abwehr* in the name of "Smit" and one issued by *Abwehrstelle* Hilversum. Only when taken into the police station he revealed his true identity. The SD still did not trust him and incarcerated him. Alfons used again and again the excuse that he as an *Abwehr* agent was trying to penetrate the Resistance. In the *Acacia Bar* he was to meet a British officer. This time Alfons wasn't so lucky. One day before the Germany army capitulated in The Netherlands his superior, his ill brother Wim, came to rescue him and got him somehow out of detention.[220]

Was Alfons at the end of the war an *Abwehr* specialist as *Stern* journalist Kai Hermann described him in 1984. No! Alfons thankfully made use of the chaotic lawless days before The Netherlands was fully liberated. As *Abwehr* agent he could allow himself certain liberties which he fully exploited. No one had any control of this young man. He travelled between Doetinchem and Alkmaar, between Utrecht and The Hague. When things did get out of hand, there was always his brother Wim to help him out.

Wim was still ill. He hardly left the house and when he walked he had to make use of crutches. In this state Louis Kuitenbrouwer met him on 28 April in Utrecht. Three days later Hitlers' death was announced. Wim was devastated. Then heard his brother was in trouble. Despite his misery, he got in to his Opel and "liberated" Alfons from the hands of the SD on 4 May 1945 in The Hague. On 5 May the German army capitulated in The Netherlands. Alfons and Wim said goodbye to their comrades and father in Utrecht: Huib Klompe, Hans Schild and Sassen senior. It was every man for himself. The brothers knew where to go.

On their way to Alkmaar they had a stopover in Amsterdam. They stayed over at Hakki Holdert. The next day, 6 May, the BS (Netherlands forces of the interior) had surrounded the *Telegraaf*-building and gave the staff a chance to leave. Wim and Alfons continued their voyage to Alkmaar. Lucky again.

In Alkmaar the boys were received by Anthony Mertens and Eddy Conijn. Wim was put safely in the home of the family Boot and Alfons would stay that night at De Bie's place. A deal was a deal. De group Mertens, De Bie, Eddy Conijn and Wim Sanders kept their word and now they had to think of a plan how to protect these men. Alfons would cause no problems. Nobody knew him. Wim was different. He was a known collaborator and a wanted man. The Field Security (FS) was looking for him. They were considering declaring Wim a casualty of war. Once officially declared dead he would be taken off the wanted list and no criminal investigator would be looking for him. The other way was to wait until everything quieted down.

As soon as the roads were opened up, roadblocks removed and border checks controls loosened up, Wim could be lead southwards, to Spain. But before any action could be taken Wim Sassen was betrayed by his own fiancée, Miep.[221]

Liberation of Holland

Recruted by the Secret Services

Alfons, on the contrary, found his Maecenas: "*After the capitulation I went to Pierre de Bie in Alkmaar. On about 8 May I went accompanied by Eddy Conijn (second in command of POD Alkmaar) to Sanders, the head of the bureau of Dienst Politieke Misdrijven (Office of Political Offenses) in Amsterdam. After I had told Sanders my whole history, Sanders asked me to work for him. I was assigned to track down former members of the Abwehr who were not yet identified in the detention centres in The Netherlands. Sanders issued me an ID card in the name of "Pierre van Aalst", a name which I had chosen myself. This chef gave me the authorization to, in coordination with the Canadian Field Security, round up remnants of the German espionage service (Bulang and Stelle Protze) in The Netherlands. After some intensive weeks we indeed succeeded.*"[222]

Sanders confirms that he protected Alfons: "*I met Fonske through the mediation of three well known men; Pierre Colaris (de Bie) 62 Tolstraat Amsterdam, chef KP Noord Holland in Alkmaar, E. Conijn chef KP in Alkmaar, later he became chef POD Alkmaar and Mertens, secretary of the board of De Linie. They introduced him because he was under command of Werner Bulang at the*

Abwehrstelle Driebergen. When he was presented I found him useful to recruit him for Dienst Politieke Misdrijven in order to help us track down agents of the Abwehrstelle. Due to my intervention Alfons Sassen was released. Fonske was supervised by Roel de Jong."[223]

Alfons was indeed introduced to Sanders on 8 May 1945 in Amsterdam. Wim Sanders worked closely with the *Canadian Field Security* (CFS). The CFS enjoyed complete authority for tracking down and interrogating SD and other German officials. Once questioned, these individuals were handed over to the *Militair Gezag* (Dutch Military Authority). Alfons debriefed Sanders and the Area Security Officer of the *British Field Security Service* (BFSS) captain *R. Douthwaits* about all he knew on the Bulang organisation.

The intel was of such quality that Sanders decided to authorize Alfons to work with the CFSS (Captain Robertson) in order to round up the espionage network. His task was to search detention centres (Den Helder, Wieringen and IJmuiden) for hidden SS, SD and *Abwehr* officials whose true identity had not been established yet. In total, he assisted in the arrest of 30 *Abwehr* officials among which his chef Bulang, as well as Schramm and Lange. In return for his cooperation, Alfons received an ID card in the name of Pierre van Aalst and a certificate of political reliability. There were limits, however. Alfons couldn't go just anywhere he wanted. At the back of his temporary ID card, Douthwaits wrote: "*Any question in regard to this man should be referred to Captain Douthwaits, area Security Officer, 126/5 Apollolaan Amsterdam, he is ordered not to leave the Canadian area.*"[224]

Alfons enjoyed his freedom in section Amsterdam. He was wearing a uniform of the BS. He did not receive any wages but could declare his expenses at the BNV (Bureau of National Security), such as the use of his motorcycle. His employers saw him as a useful informer who was prepared to expose werewolf-networks in and outside The Netherlands.

Sanders concealed Alfons from other investigation services. The criminal tribunal in Arnhem was looking for him: "*By article 18 of the Tribunal decision of 9 August 1945, the undersigned* Ferdinand Karel Rudolf Clemens Sassen, *by profession secretary of the Tribunal in Arnhem, living in Nijmegen, 1 Beekmansdalseweg, hereby reported that the Dutch national A. Sassen, last known address in Breda, 30 Rustlandstraat, has acted against the interest of the Dutch people or harmed the Resistance in favour of the enemy or complicits by becoming a member of the NSB, his enlistment to the SS as a SS war correspondent. Undersigned Nijmegen 8 August 1945.*"[225]

Intrigues within the Security Services
In the meantime, Sanders left the *Dienst Politieke Misdrijven* (DPM) for the position as Chef (CI) Central Intelligence, a section of the BNV. The transition had consequences for Alfons too. Because of his excellent cooperation in dismantling the Bulang organisation, Alfons was officially recruited as special agent no. 210. His new mission was to infiltrate the werewolf centres in Germany.

[Alfons :]"*When I, as a special agent, was still attached to the BNV, I was ordered to make a schedule of all possible S (sabotage) targets and activities of underground werewolf cells in Germany. My first focal point was Wipperfürth. From this area I would gradually work on each cell.*" This was first put to the test in Amsterdam and surroundings. Alfons was, at the end of 1945, just nineteen.[226]

The area of interest of the BNV in the mean time had changed. Its main focus was the fear of a possible communist threat. The Resistance groups of the left had, during the war, gained immense popularity. These underground movements suffered the most from German repression. The BNV wanted to neutralize this group. It wanted to chart its (communist) influence in The Netherlands. Alfons was assigned to penetrate leftist and anarchist movements and report on them. The BNV was extremely interested in the support the communists received from abroad. On top of this, it wanted to seize all concealed arsenal depots which the leftist Resistance had build up during the war.

Alfons worked from within as a mole or penetration agent under his alias "Pierre van Aalst". He became an official member of the communist association *Vrienden van de Waarheid* (Friends of the communist daily *De Waarheid*) and of *Spartacus*, the anarchistic union. During a rally, Alfons heard about the preparation of a general strike in Maastricht: "*As a member of the association of Vrienden van de Waarheid I was informed of the upcoming strike in the mines. I reported this to Sanders, who on his part sent me to police inspector De Jong. De Jong ordered me to go south to retain as much information about this strike. I went to Maastricht and visited the family of my brother's wife Fisette. They knew my past as an SS man and did not believe I was working for a Dutch organisation. In order to gain their trust I showed them my papers I received from Sanders and told them I was willing to the local police.*"[227]

Things took a turn for the worse. He got arrested on 7 or 8 July 1945 by the municipal police, after a family member (Paula Fisette) denounced him as a member of the *Waffen SS*. Fisette did not trust Alfons at all. To prove the contrary, he did go to the police, and was arrested immediately. The documents in his possession raised many questions. How was it possible that a former SS man worked for the national police? Alfons was handed over to the American CI/IPW Team 206, G2 Section Chanor Base Section APO 562. There he was interrogated by *Kurt D. Elle*, at that time a special agent in charge of the IPW (Interrogation of Prisoners of War) team 206.

Kurt D. Elle recommended: "*That subject held at Maastricht is pending determination of his status (POW or spy). That it be considered that subject is court-martialled through PW channels being accused of espionage, that this report be forwarded to higher headquarters for a determination as to why a former SS man and a member of the German espionage system can be employed by the Dutch Secret Service that in case of a court martial Wim Sanders and Pierre de Bie (at present employed at the office of the political police (POD) and Service for Political Crimes (DPM)) be summoned to testify as witnesses and finally that this office be instructed to be the disposition of subject. Undersigned Kurt D. Elle, MIS.*" Case officer *Cornelis Karel*, district leader Gennep Bergen (no.31 Gewest Limburg) BNV section A was ordered to assist: "*The suspect was kept in custody for the mean time until his identity and assignment were verified. His statement of him coming down south in order to report on the anticipated strike did not make sense, because the strike happened a week ago. He claimed he had received his false ID card from Sanders after the liberation of The Netherlands and that his superior Sanders had not had the time to issue him an ID card of the BNV. Second, he immediately revealed his mission to the investigating officer of the CIC, two members of the POD section Maastricht and two Dutch interpreters working for the CIC. He also claimed Sanders used to be a member of the German espionage and Abwehr. He went on mission carrying a Lee revolver which he had kept since his SS time. The subject was in possession of several identity papers which made a suspicious impression, and were totally unnecessary for an agent of the national secret service:* an ID card issued by Sanders, several letters of the POD, NBS and a *Certificate of political reliability, Alkmaar written by Mertens and chef POD Alkmaar E. Conijn, stating:" Herewith we certify that Alfons Sassen joined the Abwehr on our emphatic request and that after the liberation he did useful work in cooperation with the POD and that by this activity, through mediation with the FSS, it was possible to arrest the whole group of Bulang. It appeared to us that when some of the members of this A stelle were arrested at Den Helder, as these members already suspected Alfons and recognised him they said to each other "Also war der Sassen doch bei der Ondergrondse." This somewhat adventurous youth has been educated in a completely "wrong" entourage and therefore was not able to form a personal opinion about political questions. He has done much good work for the allied cause, and has also risked a lot, so that we willingly plead to give him another chance. Undersigned A. Conijn, A. Mertens, 2 December 1945."*[228]

It got even worse. Alfons remained in custody despite Sanders' intervention. Sanders himself became subject of investigation: "*On 8 July 1945 I (Alfons) was arrested by the CIC in Maastricht and put in the American MP prison. I was interrogated by 2 CIC men (German Jews). They verified my papers and stated that I, as a British intelligence man, was not allowed to enter the American zone without having first informed the American headquarters in Brussels. Then I was sent back to my cell. The next day I was questioned again about my falsified papers in the name of "Van Aalst". I asked them to verify their authenticity. The documents I carried: a false identity card, an identity card of the POD, an identity card of the POD Alkmaar and a statement of IP de Jong, stating I was on mission on behalf of the BNV. At night they dragged me out of my cell again and brought to these two CIC men. I immediately realized they were under the influence of strong liquor.*

One of them came up to me and shouted: "Und jetzt Schweinehund wirst du die Wahrheit sagen, sonst werd ich einen jüdischen Metzger holen, der dich bestimmt gerne zusammenhaut." He hit me several times with his club. I then was left alone for a week, until they wanted to interrogate me again. Present were the two CIC officers and a 2nd *lieutenant who revealed himself as an agent of the BNV. I did not know this person. This lieutenant was very friendly and sympathetic. Even the attitude of the CIC men had changed remarkably. So I realised that I was either no longer a suspect, or a game was being played. It soon became clear it was the latter. The CIC men said that major Sanders had written an open letter to their section asking for his release. I had to understand of course that they would not answer it. Weren't they an official organ to* *which he could hand in an official request for his release or was he trying to cover himself like he did by sending me on mission with falsified papers? Then the 2nd lieutenant started his story. He first wanted me to be recruited by the CIC. I then had to explain everything I knew about major Sanders, in particular with regards to his work for the German espionage service. I told them I did not know anything about this period. The 2nd Lieutenant told me that major Sanders had got rid of the best performing employees of the BNV and exchanged them for all sorts of obscure people. They wanted to put an end to it. He therefore asked me if I would be prepared to make a false statement that Sanders indeed had performed duties for the Abwehrstelle. In the mean time I had been in custody for several weeks. Then suddenly I had to appear in the office of the CIC where the two young military men and Lt. Keers received me to be examined by the staff. I was taken to the staff of the BNS (Commander of the Dutch Armed Forces Prince Bernhard) in Apeldoorn and was again interrogated by Keers the next day, again about Sanders and his role within the Abwehr. According to Lt. Wolter Keers, a conflict had arisen between the Staff of the FSS and BNV because the BNV did not respect the international intelligence laws. Sanders, in particular, was said to have breached these rules often, because he recruited politically unreliable personnel. This whole matter wasn't about me, I wasn't the problem but the fact that former SD men were working for the BNV was a step too far."*[229]

Major Sanders was placed into custody on 2 September 1946. Alfons was transferred to camp Wezep until at the beginning of November, Lt. Keers, together with a 1st lieutenant from Apeldoorn, appeared and claimed he (Lt. Keers) was misled. The Sanders affair had been cleared and he was no longer a suspect. [Alfons:] *"My statements had been verified and all was well. It would be a matter of a few days before they would release me. Lt. Keers wanted to make clear that external powers from the left wanted to dispose of Sanders. These leftist individuals had caused the turmoil within the FSS."*[230]

Alfons knew how to satisfy his interrogators. According to Alfons, both the CIC as the successor of the BNV wanted to use him as an agent. He preferred to continue his career as special agent no. 210 for the BNV: *"I wanted to dedicate my life in the service of our country"*. The NBS, the staff of the Dutch Prince Bernard zur Lippe Biesterfeld, was quite interested in such a true patriot... the CIC therefore decided to hand Alfons over to the *Generale Staf 2* (GS2: intelligence and security) of the BNV in Apeldoorn. Within the staff of the Prince GS2 there was still doubt about Wim Sanders. There was reason to believe that during the war he had collaborated with the enemy. Alfons was asked again to make an incriminating statement about Sanders. Alfons saw his opportunity to please his new chef and was quite willing to fulfil this request. Altogether, he concocted three different accusations, but in the end, he would withdraw these statements.[231]

Sanders was arrested because of several reasons. He was suspected to be a former collaborator, of running his own private intelligence service within the BNV, and of recruiting "shady" personnel. But the most damaging accusation was his political preference. It was rumoured that Sanders was a communist. The ensuing affair meant the end of Sanders' career as an intelligence officer. He was put out of action. In his defence, Sanders denied all accusations. By now, he likely managed to figure out for which tem Alfons was playing: *"It was not known to me that Alfons Sassen worked under the alias Pierre van Aalst. In any case members of the DPM did not work under an alias, even when they worked for the BNV. That employees used an alias when working in the field goes without saying. I did not know that Alfons Sassen was referred within the DPM as agent no. 210. Alfons Sassen was successful for the DPM in dismantling the Bulang organisation, and exposing others in the internment camps of Den Helder and Ijmuiden. In Den Helder he worked for the Canadians. One day Alfons was arrested and I intervened. He was then supervised by Roel de Jong, and he was restricted to the Amsterdam area. Despite this restriction he ended up in Maastricht and was arrested by the Americans. We did not interfere and later he was taken over by the staff of Prince Bernhard where he was used to collect incriminating evidence on my person. Then the fable of me being a communist started, and Fonske exploited this affair to the fullest because his is a very clever boy. I saw him again in 1946 in a Dutch military uniform. At this meeting he produced a letter stating be was released, and of that letter I took a picture, which I handed over to Colonel Einthoven. I remember that the letter he was carrying was signed by the prosecutor J.W.M. Des Tombe... Fonske (Alfons) told me that he was instructed by Lieutenant Colonel Six (NBS) to work against me. After this visit I contacted the Public Prosecutor in Arnhem to retract his conditional release. It could well be that Fonske disappeared after this, but I cannot be sure."*[232]

Wim Sanders declared later that the intelligence Alfons had gathered usually contained a high dose of fantasy, although his reports did end up on the desks of the BNV, CVD, POD and PRA.

Sanders knew much more than he revealed about the Sassen boys. Not only did he know Wim and Alfons Sassen personally, but he also knew that the other family members had worked for the German Intelligence Service.

Penetration agent Alfons

After two months of detention, Alfons was transferred into custody at Harskamp, a civilian and SS internment camp in The Netherlands. Supervising chef was investigator *A.J.P. Besselink*. Alfons was no ordinary detainee. He was used to spy on and expose members of the Nazi underground movement whose true identity wasn't yet established.

Besselink was also aware that an organisation operating from within the camp was helping political delinquents and former SS men to escape to Germany and Spain. The members belonged to a secret underground werewolf organisation whose goal it was to regroup fanatical Nazis and resist Allied domination. This clandestine organisation had organised itself already in several internment camps. Some members of the SS had had themselves arrested on purpose in order to recruit former SS and SD officials from within these detention-centres like Harskamp.

During a raid in nearby Ede, a large arms depot was discovered and Alfons had to find out where the weapons originated: *"First I was ordered to gather intelligence on unreliable guards while at the same time I had to discover more about the smuggling of arms in a nearby location."*[233]

Alfons' supervisor Besselink wanted to take it even a step further. He wanted to create a small team specialised in tracking down werewolf organisations in Western Europe. To realise this, he needed men who had knowledge of these kinds of networks and who were willing to dismantle them. Alfons became one of those team members. As MP Sergeant with pay book in the name of "Alfons Beaumont", agent no. 210 set off. In turn for his cooperation, Alfons gained liberties to move about outside the internment camp. He even stayed at the house of his commander 127 Nieuw Millingen (Amersfoort - Apeldoorn). Commander Besselink was convinced that Alfons was a reliable instrument to dismantle werewolf organisations: *"Alfons declared he could verify the network of the werewolf organisation in the Ruhr, starting in the city of Wuppertal. For that purpose he had to illegally cross the Dutch-German border. Once in the al zone, he could contact the Allied headquarters stationed in the Ruhr area. He speaks fluent German and looked quite innocent because of his youthful fresh face. Most likely he is very useful to penetrate the new organisation of NEUROP This new underground movement tries to reorganise the known werewolf organisations together with other specially selected secret agents recruited from the former SS, SD and other Nazi formations."*[234]

In December 1945, Alfons and commander Besselink undertook a trip to Belgium. There they contacted an officer of the Spanish Secret Service (S.I.E.: *Servicio de intelligencia Española*) who called himself "Pax". This "Pax", whose true identity was *Martin Aurelio Martines*, was well informed about the activities of the *International Brigade* (communist) in Europe. Through his connections, he had heard of the upcoming strike in the Rotterdam harbour, and revealed the leading names of the *Eenheidsvakcentrale* who were planning the strike. Through his connections, Alfons also heard of a possible assassination attempt on then Dutch Prime Minister *Willem Schermerhorn*. The airplane in which he would travel to London, was allegedly sabotaged.[235]

On 1 February 1946, secret agent no. 210 reported: "*In France, Belgium, England and The Netherlands the communists are currently working hard on the resurrection of the International Brigade.*" Alfons performed outstanding work. In the Haarlemmmerstraat in Amsterdam he tracked down a concealed arsenal. In The Hague he located a clandestine wireless transmitter (W/T set of 20 kW). In Belgium he reported on the BNV section in Brussels. During that time he met his brother while he was on the run. Alfons was seen at that time in the uniform of a Dutch sergeant, accompanied by another Dutch man. Who unknown. Maybe Besselink.

On the run
In March 1946, on a trip to The Hague together with Besselink, Alfons "fled". His escape, (if it can be called as such since at the time there was no reason for it) is

veiled by mystery. Alfons: "*After my escape from Harskamp I left for Belgium. There I met my brother Wim, who was in hiding. I told him that at least ten investigators of the BNV were after him in Brussels. I wanted to scare him hoping he would leave Belgium.*" [236]

The two brothers met on 8 March 1946 to be exact. Alfons obtained the address of one of Wim's many safe houses in Antwerp (Monastery, 23 Ploegstraat) from Anthony Mertens and Miep van der Voort. Wim had used his old contacts with the NIR and *Europa Sender* to find refuge. The sister of Paul Douliez, *Yvonne Douliez* (10 Pesthoflei) was one of these contacts in Antwerp. In March 1946, Wim had moved to Brussels where Miep rented him an attic in the Phillip le Bonstreet in Brussels. When Alfons met Wim, the latter was accompanied by a certain *J. Nijs*, a former fellow student and collaborator at the NIR. During their encounter, Wim mainly complained about hi money shortage. Alfons did not stay for long. He left for Amsterdam by train. In the Dutch capital he knocked at the door of a known friend: "*I left a suitcase at Pierre Colaris (*de Bie*), 62 Tolstraat Amsterdam. In this case with a zipper were my clothes, which I needed badly, and an American Tommy machine gun 11m. The mentioned suitcase was not placed in the dwelling of Colaris but at his friend's place. On 10 March 1946, together with this suitcase, I went to Pierre Colaris' house. He could not take me in, and instead took me to some friends nearby the Tolstraat. At night I went for a walk. In a cafeteria I spotted someone of the investigators of Harskamp, upon which I ran off.*"[237]

Arrested

A week later, on 15 March 1946, Alfons Sassen was arrested in Breda. He was found "naked from the waist down", in bed with another young man, *Petrus Antonius Lambertus De Jong*. De Jong was the same man at whose home Alfons had sought sanctuary in 1943 when called to fulfil his duties in the *Arbeitseinsatz*.

The PRA investigators took Alfons to the penal institution *De Koepel* in Breda. On Easter Saturday (20 April 1946) he was first transferred to detention camp Hoogerheide and, through the intervention of Besselink, again to Harskamp in July 1946.

Alfons was subsequently interrogated in Breda as well as in other two detention centres by the Public Prosecutor from Zutphen, *J.J. Lammers*, and by an investigator of the *Directoraat Generaal Bijzondere Rechtspleging* (DGBR), detective Edo Westendorp. They wanted to know more about Alfons' anti-communistic activities and even more so about his fugitive brother Wim. The following period is somewhat chaotic. Alfons stayed at Harskamp for about two months, following which he was transferred to detention centre Milligen nearby Apeldoorn. *"I left Milligen at the end of September when the whole centre was relocated to detention centre Avegoor (September 1946)."*

The contributions of agent no. 210 had been of considerable importance, and this was rewarded. On 1 August 1946, Alfons Sassen was removed from the list of wanted persons. Four months later, on 15 November 1946, he was released from custody at detention centre *Avegoor–Ellecom*. He was, though, placed under supervision of Besselink and Lammers.

On 26 November 1946, the Public Prosecutor J.J. Lammers (Boggelaan Warmsveld) wrote to colleague *T.J.G. Baron van Voorst tot Voorst* that he had recruited a most valuable operative (penetration agent): "*Hereby a copy of the release from custody of A. Sassen. We can start immediately with different cases concerning the Communist Party and this young man could help us with it. When I will visit you in Den Bosch we can discuss this matter more in detail. Many thanks for you kind cooperation, Yours sincerely Lammers.*"[238]

Between 1946 and 1947, Alfons lived in both Besselink and Westendorps' homes, always protected by one or the other. Alfons knew perfectly well how to play these two supervisors. Until 6 April 1947, Alfons was carrying out missions for Lammers and Westendorp in Belgium and The Netherlands. His task was to monitor the communist activities in both countries. After this assignment Alfons, instigated by the Spanish secret agent "Pax", moved to Bentheim, Germany. According to Pax, the communist movement had discovered the true identity of secret agent Alfons. They were after him and wanted to finish him off. Alfons subsequently used his contacts within American Secret Services to get posted in Germany: "*In Germany I worked for the Intelligence Section Hannover, under captain Smit, until the midst of June, I was on special mission for both the SIE (Servicio Información Español) and Section Hannover to Zürich (Switzerland). Three days later I left Switzerland and went to the French zone; at Sullingen (nearby Schaffhausen) I was arrested by the French Gendarmerie, because they found several identity papers in my possession. They suspected me of being a spy. I was transferred to Lör-*

rach, where the Bureau Territorial, Deuxième (II) Bureau - the French Intelligence headquarters - was located. After being placed under custody and interrogated by the II Bureau, I was asked to work for lieutenant Meier (alias). I accepted this offer. I was to return immediately to Hannover (1 August 1946). I spent five days there, and then went back again to Lörrach. Then I was sent to Hannover again for fourteen days. I worked in Hannover and was in contact with the SIS, Captain Nichols of the Special Investigative Service Frankfurt (APO 757). Wearing an American uniform I left for Paris, and from then onwards I was on mission in Germany and Belgium. In Belgium I was in contact with the service of Veiligheid van Staat, Pierre van Pelt, 24 Luxembourg, Brussels, trying to get a photocopy of the request of a Belgian passport in the name of "Jose dos Santos", a Portuguese agent of the KIC CG2 (Communist Intern Central: Komintern), who at that time was involved with the countess Sauty de Chalon, an agent of the American Secret Services who was murdered in Belgium in 1946. This Dos Santos was the man who in 1946 was ordered to kill me. In the mean time, this man had most likely already been arrested by the II Bureau."[239]

Until 12 October 1947, Alfons' operational base was Hannover, following which he decided to return to The Netherlands. On 16 October, he left for Aachen. There he contacted (DGBR) investigator Edo Westendorp, who told Alfons to wait for him at the customs office at Vaals. Together with Public Prosecutor Lammers, Westendorp wanted to lure Alfons to the border. Alfons had left the country without permission of his supervisor Lammers. On top of that they wanted to know where he had been and more specifically what he had done during his months of absence. in particular, for which intelligence services he had worked for? On top of that all his intelligence reports were based on complete nonsense. One investigator even went to Paris to verify the contents of his reports. Nothing added up. When Alfons was confronted with these allegations, he dismissed them by saying he would personally make sure to collect all the evidence needed in support. But it was too late. Despite his objections, and stating that he was now employed by the Americans, he was arrested on the spot. A day later on 18 October 1947, he was handed over to the PRA Breda. In the penal institution of Breda his interrogation continued. His unreliable reports had cost him his career as special agent no. 210. He was sentenced to three and a half months of prison.[240]

In a report dated 22 November 1947 drawn up for the *Directoraat Generaal voor de Bijzondere Rechtspleging* (DGBR: Directorate for Extraordinary Law Enforcement), investigator Edo J. Westendorp described the intelligence gathered by Alfons as: "complete fantasy". He profiled A.C.A.M. Sassen as follows: [Westendorp :] *"In my opinion Alfons Sassen is someone with some education, has a good understanding of things, very cunning and has a thirst for sensation. It is someone with a broad imagination, easily influenced by his surroundings, good or bad. Sassen grew up in a proper environment, and has the gift to get along with all sorts of people, who he can manipulate without much resistance. It is in my opinion that Alfons Sassen should, after his conviction, be kept under close supervision, preferably by those people of the same Roman Catholic upbringing as young Alfons."*[241]

Alfons was put under supervision. At the beginning of 1948, he was handed over to the (STPD) Foundation for the Supervision of Political Delinquents, section Zutphen. He ended up in detention camp Vught, just like his father. On 1 June 1948, on the recommendation of Public Prosecutor F. Van Voorst tot Voorst of the special court of 's Hertogenbosch, Alfons was released from camp Vught. Alfons did remain under supervision of the STPD, but could move around freely.

Dominican father Franciscus
The Sassens never lost contact with one another, not even during the testing years after the war. Some of them were in detention centres, others were on the run. The lines of communication ran, among others, through Alfons' sister Francisca. After the war she married a French man and lived in Paris. Another key figure was a Dominican reverend uncle from Zwolle. He played an important role in keeping them together and cared for their spiritual guidance in times of hardship and persecution. His involvement did not go unnoticed by the POD: "*In all the Sassen files there is the mention of another key figure, a certain father called reverend Willem. Most likely family. In the after war period his name shows up regularly. In intercepted correspondence between the offspring of Sassen senior it seems he interferes with the political affairs of his children. Through this father (uncle Willem) from Zwolle several members of the Sassen family ("Sassen – units") correspond with each other in some kind of code. The intercepted mail is very hard to read because the men-*

tioned persons are indicated in a code, for example Bvb T7 and 9 Lb."²⁴²

After the war, "uncle Willem" immediately started locating the Sassen family members. Three days after Wim's miraculous "escape", the commander of interrogation-centre Fort Blauwkapel received a letter from the Dominican father: *"Zwolle 18 December 1945. An unknown person asked me, in the name of my cousin, W. Sassen, detained in interrogation centre Blauwkapel, to contact his wife (Karthäuserstrasse 4 Hildesheim (Germany)). Before I contact the British authorities I would like to know which W. Sassen is the person we are writing about. Is it the father or son (both Sassen senior as his son were called Wim) as both had collaborated during the war. Could you please be so kind as to allow the detainee to write me in order to clarify the situation. Thanks in advance. H.J.H.W. Sassen chaplain, Dominican monastery Zwolle."*²⁴³

The chaplain claimed to be writing on behalf of Paula Fisette, which could not be true. Fisette was not to be found in Germany. Moreover, unofficially, Wim and Paula had split up. After the war she was at her parents' place in Maastricht. The chaplain was playing tricks.

Who was this Dominican uncle Willem from Zwolle? Willem, full name *Hendrikus Josephus Hubertus Willem Sassen*, was born in 1887 in Dongen, a place nearby Geertruidenberg. He came from a family of five. His father was a director of a postal office. His brother *Jan*, convent-name *Augustinus*, was a known church historian who during *Operation Market Garden* became the victim of an Allied bombardment. Uncle Willem's convent name was *Franciscus,* although inside they nicknamed him "Frenske". Relatives called him *Wim* or *Willem*. Church historian *M.E. Monteiro* described him in *Godspredikers, Dominicanen in Nederland (1795-2000,* Preachers of God, Dominicans in The Netherlands) as follows: *"His reputation is somehow complex, he kept to himself and was a bit peculiar."* Monteiro believed he was involved in resistance work in the Noordoostpolder*: "Because of his contribution to the Resistance he was asked to become a member of the Commission of preliminary investigation of Political Delinquents, NSB members and other war profiteers. These were rounded up in detention centres in the Noordoostpolder, where Dominican chaplain Sassen rendered his services. He saw them more as victims of circumstances, and due to this attitude he turned into their confidant. He gave them the confidence to start a new life here in The Netherlands or abroad."*[244]

In Spain

When Alfons was released, he immediately lay low and headed for Spain. In which way he managed to reach the Iberian Peninsula is still unknown, but he did have enough contacts who could help him out. In Belgium, he had contact with *De Raad van Zwarten* (the Council of Collaborators), an organisation which helped *incivieken*, political delinquents, on the run to Spain or Germany.

On 18 February 1949, the *Foundation for the Supervision of Political Delinquents* notified the Public Prosecutor of the Special Court in 's Hertogenbosch: "*With regret we have to inform you that our supervised political delinquent A.E.C.M. Sassen, born 8 December 1926 in Geertruidenberg, left without our consent or indication of future residence. Intel has shown that he is located in Spain.*"[245]

As soon as Alfons was released from the detention centre Vught, he went to see his mother in Breda, before taking off. Whether he received help from clandestine organisations or the former resistance members Mertens, Eddy Conijn or de Bie remains guess-work. In any case, he left The Netherlands behind after 23 August 1948 and reached Spain by the end of that year. In his possession, he had temporary passport. Why he was allowed to hold such a document is again unclear. Maybe he was allowed to visit his family in France, where his sister Francisca lived: "Madrid 15 December 1948, *I have the honour to inform you excellence that Alfons Sassen, last known address Warnsveld (Zutphen), by profession reporter, has consulted the consul of the embassy in order to have his Dutch passport no. 554739, which was issued on 23 August 1948 in Arnhem by the Commissioner of the Queen in Gelderland, prolonged. There the mentioned passport was valid until 22 November 1948, only for three months. I asked the Ministry of Interior instructions with regard to its prolongation and the exact duration of it. Yesterday the above mentioned person appeared again at the premises of the embassy, and explained again that his temporary pass had expired on 22 November, expressing his wish to leave for Paris. He had the intention to leave without a valid passport and to spend two months in Paris, where he, according to his own words, had an acquaintance at the consular division of the embassy who would be willing to prolong his passport. According to Sassen, the difficulties in obtaining a valid passport are due to his father's political behaviour during the war.*"[246]

In Paris, Alfons could stay with his sister Francisca until his papers were in order. To his great disappointment, however, his request was not honoured. His determination nonetheless remained.

In August 1949, more news about his activities in Spain came to the attention of the Dutch embassy. Alfons moved to La Coruña, and called himself *Alfonso Cornelio Eduardo Sassen.* He had to report at the police station because he might have been involved in the abduction of a minor from Barcelona. In La Coruña Alfons earned his living through teaching languages. He was living with a divorced lady, and had to appear now not only because of his possible involvement of the kidnapping but also because of some dispute over rent. During the interview, he complained to the Chief of Police he still could not get a temporary Dutch passport, nor could he get a *laissez-passer* for a ticket to The Netherlands. The Chief of Police was convinced that what Alfons really wanted was an exit visa issued by the Spanish authorities, with which he could escape to Latin America. In that same conversation, Alfons suggested that he was working for the Spanish Secret Service and the Americans. Ordered by the "American government" he was tasked, as an undercover agent, to investigate the illegal import of American Dollar-banknotes into Spain. The Spanish police were, however, more convinced that he was personally involved in this smuggle-scheme.

The Dutch consul in La Coruña asked for further instructions concerning this Dutch national: *"It is very likely that the police in La Coruña has the intention to provoke an expulsion order by the Seguridad (Dirección General de Seguridad, Comisaria General Politico Social). I would kindly ask your Excellency the authorisation to revoke Sassens' passport, and to give him a one way laissez-passer to The Netherlands, and to repatriate him in the cheapest way possible."*[247]

Alfons' passport was confiscated by the police in La Coruña and handed over to the consul. It did not stop Alfons. He was still desperately looking for a way out. On 25 November 1949, the Dutch consul in La Coruña reported: *"The Dutch man ACEM Sassen had no intentions of taking up our offer to return with a laisser-passer to The Netherlands. On the contrary, he was trying his best to obtain a visa for Venezuela by the Spanish authorities. As we already are aware that the Spanish police authorities are quite willing to give so called "pasaportes especiales" to foreign political delinquents, I have asked our consul to contact the provincial authorities of Galicia to point out that Sassen is in fact Dutch and should not be eligible for such a document. As already stated by your Excellency, it is our intention to keep the expenses at the lowest and wait for the Spanish authorities to expel Sassen as an undesirable alien from its territory."*[248]

The American Secret Services had in the meantime been informed of Alfons' presence in Spain. Their report of August 1949 stated: *"A. Sassen von Babel (Bavel: mothers name), Dutch passport no. 554739 issued in Arnhem. The suspect had arrived in Spain in October 1948. He carried printed credentials CIC Bad Nauheim, which is signed by a certain Nichols, identifying Alfons as Richard Gordon, a Second lieutenant born in Chicago, Michigan, the document has a picture of Sassen and he stated he is a member of Secret Intelligence (SI) and connected to the OSS (Office of Strategic Services) The cover of the document reeds: US Army, Eucom (European Command), OSS, no.: 19356. Last known address Woverlei, Epse, Gorssel, The Netherlands. Subject approached CIC on 27 August 1947 requesting for work. But according to the available records he was not employed. He claimed he had worked for the Dutch underground movement since 1943 and after the war as special agent for Dutch counter intelligence. He left The Netherlands in April 1947 allegedly to trace Martin Bormann. He went to Berlin, then to the French zone and claimed he was forced to work for them. Sassen is at present in La Coruña where he has been involved in a case of abduction of a minor and where he seems to be living with a Spanish woman. He admitted being employed by Spanish (secret) police and has told various stories about his alleged connection with various American services, amongst others with the FBI or other agency which instructed him to discover the whereabouts of counterfeit American banknotes. His stories are second of all highly fantastic and he must be regarded as utterly unreliable."*[249] The American Secret Service report concluded he is not now in possession of a valid passport, but seems to have a document issued to him by the Spanish police, which would indicate that he is employed with that service. It is understood that he is almost destitute and that the Spanish police are trying to have him leave the country. [250]

Alfons did in fact work for the Spanish Secret Service. He was under the guardianship of General *José Moscardó Ituarte*, the hero of the military garrison Alcázar in Toledo. During the Spanish civil war the garrison was besieged by the republicans and they captured his son. Despite the risk that his son would be killed Moscardó refused to give in and sacrificed his son for God and country.

Preparing to leave
A year later, on 20 December 1950, the Dutch consul was informed that Alfons was preparing his departure to Ecuador. The Ecuadorian consulate provided him with an entry visa. A month later, on 20 January 1951, Alfons Sassen, at that time still living at General Rubin (2 bajo izquierda) in the Galician city La Coruña, wrote to the Dutch consulate: "*Highly esteemed sir consul. Some months ago my passport was sent back with the notice that my request for prolonging it had been denied. I have obtained employment with a South American contractor and wish to leave, and therefore I am kindly renewing my request for a new passport. I am a former political delinquent and have been fully rehabilitated due to my anti-communist input for the section Crabbendam of the Centrale Veiligheidsdienst (CVD: Central Security Service, successor of the BNV) and in service of the commander of the stoottroepen (military units) Bep van Kooten who was appointed by minister president Schermerhorn as charge de affaires concerning communistic agitation.*

> The Rijkspolitie (the Dutch National police internal investigation department) is fully informed of my patriotic activities.
>
> The investigation officer of the Foundation for the Supervision of Political Delinquents squire Van Asch van Wijck, who was in charge of the investigation on my person had successfully asked for my release. I have kept my citizenship rights and am a Dutch national. As such I am entitled to receive my Dutch passport and therefore I am asking you to provide me with my passport, according to my rights and the applicable laws."[251]

Alfons even presented a letter of recommendation by the managing director of the *Foundation for the Supervision of Political Delinquents* esquire *Van Asch van Wijck* dated 19 May 1948 to convince the Dutch Council he was *bona fide*. The letter provided a positive character reference and *"created a clear image of the importance of Sassens work for our country and for certain individuals. Based on my experience with Sassen, I am convinced he is a reliable person and is, in principle, an anti-communist. To me his statements, as far as I know, have been verified and are correct. I am absolutely convinced that this young man when given a proper chance will make it. I note in this regard that the national police is likewise convinced of his honesty and trustworthiness. The charges against him, as well as his work after the occupation, should be viewed in the circumstances in which they succeeded. He was a victim of circumstance and had no alternative"*.[252]

It should be noted that Alfons Sassen did not provide a copy of this recommendation letter to the consul in La Coruña, but rewrote the letter himself. It was written in his own handwriting and he adopted only the positive elements of the letter's contents. He forgot to mention, for example, that he had lost his citizenship rights for the duration of 10 years.

Was Alfons really being considered a victim of circumstance, and had he done enough penance for his "mistake" by joining the SS? In 1951 the special court of 's Hertogenbosch wasn't quite convinced. Especially taking into account the other fugitive family members whose collaboration cases were under investigation, like his oldest sister Maria: "*There is indeed a family relation between the person concerned (Maria Sassen hiding in Rome, Italy) and Alfons Sassen, it is her youngest brother and a dangerous schemer, pseudo –secret agent and a conman of considerable magnitude. After the liberation, this SS man of SS Standarte Kurt Eggers made it into the BNV, and with it had free access to Germany in an Allied uniform. He was involved with car smuggling and was arrested for other offenses. Nevertheless, from within the detention centre he made it to (detainee) private chauffeur of the Public Prosecutor Lammers. The person [Alfons] in question was homosexual and his sexual deviations played an important role during this period.*"[253]

One year later Alfons left with an exit visa that he had received from Moscardó: "*According to our correspondence with the consul in La Coruña Alfons Sassen, on 14 January 1951, embarked the British steamer "Reina del Pacifico" in La Coruña leaving for Ecuador. Sassen was in the possession of an "apatride" (Stateless person) passport which was issued by the consulate-general of Ecuador in Madrid. Because Sassen was able to leave Spain it can be said that the directorate-general for the security here has granted him an exit visa on the conditions of him being a stateless person. Nonetheless it was known, due to the previous correspondence concerning Sassen's expulsion, that he was a Dutch national.*"[254]

Next to the half-hearted attempts on behalf of the Dutch to have him expelled in 1951, the American Secret Services asked for his extradition. He was suspected of being a member of the *Sonderkommando*, a special force which during the *Battle of the Bulge* (16 December 1944 – 25 January 1945, a counteroffensive in the Ardennes) had been involved in the execution of American POWs. Alfons would later deny this allegation in an interview. He declared that he was a *Waffen SS* soldier who had fought in the Balkans, Arnhem and the Ardennes, but denied any involvement in the killing of North American soldiers. Could Alfons ever have been a *Sonderagent*, a member of the Special Forces? Most likely not. In January 1944 he received his military training, but then required a long recovery period for his various illnesses and broken foot. He then was found unfit for active service. On 20 September 1944, he was nowhere near the *Battle of Arnhem,* Alfons was in Amsterdam. In the midst of the Ardennes offensive, Alfons was at a meeting with KP Noord Holland, where he offered his services as a possible double cross agent. At the end of December 1944, Alfons was working for the *Abwehr*. From January to March 1945, he worked for the *Aktivpropaganda*, as a speaker and taking care of the distribution of the so called underground newspaper. During the last months of the war he was involved in armed robberies. He was not involvement in any battles. Alfons always had a wild imagination...

Why wasn't Alfons extradited? Was it too costly? Or was there something else going on? The answer is to be found in the correspondence of the Dutch Ministry of Foreign Affairs concerning the case of Maria Sassen.

Ecuador

Following the footsteps of Maria
Alfons was following the trail of his oldest sister. Marie, also known as Maria or Mies, had already fled to Ecuador. In May 1950 she had embarked a ship in Italy and left for her new home. The history of Maria is well documented. Her involvement for the Flemish cause interested the occupying authorities. Like the other Sassen family members, she was actively involved in the German propaganda machine. She was an ardent National Socialist, a full-blown Nazi. In January 1943, she had participated in secret missions in Antwerp and Cologne. She became be an informer of the German Secret Service *(Reichssicherheitshauptamt*; RSHA). That same year, she was recruited by *Friedrich Knolle* as an undercover agent. She was briefly trained at the spy-school *Seehof* in The Hague. After her instructions, she continued her training at Goslar, Magdeburg, Berlin, Munich and Klagenfurth (Austria).

At the end of the war, Maria worked as a *Red Cross* nurse in a *Kriegslazaret* (Field Hospital) in Almelo (Holland). When The Netherlands was liberated she did not suffer from persecutions by the public; as "*moffenmeid*" (a collaborator) her head was not shaven or marked as a "Nazi-whore". No, she was in relative safety with her sister Francisca and her mother in Hildesheim (Germany). It was there where the investigation services found her. Her address was disclosed through intercepted correspondence between the family members. Alfons former employer BNV chef Wim Sanders was informed of her location on 5 February 1946: "*To sir W. Sanders, Hotel Royal, Scheveningen. In the dwelling of 4 Karthäusserstrasse Hildesheim lives mother and two sisters of Sassen. Mother is an invalid and lives together with her daughter Maria. The second sister of the suspect, now called miss Weidenbach also lives at this address in Hildesheim.*"[255]

On 10 October 1946 Maria was arrested. She was wanted by the Dutch criminal investigation service in connection with her activities for the SD and the RSHA. On 22 October 1946 she was interrogated by The Netherlands CI Mission. She was listed in *Het Nederlands boek der opzoekingen* (the Dutch book of international search warrants for war criminals) for crimes committed against state security. On 10 November 1946 Maria was handed over to the Civil Internment Camp (CIC) Paderborn no. 5. There, she should await her repatriation to The Netherlands.[256]

In one way or another, Maria managed to escape. Three years later she was found again in Austria. Together with her partner, the German *Rolf Burk*, she went into hiding and ended up in Lindau, Austria. Burk's father lived there. The criminal investigators, however, were on their track. On 17 January 1949, Maria and Rolf Burk were nearly caught during an attempt to commit burglary in Pfunds nearby Lanbeck (Tirol). Soon after, the investigators found Burk, in a hospital in Innsbruck. Once again, the couple managed to escape. This time Rome, Italy, was their destination. Through her contacts within the former DWI, shelter was provided by professor *dr. G. Lo Verde*. A year later in 1950, they found refuge in the Instituto della Mattutina, likewise in Rome.[257]

The Dutch consulate was aware of their presence in Rome. With her false identity papers in the name of "Hendriks", Maria had tried to obtain a temporary passport or an exit visa at the Argentinean, Venezuelan and Ecuadorian- consulates. When the identity papers were verified with the Dutch consulate, their true identity and location was revealed.

In December 1950 a preliminary investigation was started into M.J.J. Sassen. She was accused of treachery, or at least implicated in the betrayal of Dutch and Belgian individuals to the German authorities, together with misdemeanours like her involvement in propaganda activities for enemy broadcasters. The Dutch ministry of Foreign Affairs also stated: "*Although sentence in absentia is possible, it is preferable to interrogate the suspect before passing such a sentence. This interrogation should, especially in light of the size of the case, and in connection with the two parallel cases of the suspect's two fugitive sisters, be dealt with by a supervising officer who is in charge of this investigation. It is also of relevance to know whether the extradition of MJJ Sassen could be effected in a short term.*"[258]

In answer to the accusations, Maria responded through her lawyer that her involvement in the repatriation of imprisoned Flemish nationalists happened *"with the knowledge of the local authorities in Antwerp, Mechelen, the Italian consul in Antwerp, the consul of Belgium in Bordeaux, the representatives of the Vichy government with the Militärbefehlshaber in Paris, the King of Belgium, the president of the French Republic Petain...furthermore I do believe that the help of prisoners and refugees not only is an act of Christianity but also "covered" by the Hague Convention."* Her assistance in the repatriation started without the knowledge or assignment of the Germans, according to Maria.[259]

She refuted the accusations of her being an SD agent of *V-Frau*. She had passed on information to the SD headquarters in Antwerp and Brussels. She commented she had always acted as an intermediary and never had the intention to lure people into a SD-trap or harm them in any other way. About her education at *Zorgvliet (Seehof)* in The Hague she stated the following: *"In summer 1943 I met Knolle of the SD in The Hague. For several weeks I did a three day course at this school, I learned to operate a W/T set a bit but never took the training very seriously."* Sturmbahnführer Friedrich Knolle met Maria in 1942 due to her contacts within the SD in Antwerp and Brussels: *"Sometime later I received a personal invitation by Knolle himself for an interview. He suggested to me that I work for him (SD) as a radio/telegraph operator. I subsequently did a course of six weeks but never was employed. Later I again received an offer of Hauptsturmführer Helmut Proebsting (Pröbsting) of The Hague to work as an SD agent and penetrate the underground movement, an offer which I never accepted. I believed in the New Order for Europe, led by Hitler, and was a devout idealist, that is why I* *worked together with the SD. My operational zone for the SD was mainly in Antwerp and Brussels."*²⁶⁰

Her statement was confirmed by H. Pröbsting: *"In April 1942, I was sent to The Netherlands to head the BdS section IIIB der SD in Utrecht, and later The Hague in the rank of Hauptsturmführer (political section). My job was to gather intelligence in The Netherlands (Referat IIIB). The first Sassen member I met was (1943) Marie Sassen, when she was in contact with Knolle chef department II and Department VI (foreign intelligence) and commander of the Sicherheitsdienst Schule Zorgvliet. In that period Marie Sassen was trained as a Funker. The intention was to make her a member of the Informationsnetz (I-netz), an organisation of telegraph operators who in case of an Allied invasion would operate in occupied territory to pass on messages by telegraph to the German intelligence service."*²⁶¹

Maria reported individuals to both Knolle and Pröbsting. At the end of the war, Pröbsting also met her brothers Wim and Alfons, who were then members of the Aktivpropaganda-section as well as members of the underground spy ring *Neurop*.²⁶²

To Maria, she did not think much of the seriousness of her crimes as a collaborator. She refuted all accusations, though she did fear persecution. Through her Italian contacts, she was looking for a way out of Europe. During that time the Dutch consul in Rome and the Ministry of Foreign Affairs were discussing Maria's case. On 16 September 1949, the consul informed the Ministry about the possibility of repatriation of M.J.J. Sassen:

> *"It seems that the procedures of extradition, according the presidential decree of 26 February 1948, are a very time consuming enterprise. It is rarely the case that the accused will, in less than six months after submitting the request, be repatriated to the concerned country."*[263]

The chance that Maria would actually be extradited was very likely small. The procedure took too long and the "cooperation" of the Italian authorities was so fruitless that Maria had enough time to plan her "escape". Indeed, this was confirmed on 4 September 1950: *"The person concerned has left this spring in about May this year to Ecuador."*[264]

On 26 May 1950, her entry visa nr. 96416 had been issued by the Consul of Ecuador in Rome. On 15 July 1950 Maria, with a temporary travel document issued by the *International Red Cross*, arrived in Ecuador. She arrived alone. During the passage her partner Burk had passed away; he was suffering the late stages of poliomyelitis. She went to Quito, and rented a place on 235 Calle Gorivar. Maria learned Spanish quickly. She soon started off as a translator. Six months later she was informed by the Aliens department that her visa would expire on 15 January 1951 (with a possible prolongation of 90 days), and that if she did not comply with the necessary documents she would be transported to the Columbian border.

Maria Burk Sassen contacted the Dutch consulate in Ecuador. They, in turn, contacted the Dutch Ministry of Foreign Affairs. On 19 February 1951, the Ministry replied as follows: *"If it is possible, keep the mentioned person in Ecuador. We do our utmost best to stimulate people to emigrate. It would be strange to repatriate unwanted people. This point of view was also taken by the head of section B. Only for West Indië (West Indies: Surinam, the Antilles, etc) we have made an exception, because we did not want to leave undesirables in our dominions."*[265]

A week later, *J.D.G. Goedhart* of the special court in s' Hertogenbosch advised the director general police commissioner in The Hague on the suspect M.J.J. Sassen as follows: "*May I inform you that repatriating this woman to The Netherlands is absolutely irresponsible. She was sentenced in absentia so therefore her prosecution and trial is not needed. Unfortunately she was not present during the preparatory inquiry; therefore the court summons is somewhat limited. Due to the character of her criminal case I believe that even the state, besides the costs of repatriation, is better off without the presence of this woman, who took part in an outstanding espionage and counter espionage course at the Skorzeny Schule (A-Schule-West, Seehof in Zorgvliet), while she had access to the highest levels of the Reichssicherheitshauptamt, the SS Hauptamt and the Abwehr. Considering also the effortless ways in which this woman travelled the world after the liberation, has surprised me. May I conclude with advising your honour not to make any attempt to repatriate these youngsters (Wim, Alfons and Maria) to The Netherlands. It is better for The Netherlands that they, in the politically tumultuous rich Latin American continent, find enough possibilities to fulfil their ambitions in order that they stay away from The Netherlands. All have lost their Dutch nationality.*"[266]

In any case Maria did get her desired *cedula* (residence permit) in 1951 in the name of *Maria Johanna Jacqueline Sassen van Bavel*, nr. 170307326, profession *comerciante* (merchant). Marital status: widow. During the following years she acted as commercial representative for Dutch and German firms. According to Dr. *A.P. van der Wiel* she acted as an intermediary for buyers of livestock: "*She imported Dutch pure bred breeding animals. Due to her import activities of Dutch cattle she even managed to receive funds (200.000 Dutch guilders) of the Dutch Ministry of Agriculture. She nearly got a contract for a Dutch firm to perform drainage works in Ecuador, but her past had caught up with her. Within the Dutch embassy in Quito, a secret book circulated stating she was a Quisling. Though in Ecuador, all doors to the presidential palace and departments were open.*" [267]

The consul informed the stock breeder of her past and concluded his message with: "*Due to the above mentioned reasons it would be obvious, that this Embassy does not wish to continue with this person, to advise you to end all contact with the above mentioned person. Signed, the ambassador, Quito, 25 January 1962.*"

[The ambassador]: "*Her business reputation in Ecuador was affected (unfavourable). It seems to me improbable that she has any valuable contacts in this country.*"[268].

Contrary to the understanding of the consul, however, the Sassen sisters did have access to Ecuador high society and their role as interpreters or intermediaries was highly valued. The Ministry of Food, Agriculture and Fisheries and the Dutch embassy in Quito concluded that business prevailed. To seal the deal (roughly 10 million Dutch guilders) it was suggested it was better to ignore her criminal past.[269]

The interests at stake were high; even the former president *Galo Plaza* (1948-1952), now a respectable member of the Ecuadorian community, was involved with the transaction. The cattle breeder who was selling the pedigree stock also asked the Dutch ambassadors' support in maintaining M.J.J. Burk Sassen as a mediator to make the deal a success, which did in fact happen in March 1964.

Georgette joins in
On 15 October 1955, a delegation from Ecuador visited Friesland, The Netherlands. It was drawn by the possible import of Frisian pedigree cattle. The delegation members were engineer *Gerardo Enriquez*, assistant manager of *Banco Nacional de Fomento* (developmentbank), *Don Ramón Espinal Mendoza*, president of the Chamber of Agriculture (Guayaquil), *Dr. Rosendo Ordonez*, Director general of the department of livestock industry and national health service for live stock of the Ministry of Economics and Agriculture, and Mrs. *Georgette Servant–Sassen*. Maria's sister Georgette, carrying the name of her deceased husband *Servant*, acted as a guide and an interpreter. For four years, she had lived in Ecuador like her oldest sister and her youngest brother Alfons.[270]

Georgette had left for Ecuador in 1951 together with *Louis Peeters*. A former NSB mayor of Maastricht and

Waffen SS volunteer for the Eastfront. They boarded the freighter "Breda", a converted *Liberty Ship*, and left Amsterdam or Antwerp to the Azores-Curacao-Aruba-Cristobal Colon (Ecuador)–Panama-channel, with destination Guayaquil (Ecuador). On board were Peeters, Georgette, daughter Ingrid and a certain Lodewijk. On arrival they immediately headed for the capital Quito. There Maria and Alfonso welcomed them. Georgette found work as a secretary and interpreter/ translator. Peeters had had a hard time to adjust in his new home country and left. Georgette stayed on and did well. She eventually decided to leave the big city behind and start a *platanera* (banana plantation) in Rosa Zárate, nearby Santo Domingo. In the 50's Ecuador was in the midst of a banana-boom and Georgette decided to take advantage of this highly commercial business. Business went well. She even became a celebrity. She wrote a bestseller describing her voyage from The Netherlands to Ecuador and her life as a *platanera*.[271] In 1955 she was asked to join the Ecuadorian delegation on their visit to The Netherlands.[272]

A year after the cattle deal, Georgette left Ecuador behind. She and Peeters moved to Bruges, Belgium). In an interview with the Dutch monthly *Elsevier (24-02-1990)*, Peeters referred to other exiled Nazis in Ecuador: "*I have met many SS who were helped by the Vatican via Genoa to reach South America.*" When Georgette and Peeters decided in 1965 to return to Europe, it seems that many other former fugitives decided like them to go home again. *"Some of us are now in Bruges my best friends."*[273]

Military instructor in San Vicente
With a letter of recommendation from general Moscardó, Alfons was able to start as an instructor at the military training centre and police college in San Vicente (Ecuador). There he taught *jiu-jitsu* and *catch-as-catch-can* to the cadets of the *Colegio Militar*. Within ten years he would attain the rank of captain.[274]

Alfons tried once more to get a Dutch passport. On 13 August 1951, the Dutch consul in Bogota (Colombia) notified the Ministry of Foreign Affairs: *"Some time ago ACEM Sassen visited the consulate to request a Dutch passport. This Sassen is indeed a nasty individual. Apparently he did not know that we were already fully briefed on his person, because he presented himself as a patriot, a "glorious" member of the Dutch National army, claiming to have courageously saved former Prime Minister professor Schermerhorn's life, etc, etc. He no longer possessed his old passport and declared he had to hand it over to chief of the Falange in La Coruña in order to be able to leave Spain. He possessed no further documents proving his Dutch nationality. I therefore declined his request for a new Dutch passport. Two days later he showed up again and advised me to complete his request. When I asked him why I should comply, he said that he possessed information about Dutch authorities who during the occupation had been as bad as the Sassen family. If I was determined not to issue him his Dutch passport, he would reveal the names of these high ranking officials and their crimes to the Dutch press. If I would comply he would keep his mouth shut. After these poor attempts to blackmail me, I showed him the door. Signed envoy extraordinary in Bogota. The vice consul B.J. Elias."*[275]

Even without a Dutch passport Alfons was doing well in Ecuador. After his career as a military instructor at *Colegio Militar,* he started his studies in chemistry. He became the owner of a chemical factory (sulphuric acid, sulphate factory) which produced products for the textile and building industry.

Advisor
During the first military junta Alfons became a naturalised Ecuadorian. He was asked to become an advisor for the President for domestic and external security affairs. Alfons: *"Due to my successful tactics, I acted as an advisor for all succeeding governments, whether it was a military junta or civilian government, except for one. In which I left voluntarily, at that time I acted as a police attaché and consul for Ecuador."*[276]

As a police attaché and military advisor on security affairs, Alfons made a rapid career as a weapon specialist. He trained anti-insurgent units and acted as a consultant for governments all over the world, including in the Middle East, and Africa. During international police conferences, he took part in study groups in which information was exchanged about the fine art of counter espionage and anti-guerrilla tactics.

Alfons was well connected. According to an interview with investigative reporter Kai Hermann, while he was not a BND agent of the Federal Republic of Germany (BRD: Bundes Republik Deutschland), he did maintain his liaisons with their intelligence officers and informants: *"Ich bin berater von der Armee. Hauptsächlich für Sicherheitsangelegenheiten. Und für Waffen.* (I am a military consultant. Mainly for security affairs and weapons)." The sale of arms was the department of his brother Wim.[277]

Alfons' involvement in the intelligence community and international arms deals started in the early sixties of the previous century. Around the same time his brother started to work for the Merex company; a cover under control of the BND/CIA. Alfons became a member of this "club" of specialists from intelligence services, neo-fascists organisations, mercenaries and arms dealers. Besides surplus army supplies, Merex also offered police training. A well known field of Alfons' expertise.[278]

The fact that Alfons was recruited by the Merex company (Merex AG) can be derived from an unpublished interview of *Michael von der Goltz* in the 1980's. In this interview, Alfons stated he was considering the supply of weapons during the Biafra-war in Nigeria (1967-1970). On top of that, he revealed he was involved in the hunt for the Argentinean-Cuban and *guerrillero Ernesto Che Guevara* in Bolivia (1967).

It did not take long before Alfons was introduced to the network of former Nazi comrades in Latin America and Europe. Supposedly, he was in close contact with the Skorzeny group; a group of Nazi-diehards, also known as the *International Negra*, who regularly met in Madrid, Spain. His most striking associate was a certain *Klaus Altmann*.[279]

Barbie, Alfons and the CIA

Klaus Barbie immediately felt at home when he arrived in La Paz: "*When I arrived in Bolivia in 1951, I saw by chance something reassuring: a parade of the Bolivian socialist Falange, whose members wore uniforms which were identical to ours. Leather coupling belts, the arm strap and the fascist salute. Later I was even able to get on friendly terms with the members of this party and studied their philosophy thoroughly. I therefore sympathized with this movement. I always helped these people whenever and wherever I could.*"[280]

Klaus Barbie's first contact person in Bolivia was Friedrich Schwend, also known as "Wenceslav Turi". Just like Barbie, Schwend received a save passage by the North American Secret Service (CIC and SCI) to Latin America. Schwend was well connected in South America. Thanks to Schwend, Barbie received a letter of recommendation which would give him access to the exiled Nazi elite on the continent: "*[t]he carrier of this letter, Klaus Barbie, is fully reliable. He was Obersturmführer in France and was sentenced to death in absentia.*" The other friend was Hans Ulrich Rudel.[281]

Barbie's career really took off when he started working for the Secret Service. That opportunity was offered when the leader of the *Movimiento Nacionalista Revolucionario* (MNR) *Victor Paz Estenssoro* was elected democratically as President. Together with another former Gestapo agent *Heinz Wolf*, they were recruited as security officers. In 1964, Estenssoro was ousted by the air force general *René Barrientos Ortuño*. The transition of power did not have any consequences for Barbie, he maintained his position. Things only improved when he then entered the obscure world of intelligence officers, weapon smuggling and mercenaries.²⁸²

In 1965 the BND recruiter of department 934 paid Barbie a visit. He was selected because of his ties with high ranking Bolivian officers. From that moment on, Barbie under the alias of *Der Adler*, no V-43118, was assigned as representative of Merex AG.

Latin America was an important market for surplus military equipment. With permission of president René Barrientos a shipping company was founded. In 1966/7 a joint venture with Friedrich Schwend was founded; *Compania Transmaritima Boliviana*. A cover. For the outside world, this was Bolivia's first shipping company…in a landlocked country! Barbie became manager. At around the same time two other annexes of Merex AG and *Gemetex* were founded too. Barbie headed the in and export firm *Estrella* SA in La Paz (Bolivia) and Friedrich Schwend of *Commercial Agricola* in Lima (Peru). Officially *Estrella* traded in quinquina bark, selling it to the pharmaceutical company *Boehringer*. In reality, however, all covers were a gateway for major arms and cocaine transactions. Under the Bolivian banner, enormous weapon purchases were clandestinely exported to those countries under UN embargo. They did not only supply the Bolivian and Peruvian juntas with arms but also dictators like Alfredo Stroessner (Paraguay), *Augusto Pinochet* (Chile) and other authoritarian regimes in the Middle East, Africa and anyone who wanted to buy large quantities of illegal arms.²⁸³

Besides his direct involvement in highly profitable illegal transactions, Barbie also acted as the security advisor for *Department 4* (Bolivian Secret Police section counter insurgency), which concerned intelligence, in particular, the section psychological warfare, the headquarters of which were located in Cochabamba. It was within this field that he met Alfons Sassen. Not only because of their respective advisory roles within the intelligence community but also because of brother Wim. Like Barbie, Wim represented the interests of *Steyr Daimler Puch*. It was a small world.[284]

According to reporter Kai Hermann, the cooperation between the Sassen brothers and Barbie was very close: "*When Barbie was preparing the upcoming coup of 1980 in Bolivia, Alfons Sassen sent him his best man, Lieutenant Pablo Hérbas Chiribogas. Sassen had assisted his colleague before. He then went to Bolivia to assist in the hunt for guerrilla-leader Che Guevara.*" On 8 October 1967, the Bolivian Army (with help of the CIA) had trapped the *revolutionario* Che in the valley of Vallegrande nearby the village La Higuera. They caught him and he was taken prisoner. The next day, on the orders of the Bolivian dictator Barrientos, he was riddled with bullets. Barbie never lost his contacts within the CIA. Could it be that Alfons was a CIA informer too?[285]

The end of Klaus Barbie
The French authorities had been looking for Klaus Barbie as of the sixties. Mid seventies they finally located him in Bolivia. Extradition was out of the question. The military junta refused to adhere. In 1978, Hugo Banzer tried

to be re-elected in the conventional democratic way. But things took a different course. In November 1979, after a succession of interim governments, *Lidia Gueiler Tejada* was chosen as the democratic president of Bolivia. Her presidency did not last very long. General Luis García Meza Tejada assembled his troops for the next coup.

Specialist in counter-insurgency Barbie was called in days before the coup. On 12 February 1980, he, Klaus Altmann Barbie (at the age of 67), was officially appointed as Lieutenant-Colonel with honourable commendation by general *Louis Acre Goméz* in the Bolivian Army. On 17 July 1980, Tejada seized power with help of drugs barons, neo-fascists and the Argentinean military. The main participants were Barbie and the "cocaine king" of Bolivia, *Roberto Suárez*. Barbie had already rendered his services to this drugs-lord back in the seventies. With a small mercenary army, better known as *Los Novios de la Muerte*, he protected Suárez' drugs trade and eliminated his rivals. This is one of the reasons why Tejada's putsch is also called the "cocaine coup".[286]

The Argentinean daily *La Nación* (17 June 2001), claimed that in 1980, Wim Sassen, in collaboration with Antonio Domingo Mingolla and Klaus Barbie, provided the AUG machineguns to Luis García Meza days before the coup. Wim was also implicated as the man who strengthened the private army of '*el rey de la cocaina*' with the sale of armoured vehicles.

The Tejada regime did not last for long. Massive corruption led to its downfall in August 1981. After years of successive military juntas, the new democratically chosen president *Hernan Siles Zuazo* assumed power.

This one lasted from 1982-1985. It brought stability to the country but it did have an unsuspected turn of events for former *SS Hauptsturmbahnführer* Klaus Barbie. The protective shield surrounding Barbie lasted as long as the juntas were in power. Once broken, there was a possibility for the French to renew their request for extradition to this democratic government. There was a chance they might adhere.

Officially, Bolivia does not extradite its citizens. The committed crimes against humanity have according the Bolivian jurisdiction expired by 1983. An alternative was found. On 25 January 1983, Barbie was arrested in La Paz and accused of fraud. He apparently disregarded to pay a tax liability of 10.000 US Dollars. While in detention, the charges were extended to illegal membership of a paramilitary group, drugs trafficking, forgery of documents and identity fraud. Especially the last misdemeanour had serious consequences. It gave the Bolivians a legal excuse to extradite Barbie as an undesired (illegal) alien. That was it for Barbie. Soon afterwards he was secretly smuggled aboard a Hercules 130 plane and flown to French territory. On 5 February 1983, in Cayenne, French Guyana, he was formally detained and taken to France. In France, Barbie was sentenced to life imprisonment and he spent the rest of his life behind bars in Lyon. In 1991 he died.[287]

Alfons exposed
In contrast to his brother Wim, Alfons preferred to keep a low profile. He was thinking about moving to Bolivia in 1984. His quiet life was suddenly com-

pletely disturbed when the German *Der Stern* reporter Kai Hermann published his sequel on *Klaus Barbie, Ein Killer Karriere* (A killer career). In part 6 (14 June 1984), Alfons Sassen's membership within the international Nazi-network was revealed. Alfons was no longer "*Der Mann im Dunkeln*", the man behind the scenes. The year before, on 26 September 1983, the German reporter had interviewed him in hotel *Die Vier Jahreszeiten* in Munich. Alfons was on his way to Saudi Arabia, and later he would continue his tour in Latin America to offer his services and offer his advice as a specialist in counterinsurgency. Alfons must have thought that the interview was just about his associate and friend Barbie.

When the Ecuadorian daily *Hoy* (07-10-1984) asked his reaction on the article of Kai Hermann, Alfons stated: "*I was a SS volunteer, not a high official of the Gestapo during the Second World War; the Sassen family is on its own in the world and there is no Sassen who has served the Gestapo or who has committed any war crimes... I have nothing to hide. I have fought in de 2WW as a SS soldier. In those armies that fought communism when I was 16 years old. I had to kill because it was my duty, but because of a promise to my mother I have saved many Jews and I do not regret my past.*" He added: "*I have travelled to The Netherlands, where they say I have been sentenced to death in absentia. I have been in Tel Aviv; I was invited by an Israeli general to visit the armed forces, because I am an expert on military affairs. I hold the highest military rank that one could get as a foreign immigrant to Ecuador.*" In short; Alfons fought with the SS, saved Jews and was sentenced to death ... he really did suffer from a wild imagination.

In the same interview he denied that he was involved in arms deals with the Ecuadorian army, and that he was in fact an arms dealer. "*I was not an military instructor and my only relationship with the FFAA (army) is because I have friends there.*" A strange reply because he, like his brother Wim, worked for the Austrian *Steyr*. When the Stern reporter visited Alfons' office in Quito there were clearly pictures of the latest armoured vehicles of Steyr exhibited on the office walls. Alfons was not there to comment, but his son Roberto received the reporters in a very friendly way. [288]

On 26 September 1983, Alfons expressed his annoyance about the Steyr business to German reporter Michael von der Goltz: *"No, no I have got nothing to do with Steyr. They always get it wrong. I tell the army what Steyr products are good. For example the pistols of Steyr are no good, not good at all. So in the third place is the Baretta. The best pistol is also an Austrian one, they are of course angry about it, but it is the Glock. That is the best. I could be the brother of my brother. I love my brother above all, but when something is not right, then I have to say that. He was in favour of the panzer. Especially the Pionierpanzer SK 105 (lightweight tank) was very useful for the army."*[289]

Concerning his role as a military advisor Alfons said to Von der Goltz: "*I do something else like my brother, for me it is important, that those governments, to my taste, are able to defend themselves at best against this international terror. That is my duty. Wherever they need me, I will stay for about three months or more and that will cost them this or that much. In those three months I train the recruits. I first select the officers and the non-commissioned officers, and mix them with international soldiers from Spain, Argentina, some Germans.like the foreign legion. There lies the strength of my role as an intermediary. In Saudi Arabia, for example, I put together an anti-terrorist-unit and trained them to fight the guerrilla fighters from neighbouring country Jemen."*[290]

Alfons Sassen was quite proud of his achievements in Ecuador. [Von der Goltz]: *"He merits his contribution on the fact that Ecuador was the only Latin American country that had been completely "guerrilla-free". [Alfons] "It is very unhealthy to become a guerrillero in Ecuador."*[291]

Alfons had his own views on Ecuadorian society, politics and the return to power of the military. He was of the opinion that the Ecuadorian people were still in the developmental stage: *"When they hardly differ from animals, one should not discuss human rights."*[292]

[Alfons:] "Cordero, der ist Zivil. Die Militärs haben jetzt gar keine Lust, an die Regierung zu kommen, da hab ich neulich mit dem Präsidenten gegegessen und da hat er mich gefragt, wieviel Zeit geben mir die Militärs noch, dein Freude, die Militärs? Militärs sind in Royal, aber es geht doch wirtschaftlich so schlecht, die sind loyal mit ihnen bis zum letzten Schritt vor dem Chaos. Da hab ich ihn gesagt, wir müssen hier in Ecuador erst eine Arbeiterklasse bilden, die ihre Pflichten kennt. Bevor wir eine Arbeitsklasse bilden können… Wenn man Gerade vom Tier kommt, dann kann man doch noch gar nicht von Menschenrechten reden, die sind da ganz hysterisch in Europa… Das ist so lächerlich…

Am 10 August tritt wieder dieser versoffene Verein zusammen, das Parlament. Da sind auch zwei Analphabeten dabei, da geht's ja los, da war noch nie so eine schlechte Koalität, sogar zwei Analphabeten. Ich habe ja solches Mitleid mit dem Land. So'n Mann der kommt bei der Masse natürlich so an, da ist einer, der gehört physisch weg, der wird ausgerottet, weil der bei der Masse so ankommt…troublemaker… die haben ja alle das gleiche Problem, die trinken, da Muss er halt unter einen Wagen kommen. Den muss man betrunken machen…"[293]

"*Cordero, he is civil. The military forces don't feel like acquiring power. I recently had dinner with the President and he asked me how much time the military, my friends, would give him. The military is loyal, but because the economy is so bad at the moment, their loyalty will last until the last step before chaos. In response, I told him that we first have to create a workers-class in Ecuador, one that knows its duties. But before we can build a worker's class…when one has just evolved from being just animals, it's not even possible to talk about human rights; they are just hysterical in Europe…it's so ridiculous. On 10 August the Parliament, a ludicrous entity, will once again gather. There are even two analphabets amongst them. I pity the country.*"

Alfons had no better opinion of Germany: "*Ich ware ja der Erste, der etwas für Deutschland tun würde, wenn das nur eine rechte Regierung hätte oder wenigstens zentrumrechts. Aber doch nicht für diese Verräterbande.*"[294] "*I would be the first to do something for German, if only there were a rightist government in place, or at least a centre-right government. But I would do nothing for this band of traitors.*"

When the magazine *Nueva (October 1984)* dug into his past, it revealed: *"The Sassen family are representatives of Steyr, Daimler and Puch. Alfons is a very respectable person in Ecuador. He has admitted that he acted as an advisor on the internal en external security since the first military junta, and also for those successive presidents, whether civil or military in nature. In addition, he also confirmed that he worked closely with the Bolivian military during the hunt for Che Guevara, and thanks to him and his work Ecuador was one of the few Latin American countries which had never known any insurgent or guerrillero activities."*[295]

About his post war period, Alfons stated (*Nueva*, October 1984): "*On 8 July 1945, I was detained by the North American Secret Service. After the war I was recruited to infiltrate a communist cell of the Resistance."* All this information can be found in the North American archives, although a large proportion is inaccessible because of "public safety".[296] About his escape he said the following: [*Nueva*:]"*After having worked briefly for this service, I left for Spain, where I joined other SS officers working for the state security of Franco. In Spain it was decided to broaden the espionage network to include Latin America; I still remained at the service of the USA and Latin America was parcelled out (among various agents).* He (Alfons) left Spain for Ecuador and offered his services to the army. There he succeeded the representative Klaus Barbie. Both were committed to the same work." On 3 October 1984, he added in Ecuadorian daily *Hoy*: "*When I was 17, I joined the SS, and at the age of 18 I had become a specialist within the Secret Service. After the war I was recruited by the North Americans. Then*

I left for Spain were I rendered my services to the Secret Service of Franco. All that time I was in the service of the USA..."[297]

Alfons explained during an unpublished the interview with Von der Goltz (1983) that as holder of a West German passport he regulary visited Munich (1970-1980) as an international expert on security matters. When Van der Goltz asked him if he worked together with certain Secret Services, for example the German, Alfons replied to Van der Goltz: *"Nein, mit der Verräterbande doch nicht, um Gottes Willen.*Not with those traitors! His friend Klaus Barbie had never lost contact with the North Americans since the moment he arrived in Bolivia. In La Paz he was always surrounded with officials of the German Secret Service. The German BND was controlled by the CIA: *"Die Amerikaner kontrolieren doch den BND, als ob das ihr eigenes Büro sei."* On the question of who used Klaus Barbie, he said: *"For Klaus Barbie there was no option. This was his only way of surviving. They had always used him."* When Von der Goltz asked who, Alfons was evasive. According the Dutch weekly *De Tijd*, he justified the cooperation of Barbie with the CIA and BND as follows: *"On the first day he arrived, Klaus went directly to the Bolivian Secret Service and told them: This is my curriculum vitae, people. I had no choice but to work for the Germans and the Americans. But I will always keep you informed. Klaus was more like a double cross agent. But he always favoured the Bolivian side."*[298]

Kai Hermann, in an article published in *Der Stern* (1984), uncovered the whole history of the close relationship between the illegal international arms trade and the international intelligence community: "*In Madrid, Skorzeny, Rudel and Degrelle started in the fifties the set up of the Fascist International, codename Die Spinne (La Araña, Sechsgestern or International Negra)... In November 1951 the police in Düsseldorf (Germany) rounded up the firm Uhrmeister Gesundheitstechnik on 32 Grafenberger Allee. The firm was a cover for the activities of Die Spinne. A certain engineer by the name of Rolf Steinbauer who occasionally worked at that location was no other than Otto Skorzeny.representatives of the Fascist International in Latin America are Klaus Barbie in Bolivia, Alfons Sassen in Ecuador, Wim Sassen in Argentina, Friedrich Schwend in Peru, Walter Rauff in Chile, Josef Mengele in Paraguay and Hans Ulrich Rudel as the section head of Latin America. From this group of members of Die Spinne, not only Klaus Barbie and Alfons Sassen maintained close contacts with the American Secret Service but also SS Obersturmführer Friedrich Schwend worked for the SCI.*" [299]

On 7 October 1984, *Hoy* magazine published an article entitled *Ecuatoriano-Holandes responde a afirmaciones de revista Stern, "Nunca he sido espia, dice Alfonso Sassen"*, by *Vicente Olmedo* in which Alfons denied his alleged role as a spy. He stated: "*I have never been a spy, nor in the service of the USA, nor of any other country, not even of Franco. The only thing I can say about it is that I have been commissioned as an advisor concerning international counter-terrorism and drugs trafficking. These false allegations which have been published is the work of the drugs mafia, which is partly German, and because the work I do is very effective in the battle against drugs. It is *a known trick of drugslords, extreme leftist movements and international terrorist to damage people like me.*"[300]

In connection with Barbie, the *Hoy* reporter asked when did Alfons visit Bolivia and whether he was really involved in the death of guerrilla-leader Che Guevara, Alfons responded: "*It is absolutely untrue that I have been involved with the death of Guevara*". He also denied all involvement with the *Black International (International Negra)* or any other fascist orientated network. According to him there was no political conspiracy or Secret Service. "*The only work I do is fighting against the illegal drugs traffic.*"[301]

Alfons said he would sue the German magazine *Der Stern* because of slander. The magazine had tried to discredit him completely. In his own words: "*It is a known tactic of the Kremlin to isolate people with this kind of disinformation completely from the outside world. It also means that even your own friends do not get the opportunity to hear the truth.*"[302]

He then stated that the *Stern* reporter never interviewed him and thinks the following had happened [Alfons :] "*because I am investigating a network of drugs traffickers. and together with Dinactie we were able to inflict some damage on the organisation by intercepting a shipment of drugs in Brussels (Belgium), they are trying to silence me. About my involvement with Dinactie I can reveal little because of current investigations.*[303]"

He even denied holding any military rank within the Ecuadorian army: "*I hold no rank within the Ecuadorian army, the only thing I do is to be at their disposal when they call for me.*" Whether he was implicated in the trafficking of arms (Steyr): *Listen, my son who is a born Ecuadorian, is a representative of this firm. I have never sold a weapon, nor will I ever sell one. Personally I do not like to live of arms deals, but my son is in his own right to be a representative of arms factories.*"

He finished the interview with: "*I have never been an advisor to any government. I have been though befriended with the also from Guayaguil originating former business man and at that time conservative president Léon Febres Cordero (1984-1988)*".[304] This same Cordero was praised by the American president *Ronald Regan* for his effort in the battle against drugs with the *Drugs Enforcement Administration (DEA)*, during the *War on Drugs*.

The publicity on Alfons did not reach only German and Ecuadorian newspapers. Questions were raised in The Netherlands too. The Dutch national Public Prosecutor contacted the American embassy in Ecuador: *Recently there appeared in October a copy of the Ecuadorian newsmagazine Nueva an article about the former Nazi of Dutch nationality Alfons Sassen. This article was a reprint of a Stern article (edition 14 June 1984). The most striking point of the Nueva–Stern article are that Sassen had been a security advisor to all Ecuadorian governments and that he maintained excellent contacts with the high ranking Ecuadorian military. One of the most convincing evidence would be that the army control drugs enforcement organisation DINACTIE (División National contra el tráfico ilícito de Estupefacientes) recently awarded Sassen with a distinction for rendered services.*"[305]

The American embassy replied that Alfons Sassen entered Ecuador in 1951 on a Spanish passport. Furthermore that there were indications that he, since 1964, was a member of a neo-Nazi organisation in Latin America. But the embassy did deny any involvement of helping Alfons Sassen to Latin America, like it was in the case with Klaus Barbie. The ambassador also stated – as far as they know - that Sassen was never involved in any activities concerning the successive Ecuadorian governments (so therefore no security advisor). But he does have connections with DINACTIE.

About Dinactie the ambassador informed that it was an unreliable drugs controller. The organisation was completely infiltrated by drugs merchants, and they actually controlled it. Pressurized by the USA the whole organisation had to be cleared and reorganised before the drugs-enforcers could count on new financial and technical assistance; a consequence of the *Hawkins-Gilman amendment* to foreign assistance which was linked to the US *Law on Drugs*.[306]

The American embassy in return asked the Dutch government was interested in the extradition of Alfons Sassen. The answer was simply no. There would have been too many obstacles to have him extradited, besides The Netherlands did not have an extradition treaty with Ecuador. More importantly the Public Prosecutor concluded in December 1984 about the ACEM Sassen case: *"To the reliability of Alfons Sassen can be in general be doubted; it is known that he, at the end of 1944 beginning of 1945, together with some very doubtful characters, using his German uniform and his service weapon, started on his own initiative looting raids. Sassen could be described around that time as a complete uncontrolled adventurer. Weeks after the liberation Alfons got arrested several times and released again in order to help tracking down Abwehr officials and agents. In that time some concessions must have been done in exchange for information: Sassen was never prosecuted for his enrolment in the enemies forces or rendering of assistance to the enemy. Nor was he convicted for the –proven- robberies. The persecutions of all these crimes have been expired. Sassen is therefore not registered as a fugitive criminal, not since 1947. Signed Brilman, Public Prosecutor.*"[307] Alfons Sassen was free to go wherever he wanted. Even in The Netherlands.

Then things quietened down a bit around Alfons Sassen, until his brother died at the age of 84 in 2002 in Chile. Six years later, on 16 August 2008, Alfons Sassen died at the age of 82 in Quito.

In remembrance his son Alfonso Sassen (1953) junior General partner *Euro American Enterprises L.L.C.* (smoking accessories) in Bellingham(USA) posted on their webpage: "*Sigma Delta USA inc is greatly saddened to announce the death of its founder, guiding force and Chairman of its Board of Directors Dr Alphonse Sassen following a prolonged illness..Speaking from Sigma Delta USA's corporate headquarters in Bellingham, Washington, Company President Alfonso Sassen referred to his father's passing as a "loss which will take some time to recover from*"[308]. A month later his funeral the life story of Alfons Sassen senior was put on the internet: *SS Sonderführer* memorial webpage. In a related internet site fathers collected Nazi–memorabilia was put on sale.[309] Items the he apparently had collected during his battlefront experience in Europe. On the memorial website his colourful career at the SS was highlighted. His post-war activities mainly described his career as a master in biochemistry. No reference was made about his past as counter-insurgency specialist, his role as a military advisor, nor his famous influential friends of his glorious Nazi past: Klaus Barbie, Friedrich Schwend and others. Little would his Nazi friends have known. This young Alfons had been boasting around he was one hundred percent *Waffen SS*. Saw action in the Balkans, Arnhem (*Operation Market Garden*) and the Belgian Ardennes. In the interview (GOLTZ) he said he hated panzer... already since the war. In which war? Alfons never fired a shot in wartime Europe. After the war he collected Nazi memorabilia to reinvent his glorious SS career.

Epilogue

In 2000 the Sassen brothers again made it to the headlines once more. This time it was because of the activities of Alfons' son Robert Sassen. In Ecuador Robert and (Alfons second son) Jan Sassen inherited the business and contacts of Alfons senior. Robert represented *Prodefensa*, a company which was founded in 1986 in Quito, and took over his father's role as an advisor for the National Police. In 1991 Jan founded *Fenix Corporation SA, equipos de defensa y Seguridad*, in Guayaquil, Ecuador. Both businesses were legitimate. So far so good.[310]

On 8 May 2001 the Ecuadorian daily *Hoy* published the first signs of corruption. The headline *Roberto Sassen es un coruptor de policias'*, (Roberto Sassen corrupted the police), revealed many secrets of his trade. Due to the scandal al contracts with the army and police were suspended. A heavy blow for *Prodefensa* because it provided not only weapons, but also armoured cars and surveillance equipment to for example the *Unidad de Investigaciones Especiales y Secretas de la Policia* (UIES), the department of special and secret investigations of the police. It got worse. Apparently the Argentinean Justice department was looking for Roberto Sassen. In 1995 he was involved in an international arms smuggling case between state-owned Argentina arms firm *Fabricaciones Militares* (FM) and Ecuadorian military officials.[311]

What could go wrong, then indeed went wrong. The armsdeal was supposed to take place through a highly profitable gateway to the former Yugoslavia. Through various fronts, different contact-persons and ghost-firms in Uruguay, Panama and Venezuela a group of Argentinean military with backing of the then president *Carlos Menem*, tried to bypass UN embargos. Between 1991 and 1995 this group of international arms smugglers sold large quantities of military hardware to countries at war, among which former Yugoslavia and Ecuador.

When the *Guerra de Cénepa*, the border war between Ecuador and Peru, started in 1995 the same contraband-group was illegally diverting a shipment of 75 tons of small arms to Ecuador. Officially it went via Uruguay to Venezuela, but in reality it arrived in Guayaquil, Ecuador. There the local population would be armed.[312]

The Ecuadorian-German Robert Sassen van Elsloo, owner of the Ecuadorian company *Prodefensa*, was assigned to act as an intermediary in the purchase of arms at the DGFM (*Dirección General de Fabricaciones de las Fuerzas Armadas Argentinas*). One of the other involved intermediaries, international arms dealer *Jean Bernard Lasnaud*, chairman of the company *Carribean Group of Companies*, had close ties with the CIA.

Officially the Ecuador and Peru were obliged to respect the protocol of Rio de Janeiro (*Tratado de Paz y Amistad*) of 1942. Argentina, a guarantor of peace, was one of those countries which ratified this treaty, breached its commitments under international law by selling weapons to Ecuador and Croatia, despite the ban imposed by the UN that forbade any arms sales to Croatia.[313]

The deal, however, was made, and under the guise of darkness the weapons were flown in to Guayaquil.

A reporter of the Peruvian daily *La Republica* got wind of the deal and made it public. Ecuador was hit twice. First of all it was a violation of the international arms embargo, secondly the arms were literary useless. The whole case was a scam. The arms had been stocked in the DGFM in Rosario for about twenty years. The munitions came from Iran, and it was so poor that after its first check it was dumped into the sea. Everyone felt conned, and accused each other of illegal trafficking of arms under false pretenses. They all wanted their money back. It got even worse when the deal became international news. President Menem was accused of corruption: money laundering, breaching of international treaties, etc. When an international investigation was mounted, many implicated persons fled the country, or died under suspicious circumstances.[314]

International warrants were issued. Robert Sassen was also wanted by *Interpol*. He was lucky, judiciary mistakes led to his release from custody. He did not wait for further investigations and instead, disappeared.[315]

In an interview held in 2000 Roberto stated he was just an intermediary in this deal. In the end the case was dropped in Ecuador. In Argentina, however, Menem and other high ranking officials were convicted. Up until that point Menem had enjoyed parliamentary immunity which saved him from prison.

Robert Sassen remains at large. *Interpol* is still looking for Robert Edgar Xavier Sassenvan Elsloo wanted for organised crime, international criminal activities, and criminal actions which involve the traffic of weapons and explosives etc.[316]

The whole affair sparked a renewed interest in the Sassen families' past. The international dailies compared the two brothers with their offspring. Now old, they tried to defend themselves, but the harm was already done. Only upon retirement, when spending their last days in tranquillity, they found their peace. Wim disappeared to Chile. There he performed his last theatre play. His exact date of death is still a mystery. Alfons died at home in Quito, Ecuador. The veil of mystery around these brothers has not ended. Since the death of Wim Sassen, several screen- and theatre plays were produced concerning his person, yet always in relation to Adolf Eichmann. Unfortunately these productions did not always reflect Wim Sassen's true colours.

Abbreviations

A.D.V.N.	Documentation and research centre for Flemish Nationalism
B.N.V.	Bureau Nationale Veiligheid; Dutch Bureau of National Security
B.H.I.C.	Brabants Historisch Informatie Centrum: Regional Archive of Brabant
B.S.	Binnenlandse strijdkrachten: Dutch Volunteer Army
CEGESOMA	Centre for Historical Research and Documentation on War and Contemporary Society
FA.M.A.	Fabricaciones Militares de las Fuerzas Armadas Argentinas: Military factory for Argentinean Army
D.G.B.R.	Directoraat Generaal voor de Bijzondere Rechtspleging: Directorate for Extraordinary Law Enforcement
D.I.	División Informaciones: Argentinean Bureau of Intelligence
Dinaso	Dietse Nationaal Solidaristen: Union of Diets National Solidarists
D.P.M.	Dienst Politieke Misdrijven: Office of Political Offenses
D.W.I.	Deutsche Auslandwissenchaftliches Institut: German Cultural Institute (RSHA)
Eximorg	Export and Import Organisation
F.A.K.	Frontaufklärungskommando: Reconnaissance unit
F.A.T.	Frontaufklärungstruppe: Reconnaissance unit
F.S.S.	Field Security Section
Gestapo	Geheime Staatspolizei: German Secret State Police
H.J.	Hitlerjugend
I.R.O.	International Refugee Organization

I.S.	Intelligence Service
I-netz	Informations-netze: Intelligence-network (stay behind)
K.E.	Kurt Eggers (SS Standarte): War Correspondents of the SS (RSHA)
K.P.	Knokploeg: Dutch Armed Resistance
K.Z.	Konzentrationslager, KZ-Lager (concentration camp)
L.O.	Landelijke Organisatie voor Hulp aan onderduikers; Dutch National Organisation (resistance) LO
L.K.P.	Landelijke Knokploegen: National Organisation of Armed Squads
N.B.S.	Nederlandse Binnenlandse Strijdkrachten, see B.S.
N.I.O.D.	Institute for War, Holocaust and Genocide Studies
N.I.R.	Nationaal Instituut voor de Radio Omroep: Belgian Broadcasting Institute
NL-HaNA	Nationaal Archief Den Haag: Dutch National Archive in The Hague
N.O.	Nationale Omroep: National Broadcasting Company
N.S.B.	Nationaal-socialistische Beweging: National Socialist Movement
N.E.S.B.	Nationale Europese Sociale Beweging: National Socialist European Movement
N.S.D.A.P.	Nationalsozialistische Deutsche Arbeiterpartei: Nazi-party
N.S.V.	Nationalsozialistische Volkswohlfahrt; National Socialist People's Welfare
M.P.	Military Police
O.D.E.S.S.A.	Organisation der Ehemaligen SSAngehörigen: Organisation of Former SS Members
O.P.	Ordo Praedictatorum, Dominican order
P.K.	Propaganda Kompagnie: Propaganda Company
P.O.D.	Politieke Opsporingsdienst; Criminal Investigative Department
P.O.W.	Prisoner of War

P.R.A.	Politieke Recherche Afdeling: Political Investigative Department
R.B.S.	Rundfunkbetreuungsstelle: Trans-European Radio Network
R-netz	Rückbleiber-netz: stay behind network
R.R.G.	Reichsrundfunkgesellschaft: Broadcasting company
R.S.H.A.	Reichssicherheitshauptamt: Reich Main Security Office
S.A.R.E.	Sociedad Argentina de la Recepción Europeos: Reception of exiles and refugees
S.A.	Sturmabteilung: Stormtroopers
S.C.I.	Special Counter Intelligence
S.D.	Sicherheitsdienst: German Security Service
S.I.E.	Servicio de Inteligencia Española: Spanish Secret Service
S.I.S.	Secret Intelligence Service
S.J.	Sociëteit van Jezus: Society of Jesus
S.O.P.D.	Stichting Oud Politieke Delinquenten: Foundation of Former Political Delinquents
S.S.	Schutzstaffel: Protective Squadron or Black Guards, Hitler's elite troops.
U.I.E.S.S.	Unidad de Investigaciónes Especiales y Secretas de la Policia: Special Secret Investigating Unit of the Police
Verdinaso	Verbond van Dietsche Nationaal-Solidaristen: Union of National Solidarists
V-mann	Vertrauensmann of Verbindungsmann: Informer
V.N.V.	Vlaams Nationaal Verbond: Flemish National Union

Family tree of the Sassen

Ancestors:

Eduard Pieter Jacob Sassen (1855-1932)1
Rosalia Catharina Maria Lammers (1863-1916)

*

Children:

Jan Coenraad Hubert Marie Wilhelmus Sassen
Maria Antoinetta Francisca Sassen (1889-1905)
Georgette Antoinette Maria Sassen (1892)
Xaverius Marie Willem Antoon Sassen (1994-1927)
Adrienne Joseph Marie Sassen (1906-1942)

*

Parents of Wim en Alfons Sassen:

Jan CHMW Sassen (Wim): Ubbergen 10-07-1884 /
Bad Wiessee 27-01-1962
Johanna Margaretha Maria van Bavel:
Geertruidenberg 04-04-1884 – Munich 28-04-1959
Married in Geertruidenberg 6 September 1910

*

Children born in Geertruidenberg:

Maria Johanna Jacquelina/Jacqueline (Mies):
01-12-1912 (Raamsdonk)
Georgette Jacoba Cornelia Maria (Gilly):
24-08-1916-2000 (Belgium)
Willem Antonius Maria (Wim, Willy):
16-04-1918 /2002 (Santiago de Chili)
Johanna Gertrudis Maria (Hansi):
08-03-1920 - ?
Francisca Josepha Maria (Cisl, Cis or Franzl):
22-08-1921 / 17-11-1995 (Munich)
Jacquelina Rosalie Maria:
04-05-1925
Alphonse (Alfons) Cornelis Eduard Marie (Fonske, Alphons, Fons): 28-12-1926 / 21-09-2008 (Quito, Ecuador)

*

M.J.J. Sassen: partner Rudolf Burk
G.J.C.M. Sassen: married to Paul Marcel Servant. 2nd partner: Louis Peeters
J.G.M. Sassen: Married Alfred Herkel Kruschel
F.J.M. Sassen: Married 15-12-1944 (Enschede) to Helmut Karl Ernst Weidenbach (22-12-1917/16-04-1945); 2nd marriage: M.L.N. Graf von Tauffkirchen zu Guttenberg, Klebing-Katzenberg und Englburg (Heidelberg 21-02-1918 – Munich 25-11-2002)

*

Willem Sassen
Marriage 1

Paula Maria Fissette (Maastricht 16-01-1920)
Wed on 27-09-1940, divorced 09-01-1947³

Children:

Godelieve Maria Hildegarde (1941 - 1994)
Diethart Jan Hendrik Cyriel (1943)
Willem Koenraad Roeland (1944)

*

Woman from Oldenburg (Germany),
extramarital affair: a son (1944)

*

Marriage 2 (Argentina):

M.J.G. (Miepje) van der Voort
Married 16 May 1952 in Mexico, divorced in 1971

Children:

Saskia Josine Maria Haremaker
(05-01-1947 The Hague)
Hadewych (Hanneke 30-12-1948 Buenos Aires)
Francisca (30-09-1955 Buenos Aires)

*

Marriage 3:

Els Delbaere
Wed in 1973 Buenos Aires, Argentina
Children:
Johannes

*

Alfons Sassen van Elsloo van Bavel
Married in Quito, Ecuador:
Ana Esmeralda Chalen Lasso

*

Children:

Alfonso
Roberto Xavier
Jan

Notes

1. From Argentina *Lucia Suarez (Telefe)* Belgium *Louis de Lentdecker (De Standaard), Maurice de Wilde, Stan Lauryssens;* Germany: *Gerd Heinemann (Stern), Kai Hermann (Stern), Michael von der Goltz,* the Hungarian *Ladislas Farago* and the North American reporter *Sam Donaldson (ABC television).*
2. Jan Sassen OP, a known Dutch church historian who died in a bombing raid during *Operation Market Garden.*
3. NL-HaNa, Justitie/ Centraal Archief Bijzondere Rechtspleging (CABR), 2.09.09, inv.nr. 31614.
4. In Belgium the *Activist Movement* was created during WWI. Their main goal was dividing Belgium into a separate Flemish and Wallonian part. *The Greater Netherlands Movement* meant the unification of all Dutch speaking countries: Flemish Belgium, Netherlands and South Africa. As the leader of the *Molenaarsvereniging Saint Victor*, Sassen senior maintained liaison with the Belgian counterpart *Syndicaal Verbond van Ambachten en Nering* (Syvian) and *Burgerstrijd*. These last two organisations had strong ties with Belgian rightist movements like the Flemish movement *Verdinaso* of Joris van Severen and *Rexist Movement* (Cristus Rex).
5. The Dominican uncles Jan and Willem Sassen were sympathisors of the *Greater Netherlands Movement.*
6. NL-HaNA, Justitie / CABR, 2.09.09, inv.nr. 31614.
7. CEGESOMA 1312/11 Wim Sassen, The danger was rooted in the fact that there was only a small difference between the popularity of NS or socialism and communism among the working class. It had the potential to turn either way. The NS could win these converted communists over.
8. Stan Lauryssens, *De fatale vriendschappen van Adolf Eichmann* (Leuven 1998) 26-27.
9. NL-HaNA, Justitie / CABR, 2.09.09, inv.nr. 31614.
10. Ad Sassen (1906-1942) journalist, anti-democratic Catholic intellectual, author and poet.
11. *Stadskrant Kijk op Veghel*, 11-05 1994 / 16-06-1994, by drs A.P. van der Wiel.
12. NL-HaNA, Justitie / CABR, 2.09.09, inv.nr. 31614.

13 Georgette worked for the Flemish radio since 1938. She recited Dutch and Flemish poetry.
14 NL-HaNA, Justitie / CABR, 2.09.09, inv.nr. 31614.
15 NL-HaNA, Justitie / CABR, 2.09.09, inv.nr. 87844.
16 CEGESOMA: SOMA 1312/11 Wim Sassen
17 NL-HaNA, Justitie / CABR, 2.09.09, inv. nr. 87844.
18 NL-HaNA, BNV, 1945 – 1946, inv nr.: 3217. NL-HaNA, Justitie / CABR, 2.09.09, inv. nr. 87844.
19 NL-HaNA, Justitie/ CABR, 2.09.09, inv.nr. 45595.
20 NL-HaNA, Justitie / CABR, 2.09.09, inv.nr. 31614.
21 NL-HaNA, Justitie/CABR, 2.09.09, inv.nr.45595
22 NL-HaNA, Justitie / CABR, 2.09.09, inv.nr. 45595. Edgar Lehembre, member of VNV. Leader of the *Algemeen Vlaams Nationaal Jeugdverbond*. Joris van Severen was executed on 20 May 1940 during the socalled "Bloodbath of Abbeville". Flemish nationalist Hendrik Borginon founded as the leader frontbeweging after WWI the movement *Vlaams Oudstrijders* (VOS). After the French capitulation he negotiated on behalf of the exiled government the repatriation of the deported Flemish in France.
23 Maria possessed a traveldocument, a *Reisbescheinigung*, stating her exceptional service in the repatriation of Germans and Dutch/ Flemish nationals which had been arrested during the first days of the war. NL-HaNA, Jus/ Politie / KJZ, 2.09.107, inv.nr. 1586. NL-HaNA, Justitie / CABR, 2.09.09, inv.nr. 45595.
24 NL-HaNA, Jus/Politie/KJZ, 2.09.107, inv.nr.1586. NL-HaNA, Justitie/CABR, 2.09.09, inv.nr.: 45595.
25 Together with brother Ad they set up a program for te NF to represent the commerce, trade and retailers within the party. Sassen senior acted as a propagandist in order to gain more adherence to the movement and to gain sympathy among the population.
26 Paula (19-01-1920/20-03-2002) was the daughter of a rich Maastricht *Lincoln-* en *Forddealer* N. Fissette. Garage *Fissette & Zn.*, Scharnerweg 165, Maastricht.There is no information on where and when they, Wim and Paula, met for the first time.
27 CEGESOMA, SOMA 1312/11 Wim Sassen
28 NL- HaNA, BNV 1945-1946, inv. nr: 3217.

29 CEGESOMA: SOMA 1312/11 Wim Sassen
30 NL-HaNA, Justitie / CABR, 2.09.09, inv.nr. 87844.
31 Directoraat Generaal voor Bijzondere Rechtspleging, Kamp Vught, 14 maart 1947, rapport JCHMW Sassen.
32 Nl-HaNA, Justitie/CABR, 2.09.09, inv.nr.45595. NL-HaNA, Jus/Politie/KJZ, 2.09107, inv.nr. 1586.
33 Maria reported cases of black market trafficking and corruption, also from within the SD like the ransom cases or briberies by SD officials. She was in contact with *Dr. Rincke, president of the German court in Antwerp.* SD chef Otto Desselman was shot dead in 1943 by an employee. Desselman was known to take bribes from the Jewish comunity. *SS-Hauptscharführer* Hans Hulmann, chief Department III, SD internal security. NL-HANA, Justitie / CABR, 2.09.09, inv.nr. 45595. NL-HaNA, Jus/ Politie / KJZ, 2.09.107, inv.nr. 1586
34 NL-HaNA, Justice/CABR, 2.09.09, inv.nr. 45595.
35 NL-HaNA, Justitie / CABR, 2.09.09, inv.nr. 45595. 4-18 juni 1941 *Ausländerkursus des Instituts Um das neue Europa*. Franz Alfred Six, head Amt VII RSHA; ideological affairs, antisemitic and –freemasonry-propaganda, the study on the morale within the occupied territory and the effect the Nazi – doctrine had upon the populace; in short the ideological conduct of war. *Die Bürgerkriege Europas undder Einigungskrieg der Gegenwart, Vorträge vor der Europa Ausländerkursus "Fragen der neuen Ordnung",* 5-19 November 1942. During this course the realization of the *New Order* was discussed the implementation of the Nazi doctrine in the occupied territories.
36 A. van Breugel, 'Nederlandse vrijwilligers voor Rostow', *Limburgs Dagblad*, 15-08-1942.
37 NL-HaNA, Justitie / CABR, 2.09.09, inv.nr. 87844.
38 NL-HaNA, Justitie/CABR, 2.09.09, inv.nr.: 87844.
39 NL-HaNA, Justitie / CABR, 2.09.09, inv.nr. 87844.
40 *Algemeen Nederlands Dagblad*, 24-12-1942, 6de jaargang, no. 51.
41 NL-HaNA, Justitie / CABR, 2.09.09, inv.nr. 31614.
42 NL-HaNA, Justitie / CABR, 2.09.09, inv.nr. 31614.
43 NL-HaNA, Justitie/CABR, 2.09.09, inv.nr.:87844
44 Orginally the SS had her own *Propaganda Korps* (PK): a

corps of war reporters of all nationalities. When the SS became the main controlling force, the SS PK was reorganised. On 9 December 1943 SS Standarte Kurt Eggers was realised. This body outranked Goebbels propaganda department and became the official military propaganda department for all occupied and neutral territories. According to Wim Sassen the Standarte Kurt Eggers (K.E.) was working closely with Amt III and possibly VI of the RSHA. As of 1943 K.E. was under controle of *Heinrich Himmler*.

45 Stan Lauryssens Archive: DGBR, PRA Breda, proces-verbaal, 28-10-1946, JCHMW Sassen.
46 The NSB- administration was of the opinion that Sassen senior was too provincial and too Catholic for the movement.
47 NL-HaNA, Justitie / CABR, 2.09.09, inv.nr.31614.
48 NL-HaNA, Justitie / CABR, 2.09.09, inv.nr.87844.
49 NL-HaNA, BNV, 2.04.08, inv.nr.3217
50 NL-HaNA, Justitie / CABR, 2.09.09, inv.nr.31614.
51 *De Waarheid*, 20-04-1945, 'Een Nazi provocatie'
52 Cammaert, A. P. M., *Het Verborgen Front, Geschiedenis van de georganiseerde illegaliteit in de provincie Limburg tijdens de Tweede Wereldoorlog.* 615: dissertations.ub.rug.nl/FILES/faculties/arts/1994/a.cammaert/06_h6-2.pdf. *Limburgs Dagblad* 16-06-1984, 'Limburgse KP in Noord Holland',
53 Correspondence L.M. Bruin: It would appear that someone betrayed Fritz, or else the SD had a lucky catch. According to Pons, the set up wasn't to capture Fritz, but to reveal the whereabouts of the Resistance funds of the *Nationaal Steunfonds* (NSF). The SD officials wanted to catch a certain Ton Millord. The deal was that the Resistance group would pay 10.000 Dutch guilders and Scharrer would be released.
54 Collection Mertens, Archive of the Dutch Jesuit Society in Nijmegen (The Netherlands), De Linie, box 3, 21b.*SS-mann Polizist, Herbert Oelschlägel, De mythe, de man*, een onderzoekje van L.M. Bruijn (Groningen 2010).
55 L.M. Bruijn, *SS-mann Polizist, Herbert Oelschlägel, De mythe, de man* (Groningen 2010) 21-25.

56 Henri Scharrer, Johannes Voskuil and Fritz Conijn were executed on 6 September 1944 in Vught.
57 Collection Mertens, Archive of the Dutch Jesuit Society in Nijmegen, *De Linie*, box 3, 21b. According to Mertens Willem Sassen was a nationalist; a true patriot: 'He never hurt or betrayed anyone. He respected the resistance.'
58 *Bormshuis-Broederband, a two monthy Flemish - Dutch magazine, year 41, no 2, March-April 2004, Antwerp, article by F. van Campenhout, Jeanne de Bruyn, 7-12.*
59 NL-HaNA, BNV, 2.04.80, inv.nr.: 3217. In the Dutch East front volunteers and the Dutch resistance Wim Sassen saw so many resemblances that he considered them to be the future leaders of the post war society. NL-HaNA, Justitie / CABR, 2.09.09, inv.nr. 31614.
60 NL-HaNA, Justitie / CABR, 2.09.09, inv.nr. 31614.
61 Collection Mertens, Jesuit Archive Nijmegen (The Netherlands), box 3, 21b
62 Joachim Fernau (11-09-1909, 24-11-1988) during the war *Kriegsberichterstatter*. In 1951 *Hauptschriftleiter der Stuttgarter Illustrierten*.
63 NL-HaNA, Justitie / CABR, 2.09.09, inv.nr. 31614.
64 *Skorpion West*: codename for the SS controle propaganda actions in the West. In 1943 on suggestion of Himmler, D'Alquin *Obersturmführer* Hans Weidemann (*Kriegsberichter*) and *Obersturmführer* Joachim Fernau (*Kriegsberichter*). The *Aktivpropaganda* was created. Weidemann became chef of this department. It's main purpose was to demoralise the enemy troops by propaganda (radio, pamphlets). After *D-Day* it was also used within the occupied territories to cause confusion among the local population and to refrain them from aiding the local resistance. Groeneveld, *Kriegsberichter Nederlandse SS-oorlogsverslaggevers 1941-1945 (Haarlem 2004)*, 282. NL-HaNA, BNV, 2.04.80, inv.nr. 3217.
65 The satirical paper *De Gil was created by the Abteilung Aktivpropaganda in March 1944.* This socalled resistance paper was imensly popular until September 1944. There was also a radio (Jazz) programm called *De Gil*. Z.A.B. Zeman, *De propaganda van de nazi's* (Hilversum 1966) 180-198. Helmut Pröbsting, former head of Abteilung

IIIB with the *Befehlshaber der Sicherheitspolizei und des SD* in The Hague, and Dr. Haagn (Ministry of Propaganda, *Hauptabteilung Volksaufklärung und Propaganda* of the *Aktivpropaganda*) were behind the development of the paper *De Gil*. Further publications were prohibited when after Dolle Dinsdag an issue appeared that was too anti German that the Pressereferent Dittmar interfered.

66 NL-HaNA, Justitie / CABR, 2.09.09, inv. nr.: 31614. Miep van der Voort (1922 Heerlen).
67 NL-HaNA, BNV, 2.04.80, inv. nr.: 3217. At the beginning of 1945 Blaskowitz replaced generaal Student of *Heeresgruppe H*. It was Blaskowitz who negotiated with general B. Montgomery about the caputilation of the 25th Army. On 4 May 1945 Blaskowitz sent his chief of staf lieutenant- general Reichelt to Wageningen where in the end the actual capitualtion was signed in the presence of general C. Foulkes and Prince Bernhard zur Lippe Biesterfeld.
68 http://dare.uva.nl/document/116970
69 *HP De Tijd*, 11-11-1978, 'Willy van der Hout'
70 Lange was attached to Kommando 306. A subdivision of FAT 365, that had its operations centre in Driebergen and was run by Hauptmann Werner Bulang. Lange operated from the Ortskommandantur in Utrecht. Together with the *Armeeoberkommando* 25, the foundations for a *Rückbleibernetz (R-netz)* (stay-behind) group were being laid
71 Driebergen nearby Utrecht. In Villa *Beukenstein*, 57 Hoofdstraat, was during the war the headquarters *Gestapo and* SD. In 1944 the FAT(*Frontaufkläringstruppe*)-units were coordinated from here as an underground movement. This staybehind or *Rückbleiber-netz* would consist of Dutch Nazis who would spy on Allied forces. This *R-netz* codenamed *NEUROP* would operate from different cities. The *R-netz* wasn't a *Wehrwolf* network. With the capitulation of Germany all R and I (Information) *Netze* – operations ceased. The FAT were also deployed by *Oberstleutnant* Giskes and later his succesor Major Kiesewetter. Both better known for their role during the *England Spiel* or *Nordpolspiel*. During the England Spiel the communicationlines between the Dutch resistance and London was

intercepted by the staff of the FAT (FAT 365 als FAK 307) in Driebergen and later Hilversum. Archief Stan Lauryssens. NL-HaNA, Justitie / CABR, 2.09.09, inv.nr. 31614
72   NL-HaNA, Justitie/CABR, 2.09.09, inv.nr. 31614
73   NL-HaNA, Justitie/CABR, 2.09.09, inv.nr. 31614
74   Groeneveld, *Kriegsberichter*, 361-362. Perry Biddescombe, *The last Nazis, SS werewolf guerrilla resistance in Europe 1944-1947* (Gloucestershire 2004) 118. This group 'Kurt Eggers' under Sternberg was also called *Kommando Sternberg*.
75   NL-HaNA, Justitie/CABR, 2.09.09, inv.nr. 31614
76   *The Sassen group was to operate after the capitulation. Therefore it would be understandable that Bulang ordered Neurop to halt all activities as an underground FAT unit. It was though in the intentions of Wim Sassen to become a werewolf unit, according to Werner Schramm. His illness and the rapid turn of events prevented this.* NL-HaNA, Justitie / CABR, 2.09.09, inv.nr. 31614.
77   NL-HaNA, Justitie/CABR, 2.09.09, inv.nr. 31614
78   NL-HaNA, Justitie / CABR, 2.09.09, inv.nr. 31614. See chapter "Has Wim turned"
79   Collection Mertens, Jesuit Archive. *De Linie*, box 3, 21b.
80   Henk Boot, address Fontijn Verschuirsstraat, Alkmaar.
81   NL-HaNA, Justitie / CABR, 2.09.09, inv.nr. 31614, 87844.
82   NL-HaNA, Justitie / CABR, 2.09.09, inv.nr. 31614, 87844. NL-HaNA, BNV, 2.04.80, inv.nr. 3217. Wim stated there was a set deal. "*This is why I left for Alkmaar on the 8 May 1945 and reported myself to the local authorities. On intervention of a certain captain James of the Field Security I was formally arrested on 8 July 1945.*"
83   Collection Mertens, Jesuit Archive. *De Linie*, box 3, 21b.
84   Sonderkommando Sternberg, - Pröbsting were known units of the Dienstelle Hendrik. Wim reported on werewolfnetworks in Leipzig and Frankfurt am Main. He also revealed intelligence of the Abwehr (Damrau) to the Canadian FS concerning the post war penetration scheme of the *International Brigade* (Communists) in Europe and the rest of the world. NL-HaNA, Justitie / CABR, 2.09.09, inv. nr.31614. CEGES: SOMA 1312/11, W. Sassen

85 NL-HaNA, Justitie / CABR, 2.09.09, inv.nr. 31614.
86 Collection Mertens, Jesuit Archive. *De Linie*, box 3, 21b.
87 NL-HaNA, Justitie/CABR, 2.09.09, inv.nr. 45595.
88 *Vrij Nederland*, 25-01-1981, 'Hoe Willem Sassen de jacht op Eichmann ten slotte won, de geheimzinnige memoires van Adolf Eichmann 3'. Het *Parool*, 10- 01-1952, 'SS'er helpen vluchten, eis weer vier maanden'.
89 *De Avondster: Katholiek Dagblad*, 31-07-1945: Het eerste Canadese leger ontbonden. Foulkes wordt chef van de generale staf in Ottawa. *Hamilton Spectator*, 30-07-1945: *Charles Foulkes came home from Europe only last week to take over at Canadian military headquarters here.*
90 NL-HaNA, BNV, 2.04.80, inv.nr.3217.
91 Collection Mertens, Jesuit Archive, De Linie, box 3, 21b.
92 *Maison de passe* is a cheap hotel. Also frequented by prostitutes and their clients. NL-HaNA, Justitie / CABR, 2.09.09, inv. nr. 31614.
93 NL-HaNA, Justitie/CABR, 2.09.09, inv.nr.31614
94 NL-HaNA, BNV, 2.04.80, inv.nr.31, 3217 *Message form, From CIB, Action 80 FS Sec, Info : 5 L of C sub Area for Provost, British Military Mission (Belgium) for CIB BNV Scheveningen: opsporingsbericht via telex. De Kaszo van Tesco: alias Hendrik – SD agent, penetrated resistance organisation. Held for interrogation at CSIC, Blauwkapel.* In 1943 Lowey Ball tried to reach Spain. He got arrested by the SD and was turned. In August 1943 he returned with a *D Sonderausweis* (traveldocument), *Marshbefehl* and *Bescheinigung to Holland.*. In Holland he was implicated in the smuggle of cigarettes and formed part of an escapeline. Both he and Henri Scharrer used the above mentioned documents for their operations. L.M. Bruijn, *SSmann Polizist, Herbert Öelschlagel, De mythe, de man* (Groningen 2010). NL-HaNA, Jus/ OMD, 2.09.106, inv.:130, NL-HaNA, Ministerie van Justitie: Beleidsarchief Immigratie- en Naturalisatiedienst (IND) [periode 1945-1955], 2.09.5026, 126.
95 NL-HaNA, Militair Gezag, 2.13.25, inv.nr. 5082. NL-HaNA, Justitie / DGBG, 2.09.08, inv.nr. 1530.
96 Bijzondere Rechtspleging, Politieke Recherche Afdeling, Breda, no.: 1786.B. Interrogation report Werner Schramm

and Wilhelm Lange, 3 August 1947 at Fort Blauwkapel.
97   *Incivieken*, Belgian collaborators or political delinquents. NL-HaNA, Justitie / CABR, 2.09.09, inv. nr. 31614. The brother of Miep, Jan van der Voort, was during the war detained in several German concentrationcamps. After the war he worked for the Americans. Her youngest brother Peter was a student in Utrecht.
98   NL-HaNA, Justitie / CABR, 2.09.09, inv. nr. 31614.
99   NL-HaNA, BNV, 2.04.80, inv.nr.3217
100 Albert Persijn (Persyn) ran a well known ratline. He escaped prison many times. In January 1946 he was arrested again, but the ratline continued to operate. Frank Seberechts, Frans-Jos Verdoodt, *Leven in twee werelden, Belgische collaborateurs en de diaspora na de Tweede Wereldoorlog* (Leuven 2009) 63-64, 110-111.
101 CEGES: SOMA, 1312/11, Wim Sassen
102 NL-HaNA, Justitie / CABR, 2.09.09, inv.nr. 45595. Dr. H. Kerken was detained in Fort Blauwkapel. He made it to the Argentina.
103 *Miranda del Ebro*, detention centre in the North of Spain. It was created during the Civil War. After the war the dentention centre harboured members of the International Brigades, stateless persons/refugees and Allied pilots. After *D-Day* also deserted German soldiers were sent to *Miranda del Ebro* and *Nanclares de Oca* (among which SS and Jewhunter Jan Olij) NL-HaNA, Justitie / CABR, 2.09.09, inv. nr. 31614.
104 NL-HaNA, BNV, 2.04.80, inv.nr. 3216.
105 NL-HaNA, Justitie / CABR, 2.09.09, inv.nr. 31614
106 NL-HaNA, Justitie/CABR, 2.09.09, inv.nr.31614.
107 CEGESOMA: SOMA 1312/11, Wim Sassen
108 NL-HaNa, Justitie/CABR, 2.09.09, inv.nr. 31614.
109 Ibedem
110 Wim Sassen was charged by the Belgian Criminal Court of having infringed article 113 and 117B (Belgian Penal Code) as a member of the *Waffen SS* and article 118 bis as war reporter and collaborator of the spoken broadcasts of Sender Brussels.
111 CEGES: 1312/11, Wim Sassen
112 Collection Mertens, Jesuit Archive, De Linie, box 3, 21b.

113 Collection Mertens, Jesuit Archive.
114 *De Waarheid*, 22-07-1950, 'Rozengracht 133, broeinest van nazi's en ex Zwart Front fascisten'.
115 Marc Lindeijer SJ, *Pater Ligthart en de zaak Roothaan. Streven naar heiligheid in het utopistisch tijdperk, 1914 – 1968* (Hilversum 2009) 291-292. Jan van Kilsdonk SJ, was known to father Ligthart. In 1947 Kilsdonk took care of Sassen senior in dentention centre Vught.
116 Frank Seberechts, Frans-Jos Verdoodt, *Leven in Twee Werelden, Belgische collaborateurs en de diaspora na de Tweede Wereldoorlog*, (Leuven 2009) 112-113.
117 *Harry van Puyenbroeck textielagenturen.* Firma *Eximorg, Export and Import* Amsterdam, 260 Singel, was founded on 1 July 1947 by H.N.J. van Puyenbroek and registered by Opdebeeck. The company traded in chemicals, glucose, paint, cardboard, paper, alcohol, electronic devises, washing machines, shoes, bycicle parts, chocolate, etc...
118 *De Waarheid*, 22-07-1950, 'Rozengracht 133, broeinest van ex nazi's, Zwart-front-fascisten'.
119 Collection Mertens, Jesuit Archive.
120 Collection Mertens, Jesuit Archive.
121 Collection Mertens, Jesuit Archive. *Vrij Nederland*, 09-10-1976, 'Mertens'. NL-HaNA, Justitie / CABR, 2.09.09, inv.nr.31614.
122 *De Waarheid*, 10-01-1952, 'Tegen redactiesecretaris van De Linie opnieuw vier maanden geëist'.
123 *Köln Rundschau, Politische Rundschau*, 16-12-1960, '*Er schrieb Adolf Eichmanns Memoiren*'.
124 *Vrij Nederland*, 18-07-1981, 'Ik heb een paspoort voor Sassen gestolen, daardoor kon hij uit Nederland komen. Dat van Sassen moet je zien in de situatie van toen', by Rudi van Meurs. B.R.C.A. Broersema, *De Linie 1946-1963, Een weekblad in handen van Jezuïeten* (Amsterdam 1978), 161. *Het Parool*, 22- 06-1951, 'Redactiesecretaris van De Linie tot 4 maanden veroordeeld': *Nieuwsblad van het Noorden*, 26-07-1979,' Onze man in Zuid-Afrika 'Geen aandeel in Muldergate'.
125 *Nieuwsblad van het Noorden*, 26-07-1979,' Onze man in Zuid-Afrika 'Geen aandeel in Muldergate'.
126 *De Waarheid*, 10 -01-1952, 'Tegen redactiesecretaris van

De Linie opnieuw vier maanden geëist'.

127 B.R.C.A. Broersema, *De Linie 1946-1963, een weekblad in handen van Jezuïeten* (Amsterdam 1978) 160-162.

128 Marc Lindeijer SJ, *Pater Ligthart en de zaak Roothaan, Streven naar heiligheid in het utopisch tijdperk*, 1914-1968 (Hilversum 2009) 613.

129 Some elements within the roman catholic church were pro fascist movement. It was prohibited to become a member of the *NSB*, and an alternative was *Zwart Front*. Many clergy saw in the SS ideological partners in the battle against communism. Archive Cees Wiebes, IISG (Amsterdam). Marc Lindeijer SJ, *Pater Ligthart en de zaak Roothaan.*, 613

130 Boersema, *De Linie 1946-1963,* 158-159, 210.

131 *Het Verzet van de Nederlandsche Bisschoppen tegen nationaalsocialisme en Duitsche Tyrannie*, ingeleid en uitgegeven door Mag. Dr. S. Stokman, OFM (Utrecht 1945) 294-295.

132 Marc Lindeijer SJ, *Pater Ligthart en de zaak Roothaan.*, 293.

133 Nicolaas Johannes 'Nico' was born on 10 July in The Hague 1920 as the only son of N.J. Haremaker and C.A. de Lance. Saskia Josine Maria Haremaker was born on 5 January 1947 in The Hague. At first Saskia was called after her stepfather. The marriage between Miep and Nico lasted between 17-08-1946 and 23-03-1948. Nico remarried in 1950 and emigrated to Soerabaja, Indonesia. NL-HaNA, Ambassade Argentinië 1955-1974, 2.05.158, inv. nr. 69.

134 F. Seberechts, F.Verdoodt, *Leven in Twee Werelden, Belgische collaborateurs en de diaspora na de Tweede Wereldoorlog*, 108-114. *Vrij Nederland*, 07 - 03 – 1992. *De Tijd*, 14 -09-1984. Uki Goñi, *The Real Odessa* (London 2002) 112 – 113, 175. ADVN, AC 121, *Leven in twee werelden.* Both Otto Skorzeny as Léon Degrelle spent some time in Ireland.

135 *Estudios migratorios latinoamericanos*, jaar 14, december 1999, no. 43, *Inmigrantes, refugiados y criminales de guerra en la Argentina de la segunda posguerra, relaciones con la Argentina de funcionarios de Vichy y de colaboradores Franceses y Belgas,* 1940-1960, door Diana Quattrocchi-Woisson,

219. ADVN, SOMA, AA 627 (Pierre Daye), 486, 487, 492.

136 *De Tijd*, 14-09-1984, 'Hoe twee Nederlandse jongens in het net van de spin belandden' and 'Werdegang'. Stan Lauryssens, *De Eichmann-erfenis*, 90 - 107. Goñi, *The Real Odessa*, 112 – 113, 175. E. Opdebeeck reached Irland that year. He became chairman of the Flemish Club in Dublin.

137 *Estudios migratorios latinoamericanos*, jaar 14, december 1999, no. 43, *Inmigrantes, refugiados y criminales de guerra en la Argentina de la segunda posguerra, relaciones con la Argentina de funcionarios de Vichy y de colaboradores Franceses y Belgas*, 1940-1960, door Diana Quattrocchi-Woisson, 219.ADVN, SOMA, AA 627 (Pierre Daye), 486, 487, 492.

138 *Autorizado desembarco definitivo de la menor Saskia Josine Maria Haremaker por expto n.: 230.001/948. Ingreso en el vapour "Adelaar" al 06-11-1948.*

139 *The publisher disposed of an international network of subscribers. Through his monthly magazine Der Weg, Fritsch informed Nazis on the run about the possibilities of leaving Europe. His very useful announcements of travel agencies, international refugee organisations like Kameradenwerke, available legal advice, as well as their own mediation offices in Buenos Aires, helped many to cross the Atlantic. For the Flemish Dutch community the monthly De Schakel (El Lazo) was issued;a magazine about art and culture in Argentina and the Low Lands (Un lazo entre el sur de América Latina y el Benelux). The owner of the editorial Dürer was Ludwig Freude. A multinacional who owned companies like CAPRI, SARE and many more firms and banks. These firms played an important role in Ludwig Freude's network. It sheltered a number of important contributors who were aiding Nazis to escape Europe. Already before the war Ludwig Freude had strong ties with the Nazi – party. Due to his support Juan Domingo Perón assumed power. When Perón was installed Ludwig Freude's son Rudi became head of the security service Centro de Intelligencia del Estado.*

140 Rudel's works were published at *Dürer Verlag* (Buenos Aires) between 1949-1952. Wim Sassens (Willem Sluyse) published at this editor own work 'Die Jünger und die

Dirnen' in 1954.
141 NL-HaNA, Ambassade Argentinië 1955-1974, 2.05.158, inv.nr. 69.
142 *On 8 October 1952, the Dutch consulate stated: 'During three or four months Wim Sassen acquired a respectable administrative function at a newly created company Fábrica de Celulosa Rio Segundo SA, the main office of which was in Calle Tucumán 439, Buenos Aires*NL-HaNA, Ambassade Argentinië 1955-1974, 2.05.158, inv.nr. 69.There is an extradition treaty between The Netherlands and Argentina (7 September 1893) but it excludes the possibility of extradition of war criminals and political delinquents, crimes that are too old (article 3), and cases where the subject has become a Argentinean citizen.
143 NL-HaNA, Ambassade Argentinië 1955-1974, 2.05.158, inv.nr. 69.
144 *Die Zeit*, 16-04-2011, 'Adolf Eichmann im Angesicht eines Massenmörders'. Stan Lauryssens, De Eichmann Erfenis, 199-200. *De Waarheid,* 22 juni 1945, 'Duitsland's derde plan tot wereldoverheersing' Wim Sassen was working for *Büssing S.A.*, Officially it imported agricultoral machinery. Main office in Braunschweig. Büssing became a part of MAN SE. Since WWI *Büssing NAG together with Daimler Benz* and *Rheinmetall made armoured cars like the Spähpanzer Luchs.* The Austrian *Steyr-Daimler–Puch produced next to cars, trucks and tractors, also (together with FIAT, Mercedes Benz, BMW) arms.*
145 The *Goodwill mission* of the Prince Bernhard. Starting on 13 March 1951. The mission arrived 26/27 March in Montevideo (Uruguay), 3-10 April Argentina, 10-17 April a visit to the lakedistrict Ruta de los site Lagos, nearby Bariloche, among which the island Huemul, and 17 left for Chile, finalizing his trip on 26 in Buenos Aires.
146 *Todo es Historia* No. 334, 'Los scientificos Alemanes y Perón' (Mayo de 1995 Buenos Aires) 9 – 22. According to Abel Basti, Prince Bernhard was via *Philips co-financer of the atomic project on the isle Huemul. If Richter succeeded Argentina would become an atomic power.* Abel Basti, *Bariloche Nazi,* 2005. *Utrechts Nieuwsblad,* 27-03-1951, 'Gereguleerde atoomenergie op een nieuwe basis'. *Utrechts*

Nieuwsblad, 17-05-1951, 'Professor Bakker naar Huemul'
147 CAPRI was also known as '*La Compania Alemana Para Recien Inmigrados*'. *A water extraction company directed by the* German – Argentina *entrepreneur Horst Carlos Fuldner.* Fuldner was heavily involved in the ratline to Latin America. Through his coverfirms Fuldner bank, CAPRI, Dürer Verlag, travel agencies, etc and other ways he managed to get technicians like Kurt Tank, scientist and other high ranking Nazis to Argentina. *In 1950, Wim also started working for CAPRI, he did not work at the main office but was assigned to remote areas like Tucumán and to Córdoba.* Goñi, *The Real Odessa*, 249. *Página 12*, 06-02-2005,'Un hombre llamado Eichmann'. Abel Basti, *Bariloche Nazi, Guia turistica, sitios historicos relacionados al nacionalsocialismo*, Edicion del autor (2005) 61.
148 Adolf Eichmann had met Erich Rajakowitsch in The Hague during the war. Both worked for the RSHA department IV-B-4, the prosecution and extermination of Jews. Rajakowitsch met Eichmann again in 1952 in Argentina. *Vrij Nederland*, 21-07-1976, 'Het ontbrekende bewijs tegen Jodenmoordenaar dr. Rajakowitsch'.
149 *Der Spiegel*, 28-03-2011, 'Triumpf der Gerechtigkeit'. *Der Spiegel*, 09-02- 2011, 'Die Akte Klaus Barbie'. Eichmann could have been located much sooner. Vera Eichmann asked for her libre de disembarco (visa) for her and her sons in Argentina. She showed the birth certificates to the German consul. An easy track to follow. Vera Eichmann, and kids, Klaus, Dieter, Horst arrived 28 July 1952 in the docks of Buenos Aires. They had left Genova by boat, *SS Salta*, to Argentina. The day before their arrival Evita Duarte Perón had died of cancer. Josef Mengele lived nearby the Sassen family, he ran a general practice. In 1957 Mengele and Rudel visited Walter Rauff in Chile. Juan Casparini, mentions in *La Fuga del Brugo* (Buenos Aires 2005) on page 72 the existance of a group photo of Mengele, Barbie, Rauff, Adolf Eichmann, Erich Priebke and José Lopez Rega who had met in Bariloche in the 50's.
150 *Der Spiegel*, 04-01-2011, 'The Long Road to Eichmann's arrest'. *Der Spiegel*, 28-03-2011,'Triumph der Gerechtigkeit'. *Der Spiegel*, 09-02-2011, 'Die Akte Klaus Barbie'.

Reinhard Gehlen, *Nu spreek ik!, Herinneringen 1942- 1971* (Baarn 1972) 132-137. The BND moved in 1947 the estate Pullach nearby Munich. Informants of the Gehlen organisation was the correspondent of the *Frankfurter Allgemeine* Fritz Otto Ehlert, and the publisher of the magazine *Freien Worts*. For this magazine Wilfried von Oven worked as chief editor in 1952. Von Oven deckared that Gehlen was one of the main financers of this magazine and even provided a printing machine; *sueddeutsche.de*, Adolf Eichmann und der BND, ´Beide Augen zu´, 14-01-2011, by Willi Winkler.

151 Kipp was a businesspartner of ex-*Luftwaffe*-piloot Dieter Menge, a dealer in scrap metal. Dieter Menge's house was a known meeting centre of Nazis like Eichmann, J. Mengele en Willem Sassen, Vgl.: Goñi, *The Real Odessa*, 307. *Der Spiegel,* 28-03-2011, 'Triumpf der Gerechtigkeit'. The taperecorder used to belong to an old friend of Wim, the former Eastfront volunteer *Pedro Pobierzym*. Jorge Camarasa, *ODESSA al sur, La Argentina como refugio de nazis y criminales de guerra*, (Buenos Aires 1996) 299 – 300. *De Volkskrant*, 4 - 2 - 1992, 'Abraham Kipp, die naam vergeet ik nooit meer'. *Haarlems Dagblad* , 4 - 10 - 1988, 'Abraham Kipp zwaarste nog gezochte oorlogsmisdadiger'.

152 *Vrij Nederland*, 09-10-1976, 'Mertens'. *Nieuw Israëlitisch Weekblad*, 22-10- 1976 , 'Nederlandse journalist Mertens hield schuilplaats van Eichmann geheim'. Correspondence Mertens – Höttl 12 -03-1956. Stan Lauryssens, 111. Former RSHA official Wilhelm Höttl, (as representative of Walter Schellenberg SD section Budapest) had evesdropped on the OSS headquarters in Bern (Switzerland). That year Anthony Mertens and Höttl met in the Austrian village Alt Aussee. Höttl revealed the presence of Eichmann in Argentina. Back in Amsterdam Mertens was invited to a "Hitchcocktailparty". He met up with Alfred Hitchcock, who was in Amsterdam to promote his last film, and suggest him a docu-movi about the "hunt for the biggest massmurderer of this century Adolf Eichmann"; *Intermediair*, 15-10-1976. *NRC Handelsblad*, 24-01-1992, 'Handel drijven met Hitler'. The CIA was informed by the Italian correspondent of Time-Life of Eichmanns presence in

Argentina (Wim Sassen had shown him the manuscript). Around the same time the CIA office in Vienna, through Höttl. was informed of Eichmanns presence in Buenos Aires.

153 *De Standaard*, 15-03-1958, Argentijns prentenboek voor Vlaanderen, 'Mañana dankzij Wim Sassen'

154 Louis De Lentdecker, serie *Argentijns prentenboek voor Vlaanderen*, 'Maniana dankzij Wim Sassen', *De Standaard*, 15-03-1958.

155 ADVN: ARR, *De Schakel*, 1, 56-69. Letter Raes aan L. Poppe. Frank Seberechts, *Ieder zijn Zwarte* (Leuven 1994) 72, 111. Anthony Mertens had moved at the beginning of 1960 to Bruges, Belgium. There he started to write for *De Nieuwe Linie*, the Belgian daily *De Standaard* and the extremely controversial rightist pro Apartheid magazine *To the Point International*.

156 Stan Lauryssens interviewed Willem Sassen in Munich. *Het Vrije Volk* 26- 11-1960, 'Life: Sassen was alleen tussenpersoon'. *Süddeutsche Zeitung*, 14-01- 2011, 'Beide Augen zu´, von Wili Winkler. Latin-Americacorrespondent of the *Frankfurter Allgemeine* Fritz Otto Ehlert, en Frederico Müller – Ludwig,the Publisher of *Die Freie Presse,* worked in Argentina for the BND. *Süddeutsche Zeitung*, 12-04-2008, ´Journalisten mit Nazi-Vergangenheit in Deutschland´. *Die Welt*, 03-04- 2011, 'Eichmann hat eine perfide Show abgezogen'. Until 1965 Wim 'our special corrspondent' of *De Telegraaf,*; *Vrij Nederland*, 25-04-1981, 'Kameraden'. *Het Vrije Volk*, 26-11-1960, 'Life: Sassen was alleen tussenpersoon'. *Berliner Zeitung*, 22-08-1998, 'Da war wirklich nix'. As off 1951 a strong alliance existed between *Der Weg* and *Nation Europa*. In 1951 Wim Sassen wrote under the alias "Willem Sluysse"a number of "open letters"to government leaders and high military among which the British prime minister *Sir Anthony Eden* and general *Eisenhower*, which were published in *Nation Europa*. In *Der Spiegel* van 30-04-1952, 'Militärische Macht Notwendig' such a letter to general Eisenhower was described as: '*Verfasser: der ehemalige holländische Waffen-SS-Soldat Dr. Willem Sluyse. Sluyse rechnet dem General ressentiment-geladen vor, daß die Soldaten der ersten "Europa-Armee", nämlich die europäis-*

chen Freiwilligen in der deutschen Wehrmacht während des Rußlandfeldzuges, heute noch verfemt und eingekerkert seien.'

157 Gaby Weber, *Radio broadcast 04-03-2011* 'The Abduction Legend or how Eichmann came to Jerusalem?' In 1959 the publisher *Der Weg* was backrupt. According to BND report Wim Sassen was befriended with the American ambassador in Buenos Aires: Gaby Weber, *Eichmann wurde noch gebraucht - Der Massenmörder und der Kalte Krieg* (Berlin 2012). *Portal Amerika21.de*, 26-05-2012, '*Das Braune Exil in Argentiniën, Wie Adolf Eichmann und andere Naziverbrecher sich über die "Rattenlinie" nach Südamerika absetzten*' by Gaby Weber.

158 NL-HaNA, Ambassade Argentinië 1955-1974, 2.05.158, inv.nr. 69: "*Sassen ist in 1941 der sogenannten Freiwilligen Legion Niederlande beigetreten und hat infolgedessen die Niederlandsische Staatsangehürigkeit verloren. Nach Mitteilung des deutschen Botschafters in Buenos Aires an den dortigen Niederländischen Botschafter wird W.A.M. Sassen, weil er während des Krieges im deutschen Dienst war, als Deutscher betrachtet. Wim Sassen besitzt einen deutschen Reisepass: NB 3404153, auf dem Namen Sassen van Elsloo, Willem Antonius Mario.Staatsangehorigkeit: Deutscher. Register: 529-60 Wohnort: München, Ausgestellt in: Grosse Kreisstadt Konstanz, 4 juli 1960., Gultig: for In und Ausland, Ungultig: am 4 juli 1965, Beruf: Journalist-Fotograf.*" Bettina Stangneth stated in *Eichmann before Jerusalem*, page 228 and 379, W.A.M. Sassen van Elsloo, by profession reporter and writer, was a German citizen 25 Augus 1956 and had moved to Konstanz (61 Schottenstrasse 61). The German political party *Bündnis 90/ Die Grünen has recently asked* (18 March 2013) in chambers about W. Sassens German identity papers issued in Konstanz and his relation with the German ambassador W. Junker; Drucksache 17/12884, *Deutscher Bundestag: Aufklärung über die Beziehungen von Bundesregierung und Bundesnachrichtendienst zu Adolf Eichmann.*

159 *De Volkskrant*, 17-12-1960,' Monument van schijnheiligheid'. The compensation of 25.000 US Dollar went to Vera Eichmann.

160 Hanna Arendt, *Eichmann in Jerusalem* (Amsterdam 2007) 375. *De Volkskrant*, 10-06-1961, 'Vervalste SS'er Sassen

Eichmanns memoires?'

161 In June 1960 friend and president of the Argentina Arturo Frondizi paid a visit to Germany. Coincidence? Germany at time was one of the five biggest contributors to the Argentinean economy.

162 *Süddeutsche.Zeitung*, 14-01-2011, 'Beide Augen zu', von Wili Winkler. *Süddeutsche Zeitung*, 12-04-2008,'Journalisten mit Nazi-Vergangenheit in Deutschland'. At *Der Spiegel* en *Stern* were pro former PK-comrades employed. Nannen and Sassen met again in 1950.

163 *Intermediair*, 15-10-1976, 'De Eichmann-erfenis. During the preparation of the Eichmann trial in Jerusalem the existance of the Sassen documents was revealed. The Mossad wanted to buy the taped manuscript for 20.000 US Dollars. Sassen wanted to sell, but not to Israel. Then the taped recordings of Eichmann statement disappeared for several decades.

164 Family members of the Shoah survivor Lothar Hermann have recently shown that their family member had informed the Argentinean authorities, the *Delegación de Asociaciónes Israelitas Argentinas* (DAIA) and the Israeli Embassy of Eichmanns presence as early as of 1954. Wiesenthal did not react to this information nor the Mossad until 1960. Why remains unclear. Gaby Weber, 'The abduction Legend or how Eichmann came to Jerusalem', *Deutschlandfunk*, 2011. Lauryssens, *De Eichmann erfenis*,175. Leo Poppe worked at the *Claridge Hotel*. *Vrij Nederland*, 25-04-1981, 'Kameraden, Hoe Willem Sassen de jacht op Eichmann ten slotte won', door M. van Amerongen. *Página 12*, 21-04-2002, 'La que Faltaba', door Raul Kollmann

165 *Dagblad voor Amersfoort*, 29-05-1961, 'Adolf Eichmann will met Jezuïet praten'.

166 Ian Black, Benny Morris, *Israel's secret wars: a history of Israel's intelligence services* (London 1991) 190-198. Irmtrud Wojak, *Fritz Bauer, 1903-1968, Eine Biographie* (München 2009) 291, 313. Gerald L. Posner and John Ware, *Mengele: The Complete Story* (New York 1986). Goñi, *The Real Odessa, How Perón Brought the Nazi War Criminals to Argentina* (Londen 2002) 64, 293, 312 – 319. Wim wasn't the only

Mossad recruit. Otto Skorzeny was recruited by the Israeli Secret Service in 1963 in Madrid (Spain).

167 Father Jan Sassen moved to Regensburg after his wife Johanna passed away. On 27 January 1962 he died in Bad Wiessee (Bayern).

168 ADVN, Doos AC 121 (*Leven in twee werelden*), Map 2, correspondence between R. Raes en L. Poppe. A.R.R., *De Schakel* 1, 56-69. Brief van Roeland Raes aan Leo Poppe, Gent 17 december 1960.ADVN: ARR, *De Schakel* 2, 70-79. Brief van Roeland Raes aan Beste Vrienden, Gent, 3 augustus 1979.

169 *Der Spiegel*, 27-10-1975, ´Waffelhandel, Post für Pullach´. *Der Spiegel*, 21-04-1986 , 'Waffenhandel, Legaler Ausweg'. *Der Spiegel*, 21-08-1967, 'Waffenhandel, Falsche Perser'.

170 Guido Knopp, *Hitlers moordenaars, de geschiedenis van de SS* (Antwerpen 2004) 275. ADVN: Archief Roland Raes, *De Schakel*, 1, 56-69. Brief van R. Raes aan L. Poppe, Gent 17 december 1960. Rudel was involved as presentative of *Siemens* together with CAPRI-director Horst (Carlos) Fuldner, in the construction of the powerplant in San Nicolás (Tucumán 1952). When CAPRI a year later was declared bankrupt, the CAPRI employees went over to *Siemens*.

171 www.foia.cia.gov/sites/default/files/document_conversions/1705143/SCHWEND,%FRITZ_0146.pdf. www.foia.cia.gov/sites/default/files/document_conversions/1705143/SCHWEND,%FRITZ_0128.pdf.

172 www.foia.cia.gov/sites/default/files/document_conversions/1705143/SCHWEND,%FRITZ_0146.pdf.

173 *Der Spiegel*, 27-10-1975,´Waffelhandel, Post für Pullach´. www.taz.de, 20-06-2011,´Codename Uranus´, by Philipp Gessler. The firm Technicom was founded on 16 August 1954, a year later (15-09-1955, after the revolution Libertadora) the company name was changed to Anguita y Tubert Technicom; www.foia.cia.gov/sites/default/files/document_conversions/1705143.

174 *Die Spinne*, also known as *La Araña* of *International Negra*. T.H. Tetens, *Het Nieuwe Duitsland en de oude nazi's* (Den Haag 1962) 76,77, 191, 192. *Clarin*, 29-02-1992, 'Un piloto salteño trajo al pais a varios jerarcas Nazis'. *Cipriano*

Pedraza, commander of the Argentinean Airline stated that he in the summer of 1947 had flown Otto Skorzeny and Hans Ulrich Rudel in a DC4 to Argentina. Often he saw Kurt Tank who would buy plane parts in Spain for the Pulqui. Many former SS found work at German companies in Argentina: *Siemens, Krupp, Mercedes Benz, Bayer.* In a memorandum of 14 October 1952 of the Argetinean Secret Serice department in Córdoba, that members of *Die Spinne* regurarly met in Zona Serrana. In Córdoba Wim Sassen received his *cedula, residence permit.*

175 NL-HaNA, Ambassade Argentinië 1955-1974, 2.05.158, inv.nr. 69. *Der Freitag*, 16-06-2011, 'Ich bin meine eigene Person'. In the same interview Saskia stated that her father Wim Sassen was never involved in any criminal act. Wim would have hated the Nazis in Argentina, like he hated Goebbels. It was Goebbels, according to Saskia, who had called for his arrest. Whether her father worked for the Mossad she did not know. These were rumours. During the war Wim Sassen became a German citizen. Due to this fact Miep van der Voort, when married to Wim, received the same nationality. Wim tried in July 1956 to retain the Dutch nationality. Which was denied. Miep van der Voort did receive a new temporarly Dutch passport, which lasted until 7 November 1962 when she became an Argentina citizen.

176 *In 1963 the exportcompany Merex AG was founded in Corseaux, Zwitserland, in 1964 other offices were opened in Bonn (Germany) and Washington DC. Smaller offices were located in Abu Dhabi, Quito, Athens, Riad, London, Paris and Rome, and more agencies were spread over North and South America*': Peter Hammerschmidt, *Deckname Adler, Klaus Barbie und die westlichen Geheimdienste (Frankfurt am Main 2014),* 250.

177 *Speciaal,* 28 – 02 – 1998. Lauryssens, 126 – 131. *Dagblad voor Noord Limburg,* 15-10-1976, 'Eichmann vertelde levensverhaal aan oud SS' er'. NL-HaNA, Ambassade Argentinië 1955-1974, 2.05.158, inv. nr. 69. El Pais, 29-01-2012, '*Se ha roto el ciclo, porque el salario del trabajador ya no permite mantener el consumo*', by Antaxu Zalbalbeascoa.

178 The Argentinean intelligence service *SIDE: Secretaria*

de Inteligencia was created in 1955. Ladislas Farago, *Aftermath, Martin Bormann and the Fourth Reich* (London 1975). Jorge Camarasa, *Odesa al Sur, La Argentina como refugio de nazis y Criminales de Guerra* (Buenos Aires 1995) 170. The *Stern*-serial by Kai Hermann appeared in 1983, was published by the Dutch weekly De Tijd, between 10-08-1984 and 14-09-1984; 10-08-1984 'Een nazibeul als moordenaar in Bolivia'; (17-08- 1984), 'Waarom Bonn Barbie niet wilde hebben'; (24-08-1984), 'La Paz 1981: de slachter van Lyon pleegt zijn laatste massamoord'; (31- 08-1984), 'Hoe de oude hap van de SS door Amerika werd gefêteerd'; (07-09-1984), 'Barbie regisseert de staatsgreep van de cocaïne generaals'; (14-09-1984), 'Hoe twee Nederlandse broers in het net van de Spin belandden'.

179 Wim had maintained contact with former president Juan Perón in Spain, where he had sought asylum. Perón resided in the Madrid quarter of *Puerto de Hierro*, a known meeting centre of Perón supporters, reporters, businesspeople, politicians and Nazis, like black market dealer, Jew hunter and pimp Andries Riphagen. Together with Hans Ulrich Rudel, in the late sixties, Wim supported the return of Juan Perón to Argentinean politics. In 1973, Perón returned.

180 Cono Sur: Argentina, Chile, Paraguay, Uruguay. Later Bolivia also joined.

181 Archive Stan Lauryssens.

182 Archive Stan Lauryssens.

183 *Het Vrije Volk*, 25-11-1960, 'Sassen in dienst bij Time-Life'. Archief Stan Lauryssens.

184 *Der Spiegel*, 19-01-2011, 'Vom Nazi-Verbrecher – zum BND agenten'. *La Nacion*, 17-06-2001, 'Mas lazos con el tercer Reich'. Uki Goñi, revealed *in The Real Odessa*, that Wim Sassen was implicated in the sale of arms to the Argentinean general Leopoldo Galtieri just before he invaded the Falklands. Goñi, *The Real Odessa*, 288, 289. Guido Knopp, *Hitler's moordenaars, de geschiedenis van de SS* (Antwerpen 2004) 275.

185 *De Tijd*, 07-09-1984, 'Barbie regisseert de staatsgreep van de cocaïnegeneraals'. *De Tijd*, 14-09-1984, 'Hoe Twee Nederlandse jongens in het net van de Spin belandden'.

186 *Freedom of information act (FOIA) nazi war crimes dis-*

closure act, declassified and approved for release by the Central Intelligence Agency, date 2001: http://www.foia.cia.gov/sites/default/files/document_conversions/1705143/SCHWEND,%20FRITZ_0128.pdf

187 On 13 May 1947 his father Jan Sassen was sentenced to 10 years in prison by the Criminal Court of Breda. On 5 May 1952 he was released from detention.

188 Even official websites dedicated to Saskia Koob-Sassen state she was born in 1949. Fact is though, she was born on 5 January 1947 in The Hague as Saskia Haremaker. We all rewrite our own history. NL-HaNA, Ambassade Argentinië 1955-1974, 2.05.158, inv.nr. 69.

189 *El Pais,* 29-01-2012, 'Se ha roto el ciclo, porque el salario del trabajador ya no permite mantener el consumo´, by Antaxu Zalbalbeascoa.

190 Gaby Weber, *Disinformation – The wanted historical lie of the Mossad,* 2015

191 NL-HaNA, BNV, 2.04.80, inv.nr. 3216. NL-HaNA, Justitie / CABR, 2.09.09, inv.nr. 87844.

192 NL-HaNA, Justitie / CABR, 2.09.09, inv. nr. 87844. David Barnouw, *Van NIVO tot Reichsschule, Nederlandse meisjes in Duitse vakantiekampen zomer 1940* (Den Haag 1981) 34, 50, 94.

193 NL-HaNA, Justitie / CABR, 2.09.09, inv.nr. 87844.
194 NL-HaNA, Justitie / CABR, 2.09.09, inv.nr. 87844.
195 NL-HaNA, Justitie / CABR, 2.09.09, inv.nr. 87844.
196 NL-HaNA, Justitie / CABR, 2.09.09, inv.nr. 87844.
197 NL-HaNA, BNV, 2.04.80, inv.nr. 3216.
198 NL-HaNA, Justitie / CABR, 2.09.09, inv.nr. 45595.

199 The address of Alfons in Berlin SS-*Schütze E Zug, SS-Standarte Kurt Eggers,* Heimatstrasse 27 Berlin-Zehlendorf. SS-number: 5504. Fons had bloodsign O. He recovered in Holland from his foot. His sister Hansi Sassen worked at that time for the *Kriegsberichter Abteilung* in Berlin, her fieldnumber was: 33245. In Breda she had worked at the *Wehrmachtskommandantur* as an interpreter. At the end of the war she volunteered as a nurse in a fieldhospital; *Kriegslazarett 686,* in Enschede.

200 *Hauptmann* Helmut Karl Ernst Weidenbach, 22-12-1917 Dortmund – 16 April 1945 in Oberbrackendorf, Harz.

Married Francisca Sassen on 15 December 1944 in Enschede (Holland). Mother Johanna Sassen van Bavel was treated for her illness in a health resort in Hildesheim. NL-HaNA, Justitie / CABR, 2.09.09, inv.nr. 31614, 87844.
201 NL-HaNA, Justitie / CABR, 2.09.09, inv.nr. 31614, 87844.
202 The *Beauftragte* of the *Reichskommissar* in Utrecht asked him to become temporary / substitute burgomaster of the municipality of Oudenrijn in Autum 1944.
203 NL-HaNA, Justitie/CABR, 2.09.09, inv.nr.:31614
204 NL-HaNA, Justitie / CABR, 2.09.09, inv.nr. 87844. *Vlaanderen Vrij Radio*: part of *Aktivpropaganda, Kampfpropaganda West*: Scorpion.
205 Stadsarchief Amsterdam, EVOPR0014000091/92. NL-HaNA, Justitie /CABR, 2.09.09, inv.nr. 87844.
206 NL-HaNA, BNV, 2.04.80, inv.nr. 3216.
207 NL-HaNA, Justitie / CABR, 2.09.09, inv.nr.31614. Alfons was instructed by Pierre de Bie to gather Intel on the Abwehr members in Holland. Johannes Maria Pieter "Pierre" de Bie alias Colaris, born on 23-07-1920 Maastricht 08-01-2001. NL-HaNA, Justitie / CABR, 2.09.09, inv.nr. 87844.
208 NL-HaNA, Justitie / CABR, 2.09.09, inv.nr. 31614. NL-HaNA, BNV, 2.04.80, inv. nr. 3216. According to a report of the BNV Herman Lange was an informant of Wim Sanders. FAT's collect military and other usefull Wehrmacht Intelligence by using Dutch spies and informants who crossed the lines (line-crossers)
209 Archive Stan Lauryssens: interrogation report Helen Skrodzki.
210 NL-HaNA, Justitie / CABR, 2.09.09, inv.nr. 31614 and 87844.
211 NL-HaNA, Justitie / CABR, 2.09.09, inv.nr. 31614.
212 NL-HaNA, Justitie / CABR, 2.09.09, inv.nr. 87844.
213 NL-HaNA, Justitie / CABR, 2.09.09, inv.nr.31614
214 NL-HaNA, Justitie / CABR, 2.09.09, inv.nr. 31614. NL-HaNA, Justitie / CABR, 2.09.09, inv.nr.87844. *Hauptmann* Werner Bulang was head of *Sonderstab Wehrmacht* AOK in Driebergen, *Villa Beukenstein*. From this place the FAT was coordinated. Lange belonged to Kommando 306,

a unit of FAT 365 (Driebergen).
215 NL-HaNA, BNV, 2.04.80, inv. nr. 3216
216 NL-HaNA, Justitie / CABR, 2.09.09, inv.nr. 112110., NL-HaNA, BNV, 2.04.80, inv.nr. 3216.
217 NL-HaNA, Justitie / CABR, 2.09.09, inv.nr. 87844. After the war there were many gangs operating, claiming their robberies were in the name of the resistance. Among them many *V-männer*, informants of the SD or *Abwehr*. F. de Boer, *Een naoorlogse moord in mei '45* (Soesterberg 2006), 68, 74.
218 NL-HaNA, Justitie/CABR,2.09.09, inv.nr. 45595.
219 NL-HaNA, Justitie / CABR, 2.09.09, inv.nr. 31614.
220 5 May Liberation day (Holland) , 8 May the complete capitulation of Germany. NL-HaNA, BNV, 2.04.80, inv. nr. 3217. NL-HaNA, Justitie / CABR, 2.09.09, inv.nr. 87844.
221 NL-HaNA, BNV, 2.04.80, inv.nr.3216.
222 NL-HaNA, Justitie / CABR, 2.09.09, inv.nr. 87844.
223 Ibedem.
224 NL-HaNA, Justitie / CABR, 2.09.09, inv.nr. 31614.
225 NL-HaNA, Justitie / CABR, 2.09.09, inv.nr. 31614.
226 Inspector first class *Johan Gottlieb Crabbendam* was until April 1941 head of the documentationsection of the police in The Hague. An intelligence service which collected information on Jews, communists and resistance members and passed this information on to the SD and Abwehr. After the war it seemed he had worked for the resistance...: Ton Biesemaat, *Van Atjeh tot Uruzgan* (Soesterberg 2012) 103-105. NL-HaNA, Justitie / CABR, 2.09.09, inv.nr. 87844. Alfons volunteered in trying to locate the clandestine werewolf groups Herkenrath, Wupperthal, Wipperfürth, Essen, Düsseldorf, Cologne, furthermore he briefed them on *Sonderstab* OKW and Skorzeny.
227 NL-HaNA, Justitie / CABR, 2.09.09, inv.nr. 31614.
228 NL-HaNA, BNV, 2.04.80, inv.nr.3216.
229 NL-HaNA, BNV, 2.04.80, inv.nr. 3216
230 NL-HaNA, BNV, 2.04.80, inv.nr. 3216. CIC: *US Army Counter Intelligence Corps.*
231 NL-HaNA, Justitie / CABR, 2.09.09, inv.nr. 87844.
232 Gerard Aalders, *Leonie, Het intrigerende leven van een Ned-*

erlandse dubbelspionne (Amsterdam 2003) 275. Gerard Aalders and Coen Hilbrink, *De affaire Sanders spionage en intriges in herrijzend Nederland* (Den Haag 1996) 48, 243. IISG, Amsterdam, *Collection Cees Wiebes*, box 1 (espionage and IS). Squire Pieter Six van Hillegom suspected Sanders being a communist. Philip Dröge, *Beroep: meesterspion. Het geheime leven van Prins Bernhard* (Amsterdam 2001) 122, 137-138. Sanders a former police investigator in Enschede, was succeeded by Antony Berends. It was rumoured that Sanders during the war was involved in the arrest of Jews, Black market traffickers and Jehova's.

233 NL-HaNA, Justitie / CABR, 2.09.09, inv.nr. 112110. *De Tijd* 10-12-1945, 'Razzia bij Harskamp. Wapens en munitie in beslaggenomen'.

234 Perry Biddiscombe, *The last nazis. Het Kompas*, oud illegaal blad, no 7 derde jaargang, 'Ondergrondsverzet door A Michie'. *De Uitkijk*, oud illegaal blad (Haarlem) zaterdag 28 juli 1945, no. 23. NL-HaNA, BNV, 2.04.80, inv. nr.3216. Alfons knew the chef of the transmitter in Wippenfurth, generaal Bümer, and the werewolfcommander, general Friedrich Wilhelm Abel. *Hauptscharführer* Abel used to work with the Skorzeny group. NL-HaNA, BNV, 2.04.80, inv.nr. 3733

235 NL-HaNA, Justitie / CABR, 2.09.09, inv.nr. 112110. NL-HaNA, Justitie / CABR, 2.09.09, inv.nr. 87844.

236 NL-HaNA, Justitie / CABR, 2.09.09, inv.nr. 87844.

237 NL-HaNA, Justitie / CABR, 2.09.09, inv.nr. 87844.

238 NL-HaNA, Justitie / CABR, 2.09.09, inv.nr. 112110. On 15 November 1946 Alfons Sassen was released.

239 NL-HaNA, Justitie / CABR, 2.09.09, inv.nr. 87844. P. van Pelt was the investigating officer during the Wim Sassen case in Brussels and interviewed Wim. Wim was questioned about the *Wehrwolf* network of Damau by colonel Mampuys, TI Dienst, for the investigating judge P. Blero; CEGESOMA: SOMA 1312/11 Wim Sassen..

240 NL-HaNA, Justitie / CABR, 2.09.09, inv.nr. 87844. In 1946 espionage agents were called for active service for the American Army in Germany, their mission is to neutralize other spy (Intelligence) services of other countries. Keesings Historisch Archief, no 802, 6982, 27 – October – 2

November 1946. Overview Alfons detention centres before his final escape to Spain: 8 May 1945 BNV Sanders – 7 July 1945, GS II, Harskamp, escaped March 1946, 15 March detained in Limburg, transferred to penal institution Breda, detention centre Hoogerheide 20 April 1946, Harskamp July 1946, Nieuw Milligen September 1946, Avegoor 15 November 1946 till 6 April 1947 recruited as penetration agent in Holland, Belgium and Germany. June 1947 – 18 October 1947 Germany, France, Switzerland, arrested finally at the German – Dutch border in Vaals, detained inVught till 1 June 1948, under supervision of the STPD in Zutphen released from custody.

241 NL-HaNA, Justitie / CABR, 2.09.09, inv.nr. 87844.
242 NL-HaNA, Justitie / CABR, 2.09.09, inv.nr. 31614. NL-HaNA, Jus/ Politie / KJZ, 2.09.107, inv.nr. 1586. During the war Francisca worked for Zender Bremen.
243 NL-HaNA, BNV, 2.04.80, inv.nr. 3217.
244 M.E. Monteiro, *Godspredikers: Dominicanen in Nederland (1795-2000)* (Hilversum 2008) 384-385. *De Tijd*, 31-10-1938, Pater H. Sassen, 'De aalmoezenier der werkverschaffing 25 jaar priester'. H. J. H. W. (Wim) Sassen o.p., "Franciscus" (1887 Dongen - 1955 Nijmegen).
245 NL-HaNA, Justitie/CABR, 2.09.09, inv.nr. 112110.
246 NL-HaNA, Gezantschap Spanje, 2.05.86, inv.nr.660.
247 NL-HaNA, Gezantschap Spanje, 2.05.86, inv.nr.660.
248 NL-HaNA, Gezantschap Spanje, 2.05.86, inv.nr.660.
249 NL-HaNA, Justitie/CABR, 2.09.09, inv.nr. 87844, NL-HaNA, Gezantschap Spanje, 2.05.86, inv.nr.660.
250 The address was of Public Prosecutor in Zutphen JJ Lammers. Alphons stayed at his place while he was questioned about intelligence and communist movements in Holland. Investigator Edo Westendorp and Besselink worked for Lammers. NL-HaNA, Justitie / CABR, 2.09.09, inv.nr. 87844.
251 NL-HaNA, Gezantschap Spanje, 2.05.86, inv.nr. 660. Inspector Bureau B, Major Crabbendam was head of the Political Intelligence Section who informed the government on extremist ("red") movements in Holland. Crabbendam reported on Sanders to his superior BNV chef Louis Einthoven.

252 NL-HaNA, Gezantschap Spanje, 2.05.86, inv.nr. 660.
253 NL-HaNA, Jus/ Politie / KJZ, 2.09.107, inv.nr. 1586
254 NL-HaNA, Gezantschap Spanje, 2.05.86, inv.nr. 660. *Archief Peter Hammerschmidt.* The British steamer Reina del Pacifico was in business until April 1958. Main destination Latin America: Liverpool, La Rochelle (France), Vigo (Spain), Hamilton (Bermuda), Nassau (Bahamas), Havana (Cuba), Kingston (Jamaica), Panama Canal, Guayaguil (Ecuador), Callo (Peru), Antofagasta (Chile) and Valparaiso (Chili). San Sebastian, Bilbao, La Coruña and Vigo were known ports for fleeing Nazis, emigrating Jews and stateless persons.
255 NL- HaNA, BNV 1945 – 1946, inv nr.: 3217.
256 NL-HaNA, Justitie / CABR, 2.09.09, inv.nr. 45595.
257 During the war Maria had contact with J. de Rossi del Arno, *Vice Presidente del Concorso del Grana*, Talia Tede, Rome; Professor dr. G.M.S. Lo Verde, *Cabinetto del presidente della camera dei Fasci e della corporazioni*, Rome; Prof. Maria Castellani, *Commissario Nazionale ANFAL*, Via Toscane 5, Rome. NL-HaNA, BuZa / Gezantschap/Ambassade Italië (Rome), 2.05.289, inv.nr. 1389. Veiligheid van Staat, T.I. Dienst Post Nienburg, 20-11-1946.
258 Investigating prosecutors were looking for Maria (Mies) because of her activities for the SD NL-HaNA, BuZa / Gezantschap/Ambassade Italië (Rome), 2.05.289, inv. nr. 1389. NL-HaNA, Justitie / CABR, 2.09.09, inv.nr. 31614. The alias "Hendriks"was given to her at Seehof.
259 NL-HaNA, BuZa / Gezantschap/Ambassade Italië (Rome), 2.05.289, inv.nr. 1389.
260 NL-HaNA, Jus/ Politie / KJZ, 2.09.107, inv.nr. 1586
261 Helmut Pröbsting, former chef of department III B at the *Befehlshaber der Sipo* en SD in The Hague. NL-HaNA, Justitie / CABR, 2.09.09, inv.nr. 45595.
262 NL-HaNA, Jus/ Politie / KJZ, 2.09.107, inv.nr. 1586. NL-HaNA, Justitie / CABR, 2.09.09, inv.nr. 45595. NL-HaNA, Justitie / CABR, 2.09.09, inv.nr. 31614. Helmut Pröbsting together with Dr. Haagn of the *Aktivpropaganda* supported the daily *De Gil*. The paper was issued by the *Hauptabteilung Volksaufklärung und Propaganda* of the *Reichskommissariat*. In the last phase of the war Pröbsting was

a member of a *Sonderkommando*. A subunit of *Dienststelle Hendrik* (*I-netz*) in Apeldoorn.
263 NL-HaNA, BuZa / Gezantschap/Ambassade Italië (Rome), 2.05.289, inv.nr.1389.
264 NL-HaNA, BuZa / Gezantschap/Ambassade Italië (Rome), 2.05.289, inv.nr.1389.
265 NL-HaNA, Jus/ Politie / KJZ, 2.09.107, inv.nr. 1586.
266 NL-HaNA, Jus/ Politie / KJZ, 2.09.107, inv.nr. 1586.
267 Collection Bas Zijlmans: drs. A. P. van der Wiel, *Kijk op Veghel*, 11 -16 mei 1994. In 1961 Maria Burk Sassen would also be involved in the exploitation of oilfields in the provinces Los Rios and Cotopaxi.
268 NL-HaNA, Gezantschap Ecuador, 2.05.77, inv.nr. 74, 106. Georgette Sassen married in the war Paul Marcel Servant.
269 NL-HaNA, Gezantschap Ecuador, 2.05.77, inv.nr. 106.
270 *Leeuwarder Courant*, 26-10-1955, 'Delegatie uit Ecuador brengt Friesland oriëntatiebezoek' . *De Friese Courier*, 15-10-1955, 'Commissie uit Ecuador is gast van het Stamboek
271 Georgette Sassen, *Ponchos, zhanzas y bananos*. (Quito1960), 227. Paul Bronzwaer, *Maastricht en Luik bezet, een comparatief onderzoek naar vijf aspecten van de Duitse bezetting van Maastricht en Luik tijdens de Tweede Wereldoorlog* (Hilversum 2010) 124.
272 NL-HaNA, Justitie / CABR, 2.09.09, inv.nr. 75042. Hans Schippers, *Zwart en Nationaal Front, Latijns georiënteerd rechtsradicalisme in Nederland (1922-1946)* (Amsterdam 1986) 362. Joost de Haas en Charles Sanders, 'Alles voor het vaderland', *Elsevier* 24-02-1990. Stan Lauryssens in *De fatale vriendschappen van Adolf Eichmann*, 117. NL-HaNA, Justitie / CABR, 2.09.09, inv.nr. 75042. Nationaal Archief, Den Haag, *Rijksinstituut voor Oorlogsdocumentatie* (RIOD): Serie Dubbelen, 1933-1966, nummer toegang 2.14.08, inventarisnummer 921.
273 Joost de Haas en Charles Sanders, 'Alles voor het vaderland', *Elsevier*, 24-02- 1990. Archief Stan Lauryssens.
274 Personal archive Peter Hammerschmidt
275 NL-HaNA, Gezantschap Spanje, 2.05.86, inv.nr. 660.
276 NL-HaNA, Jus/OMD, 2.09.106, inv.nr.:269.

277 Unpublished interview by Michael von der Goltz (1983): Archive Peter Hammerschmidt.
278 Ken Silverstein, Daniel Burton Rose, *Private Warriors* (NY 2000) 122-124. Mertins had representatives in Iran, Saudi Arabia, North Africa and Latin America. Many of these arms came from the surplus Bundeswehr depots, but the company also sold surplus military equipment from other countries like France, Great Brittany and Holland. Merex offered also the organsiatuion and training of the police force. Alfons'business card showed: Alphonso Eduard Sassen van Elsloo van Bavel, agent for the offices in Monaco, Germany, Buenos Aires and Quito.
279 Louis Peeters met Skorzeny when he and Georgette moved to Barcelona Spain (1964-1972).
280 Cit. from Magnus Linklater, Isable Hilton, Neal Ascherson, *Het Barbie Dossier, Het Vierde Reich* (Utrecht 1984) 281.
281 Linklater, Hilton, Ascherson, *Het Barbie Dossier, Het Vierde Reich* (Zwolle 1984) 288-294. *Algemeen Dagblad*, 08-02-1983, 'We wilden hem doden'. IISG, collection Ton Regtien, inv. nr.: 384, Klaus Barbie.
282 In Bolivia there were two fascist movements active; MNR and the *Falange Socialista Boliviana*. Barrientos died in a helicopter crash in April 1969.: Linklater, Hilton, Ascherson, *Het Barbie Dossier, Het Vierde Reich (*Zwolle 1984*)* 279-294, 307, 321. Alfredo Serra, *Nazis en las sombras, siete historias secretas* (Buenos Aires 2008) 85.
283 Both Klaus Barbie and Alfons represented the pharmaceutical concern *Böhringer* (*Boehringer*) *Pharmazeutischen Werke* in Quito. It's main office of Böhringer was in Mannheim. http://www.raremilitaria.com/sassen_001.htm according to this website Alfons Sassen was a doctor in chemistry. Former SS colonel Walter Rauff arrived in Ecuador in 1949. In Quito he represented the Wuppertal pharmaceutical company *Bayer*, the American *Pharma – Multis*, and other companies like *Mercedes Benz, Opel and* the German- Ecuadorian company *Moeller – Martinez until he moved to Chile in the 60s.* According to Shraga Elam of the Israëlian daily *Haaretz, In the Service of the Jewish State*, 29-03-2009, Rauff was recruited by the Mossad in the 50s.

As of 1958 till 1962 he worked for the BND until his arrest in Chile: http://www.cbgnetwork.org/4442.html. *Der Spiegel*, 26- 09-2011, 'Geheimdienste, Treuerfreund'. *Der Spiegel*, 30-09-2011, 'CIA Akten über SS-mann'. www.taz.de, 20-06-2011, 'Codename Uranus', door Phillippe Gessler. '*Noch brisanter aber ist, dass Schwend Anfang der sechziger Jahre mit Barbie und Rudel ein Unternehmen gegründet hatte: "La Estrella", der Stern. Auch der Estrella-Mann Otto Skorzeny rutschte in das Merex-Unternehmen.. Der BND war den CIA-Akten zufolge "sehr interessiert" an den Kontakten des Merex-Mannes mit "Rudel und anderen im Ausland lebenden Deutschen, die gegenwärtig in Lateinamerika" wohnten.*' Vgl.: *Der Spiegel*, 27-10-1975, 'Waffenhandel, Post für Pullach'; '*Merex habe Flugzeuge, Geschütze, Maschinengewehre, Panzerfäuste, und Minen aus Bundeswehrbeständen in Spannungsgebiete verkauft und so Kriegswaffenkontroll- und Aussenwirtschafts-Gesetz verletzt.* Linklater, Hilton and Ascherson, Het Barbie dossier, 307.

284 *Algemeen Dagblad*, 19-02-1983, 'Weer slachtoffer Barbie'. *Algemeen Dagblad*, 08-02-1983, 'We wilden hem doden'. *De Tijd*, 14 -09- 1984,'Hoe twee Nederlandse jongens in het net van de spin belandden'. *De Waarheid*, 12 - 12 - 1989, 'Hollandse SS'er brengt Ecuador in opschudding'. Address of (Alfons) Sassen firm in Ecuador, *Maquiec Cia Ltd*, 9 de Octubre 520-530, Quito Ecuador, tel: 552832, other contactaddresses in Monte Carlo, München and Buenos Aires. His visiting card said: *Busy SA*, Leoandro N. Alem 424, 1003 Buenos Aires.

285 *De Tijd*, 14-09-1984,'Hoe twee Nederlandse jongens in het net van de spin belandden'. *De Tijd*, 10-08-1984, 'Een nazibeul als moordenaar in Bolivia', door Kai Hermann. *De Tijd*, 07-09-1984, 'Barbie regisseert de staatsgreep van de cocaïne-generaals', door Kai Hermann. Jean Cormier, *Che Guevara, een biografie* (Amsterdam 1996) 414-415. *Der Spiegel*, 07-11-1983, 'Selbst Verkloppt'.

286 De French knew around 1960 of Barbie's presence in Bolivia , www.derechomilitar.info: casos para el estudio (III) *El proceso Barbie*, door Miguel Alía Plana. *La Nación*, 17-06-2001, 'Más lazos con el Tercer Reich'.Archive Peter Hammerschmidt: Interview Michael von der Goltz: Wim

Sassen had advised Klaus Barbie, just before his detention, to contact Alfons Sassen. "You will be safe there". Some police official even had offered his own hacienda. But it was too late.

287 Jacqueline Wesselius, Lambiek Berends, *Barbie, Misdadiger tegen de mensheid, een ooggetuigenverslag* (Amsterdam 1987) 114. *Algemeen Dagblad,* 08-02-1983, 'We wilden hem doden'. IISG, Amsterdam, Collection Ton Regtien, inv.nr.: 384.

288 NL-HaNA, Jus/ OMD, 2.09.106, inv.: 269. *Hoy,* 03-10-1984, 'Ex espia nazi en Ecuador'. *Hoy,* 07-10-1984, 'Nunca he sido espía, dice Alfonso Sassen'. *El Comercio,* 08-02-1983, 'Otro nazi estaría en el Ecuador'. *El Comercio,* 08- 02-1983, 'Fui de la SS dice Sassen'. *El Comercio,* 10-02-1983, 'Desechan posibilidad de que ex nazi viva en el Ecuador'.

289 Unpublished interview by Michael von der Goltz (1983): Archive Peter Hammerschmidt.

290 Archive Peter Hammerschmidt. Michael von de Goltz, interviewed Alfons Sassen in Munich 26 September 1983.

291 '*Da ich so viel Erlog gehabt habe mit den Guerrillas, die Vermeidung einer eventuellen Guerrilla in Ecuador, das ist das einzige Land, das keine Guerrillas hat... bei uns scheint es sehr ungesund zu sein, Guerilla zu werden...*(I have been very successful in the counter guerrilla operations that it is better not to become a guerrillero in this country): Alfons in interview on 26 September 1983 with Von der Goltz.

292 Archive Peter Hammerschmidt. Michael von der Goltz, interviewed Alfons Sassen in Munich 26 September 1983.

293 Archive Peter Hammerschmidt, Michael Von der Goltz interviewed Alfons Sassen in Munich 26 September 1983.

294 Ibedem.

295 Ibedem. Alfons said he at one time was consul in Bilbao (Spain) for some time and travelled Europe while attending international police congresses.

296 NL-HaNA, Jus/ OMD, 2.09.106, inv.: 269.

297 *Hoy,* 03-10-1984, 'Ex espía nazi en Ecuador'. Alfons had a broad imagination. During the war he was a boy with a poor health, who never saw action on the East front. He never saved any Jew. If not it would have been recorded.

His heroic acts, the penetration of the resistance and treason. During the last months of the war he abused the power vacuum with a gang of robbers to assault defenceless people. After the war he eagerly took the opportunity of the growing anti communist sentiment by taking the role as an expert on werewolf organisations and getting assigned as an undercover agent for several intelligence services in Western Europe. Soon they realised that many reports were based on fantasy. His true carreer started in Ecuador.

298 *De Tijd*, 14 -09- 1984, 'Hoe twee Nederlandse broers in het net van de Spin belandden'. Alfons was naturlized Ecuadorian in 1965.

299 *Der Spiegel*, 19-01-2011,' Klaus Barbie von Nazi-Verbrecher zum BNDAgenten'. *De Tijd*, 14-09-1984, 71-76. The organiser and financial leader of the Group was Otto Skorzeny, Hans Ulrich Rudel and Alfons Sassen. They were the most important representatives of the *Black International (International Negra)* in Latin-America. Walter Rauff was recruited by BND agent Oebsger-Röder (former SS, and *Spiegel*-reporter) in 1958. Wolfgang Schwanitz, 'Nazis on the run', *Jewish Political Studies Review*, 01-04-2010. Shraga Elam, 'In the Service of the Jewish State', *Haaretz*, 2-03-2007. *Der Spiegel*, 26-09-2011,'Treuer Freund, door Klaus Wiegrefe'.

300 Vicente Olmedo, 'Ecuatoriano-Holandes responde a afirmaciones de revista Stern "nunca he sido espia"'; *Hoy*, 07-10-1984.

301 *Hoy*, 07-10-1984 , "Nunca he sido espia, dice Alfonso Sassen"

302 *Hoy*, 07-10-1984 , "Nunca he sido espia, dice Alfonso Sassen

303 *Hoy*, 07-10-1984 , "Nunca he sido espia, dice Alfonso Sassen

304 Ibidem

305 *Hoy*, 09-09-1984, 'El captan Alfonso Sassen fue condecorado en el grado de caballero por la Dinactie, organismo de la Procuraduria General del Estado'. 'El acto tuvo lugar en uno de los salones del hotel *Alameda Real*'.

306 NL-HaNA, Jus/ OMD, 2.09.106, inv.:269 During that

time human rights watch were aware that torture, murder and other violations took place under his presidency. The North American president Reagan supported also this the pistol wielding and horse breeding businessman from Guayaguil León Febres Cordero. He was an ally in the battle against drugs. Alfons Sassen wasn't able to silence the Ecuadorian urban guerrilla group of Alfaro Vive Carajo (Guayaquil) for his friend. A special elite force of members of the Unidad de Investigaciones Especiales (UIES) and the Servicio de Investigación Criminal (SIC-10) was set up to neutralize guerrilleros. Both Alfons as his son Roberto Sassen did business with Uies.*New York Times*, January 17, 1987, 'Ecuador troops kidnap president and trade him for failed general'. *New York Times*, 13-03-1988, 'Reports finds Ecuador rights abuses rose sharply'. *Hoy*, 07-10-1984, 'Nunca he sido espía, dice Alfonso Sassen'.

307 NL-HaNA, Jus/ OMD, 2.09.106, inv.:269. All Sassens of Geertruidenberg were seen as political delinquents, not as war criminals.

308 http://www.sigmadeltausa.com/sigma_delta_010.htm

309 www.raremilitaria.com/sassen_001.htm

310 Roberto Edgar Xavier Sassen van Elsloo, 14-8-1954 (Pinchincha/ Quito). Studied in the 70s in Germany, technical school, and then in USA. In 1976 returned to Ecuador and became the Glock representative and international armsdealer. He also supplied the Ecuadorian police force. Jan Hendrik Bernardo Sassen van Elsloo Otcro, also like his brother Roberto (in Quito) South American distributor of Remington (light-arms manufacturer) in Guayaquil.

311 *Hoy*, 08-03-2001, 'Sassen es un corruptor de policias'. *Hoy*, 21-06-2005, 'Los equipos donados por Sassen fueron a las bodegas de Unase'.

312 *Guerra de Cenepa* or *Guerra del Cóndor* in 1991. *Clarín. com*, 15-08-1998, "*Guerra del Cóndor*, las armas delsentido común'. *Clarin digital*, 12-05-1996, "las armas secretas'. *La Nación*, 18-12-2002, 'Un empresario ecuatoriano dijo que el traficante Lasnaud mintió.'

313 *El Comercio*, 07-12-1999, 'El tiro por la culata.' Through the cover firm Hayton Trade, a Uruguayan society, representative of Fabricaciones Militares (DGFM) in Venzuela,

the arms shipment reached Ecuador. During the war between Ecuador and Peru the president Sixto Durán Ballén decided to arm the civilian population, hence the deal. Sassen and his associates were recruited to make this deal. Through Lasnaud contact was made in January 1995 with the Argentinean colonel Edgberto Gonzales de la Vega, the commercial representative of the Argentinean DGFM, the traiding company of the Ministry of Defence. UIESS: a police unit specialised in countering organised crime and drugs traffic. *Página 12*, 19-10-2002, 'El respaldo Legal de Menem'. *La Nación,* 17-06-2001, 'Surge la conexion de los nazis croatas'.

314 *Clarin Digital,* 12-05-1996, 'Las armas secretas'. *La Nación*, 24-04-1999, 'Toman declaración a un testigo clave.' Lasnaud stated that 'Roberto Sassen officially hired me as mediator with Horacio Estrada to get the order for Prodefensa'. *La Nación*, 25-02-2005, 'Detenciones en Ecuador por la venta de armas'. *La Nación*, 11-12-2002, 'A Ecuador llegaron armas obsoletas'. *La Nación*, 07-12-2002, 'Lasnaud declaró que el gobierno de Menem conocía el envío de armas'. *La Nación*, 18-10-2002, 'Un traficante dijo que Menem respaldó la venta de armas a Ecuador'. *La Nación*, 24-04-1999, 'Oscuro eslabón que acentuó sospechas'. *La Nación*, 27-04-1999, 'Crecen las dudas sobre la muerte de Estrada'.

315 *La Plata,* 19-05-2001, 'Balza está contra las cuerdas por las armas'. Roberto Edgar Xavier Sassen van Elsloo Otero and Cesar Bolivar Torres Herbozo versus Ecuador, Petition 183/02, Report no. 70/02, Inter-Am. CHR, Doc. 5 rev. 1 at 284 (2002) On 25 June 1999 Interpol Argentina issued a warrent against R. Sassen concerning the arms deal with Ecuador.

316 *El País*, 13-06-2013, "El expresidente Carlos Menem condenado a 7 años por trafico de armas. *La Nación*, 13-06-2013, "El kirchnerismo va a bloquear los pedidos de desafuero de la oposición Politica'. *Página 12,* 14-06-2013, 'Siete años de prisión efectiva'.

Documentary Sources

Archives

Dutch archives:
Jesuit Archive in Nijmegen, Linie-Archief, Paters Barten en Baltussen
Collection Bas Zijlmans
International Institute for Social History (IISG) Amsterdam
National Archives, The Hague
Institute for War, Holocaust and Genocide Studies (NIOD) Amsterdam
City Archive Amsterdam

Belgian archives:
Documentation and research centre for Flemish Nationalism, Antwerp (ADVN).
Centre for Historical Research and Documentation on War and Contemporary Society, Brussels (CEGESOMA).

Unpublished sources:
Embassy of Ecuador
Peter Hammerschmidt: correspondence
Stan Lauryssens: archive
L.M. Bruijn: archive
Prof. D.F.J. Bosscher: correspondence
Gaby Weber: correspondence

Bibliography

Aalders, Gerard, en **Hilbrink**, Coen, *De Affaire Sanders, spionage en intriges in herrijzend Nederland*, Sdu Uitgevers, Den Haag, 1996.

Amerongen, M van., *Eins zwei drei... rechts! Op mars naar het Vierde Rijk?* Baarn, 1967.

Barnouw, David, *Van NIVO tot Reichsschule, Nederlandse meisjes in Duitse vakantiekampen zomer 1940*, Sdu, Den Haag, 1981.

Basti, Abel, *Bariloche Nazi, Guía turística, sitios historicos relacionados al nacionalsocialismo*, Ed del autor, 2005.

Biddescombe, Perry, *The last Nazis, SS werewolf guerrilla resistance in Europe 1944-1947*, Tempus Pub., Gloucestershire, 2004.

Boersema, B.R.C.A., *De Linie, 1946 - 1963, Een weekblad in handen van Jezuïeten*, Apa Holland Universiteitspers, Amsterdam, 1978.

Bronzwaer, Paul, *Maastricht en Luik bezet, een comparatief onderzoek naar vijf aspecten van de Duitse bezetting van Maastricht en Luik tijdens de Tweede Wereldoorlog*, Maaslandse monografiën/ 73, Verloren BV, 2010.

Brilman, P.M., *Trema, 3 maart 1986, Een strafrechtelijke nalatenschap.*

Bruijn, L.M., *SS-mann Polizist, Herbert Öelschlagel, De mythe, de man*, Groningen 2010.

Bruijn, L.M., *Het wondere leven van Toontje Mertens, Fascist, Verzetsstrijder, Publicist en Katholiek zi-*

jnde een korte biografie van M. Theodorus Antonius Mertens, Groningen 2010.

Buchrucker, Christián, *Nacionalismo y Perónismo, La Argentina en la crisis ideológica mundial (11927 - 1955)*, Editorial Sudamericana, Buenos Aires, 1987.

Black, Ian, en **Morris**, Benny, *Israel's secret wars: a history of Israel's intelligence services*, Hamish Hamilton Ltd, London, 1991.

The Naumann Plot, Evidence from the Impounded Documents, **The Wiener Library** (Londen juli 1953).

Roberto Edgar Xavier Sassen van Elsloo Otero and Cesar Bolivar Torres Herbozo versus Ecuador, Petition 183/02, Report no. 70/02, Inter-Am. CHR, Doc. 5 rev. 1 at 284 (2002).

Camarasa, Jorge, *ODESSA al Sur, la Argentina como refugio de nazis y criminales de Guerra*, Planeta, Buenos Aires, 1996 (1995).

Casparini, Juan, *La Fuga del Brugo*, Grupo Editorial Norma, Buenos Aires, Argentinië, 2005.

Cesarini, David, *Eichmann, De definitieve biografie*, Uitgeverij Anthos, Amsterdam, 2005.

Chairoff, Patrice, *Dossier Néo-Nazisme*, Préface de Beate Klarsfeld, Éditions Ramsay, Paris, 1977.

Cormier, Jean, *Che Guevara, een biografie*, BaBylon-De Geus, Amsterdam, 1996

Crassweller, Robert D., *Perón and the enigmas of Argentina*, Norton & Company, New York, 1988 (1987).

Dedeurwaerder, Joris, *Professor Speleers, een biografie*, Perspectief Uitgaven, Antwerpen, 2002.

Dröge, Philip, *Beroep Meester Spion, Het geheime leven van Prins Bernhard*, Uitgeverij Vaassallucci, Amsterdam, 2002

Eck, D. van, *Berechtiging van oorlogsmisdadigers en de gronden voor een internationaal strafrecht*, Dekker & van de Veght N.V., Nijmegen, 1947.

Farago, Ladislas, *Het Spel van de Vossen*, Uitgeverij Nieuwe Wieken BV, Uithoorn (1971) 1972.

Farago, Ladislas, *Aftermath, Martin Bormann and the Fourth Reich*, Hodder and Stoughton, London, 1975.

Garbely, Frank, *Evitas Geheimnis, Die nazi's, Die Schweiz und Peróns Argentinien*, Rotpunktverlag, Zürich, 2003.

Gehlen, Reinhard, *Der Dienst, Erinnerungen 1942 – 1971*, von Hase & Koehler Verlag, Mainz-Wiesbaden, 1971.

Gehlen, Reinhard, *Nu spreek ik!, Herinneringen 1942-1971*, De Boekerij, Baarn, 1972.

Goñi, Uki, *The Real Odessa, How Perón Brought the Nazi War Criminals to Argentina*, Granta Books, Great Britain, 2002.

Gotovich, J., *Nazi's op de vlucht naar Argentinië*, Spiegel Historiael, februari 1986.

Govers, *Corridor naar het verleden, Veghel een snijpunt in Oost Brabant 1940-1945*, Uitgeverij De Kempen BV, Hapert, 1983.

Groen, Koos, *'Er heerst orde en rust...', Chaotisch Nederland tussen september 1944 en december 1945*, Uitgeverij B. Gottmer, Nijmegen, 1979.

Groen, Koos, *Landverraad, De berechting van collaborateurs in Nederland*, Unieboek, Weesp, 1984.

Groen, Koos, *Als slachtoffers daders worden, De zaak van joodse verraadster Ans van Dijk*, Ambo, Baarn, 1994.

Groeneveld, Gerard, *Kriegsberichter, Nederlandse SS-oorlogsverslaggevers 1941-1945*, Uitgeverij van Tilt, Haarlem, 2004.

Heyrman, P., *1918-1940: Middenstandsbeweging en beleid in België, Tussen vrijheid en regulering*, Leuven, Universitaire Pers, 1998.

Hammerschmidt, Peter, *Deckname Adler, Klaus Barbie und die westlichen Geheimdienste*, S. Fischer Verlag, Frankfurt am Main, 2014.

Hopman, Jan, *Zwijgen over de Euterpestraat, Op het hoofdkwartier in Amsterdam gingen in 1944 verraad en verzet hand in hand*, Free musketeers, Zoetermeer, 2012.

Iddekinge, P.R.A van / **Paape**, A. H., *Ze zijn er nog...* De Bezige Bij, Amsterdam, 1970.

Jackisch, Carlota, *El nazismo y los refugiados alemanes en la Argentina 1933 - 1945*, Editorial de Belgrano, Buenos Aires, 1989.

Jansen, Dr. Hans, *De Zwijgende Paus? Protest van Pius XII en zijn medewerkers tegen de Jodenvervolging in Europa*, Uitgeverij KOK, Kampen, 2000.

Jansma, T.J., *Het bezettingsrecht in de praktijk van de Tweede Wereldoorlog, Proefschrift*, uitgeverij H. Veenman en Zonen, Wageningen, 1953.

Jong, L. de, *Het Koninkrijk der Nederlanden in de Tweede Wereldoorlog*. Parts 2, 4, 5, 6, 7, 9, 10, 12. Martinus Nijhoff, 's-Gravenhage, 1970-1982.

Jong, R. de., *De Spaanse burgeroorlog*, Bert Bakker/Daamen NV, Den Haag, 1963.

Kikkert, J.G., *De zeven levens van 'The Cat', een halve eeuw contraspionage in oorlogs- en vredestijd*, Uitgeverij Aspekt, Soesterberg, 2003.

Knopp, Guido, *Hitlers moordenaars, de geschiedenis van* *de SS*, Manteau, Antwerpen, 2004.

Lauryssens, Stan, *Opmars naar het Vierde Rijk*, Wetenschappelijke Uitgeverij, Amsterdam, 1975.

Lauryssens, S., *De Eichmann-erfenis*, Manteneau-INFO, Brussel & Den Haag, 1976.

Lindeijer SJ, Marc, *Pater Ligthart en de zaak Roothaan. Streven naar heiligheid in het utopistisch tijdperk, 1914 – 1968*, Uitgeverij Verloren, Hilversum, 2009.

Lingen, Joost van, Niek Sloof, *Van verzetsstrijder tot staatsgevaarlijk burger, Hoe progressieve illegale werkers na de oorlog de voet is dwarsgezet*, Anthos, Baarn, 1987.

Linklater, Magnus / **Hilton**, Isabel / **Ascherson**, Neal, *Het Barbie Dossier, Het Vierde Reich*, Bruna, Utrecht, 1984.

Martinez, Tomas Eloy, "Perón and the Nazi criminals", *Latin American Program*, The Wilson Center, Washington, 1984.

Meding, Holger M., *Flucht vor Nürnberg? Deutsche und Österreichische Einwanderung in Argentinien 1945 - 1955*, Böhlau Verlag, Keulen, 1992.

Middelburg, Bart, **ter Steege**, R., *Riphagen De Amsterdamse onderwereld 1940 - 1945*, Uitgeverij De Arbeiderspers, Amsterdam, 1990.

Middelburg, Bart, **ter Steege**, René, *Riphagen 'Al Capone', een van Nederlands grootste oorlogsmisdadigers*, Uitgeverij L. J. Veen, Amsterdam, 1997.

Monteiro, M.E., *Gods predikers: dominicanen in Nederland (1795-2000)*, Uitgeverij Verloren, Hilversum, 2008.

Mouton, M.W., *Oorlogsmisdrijven en het Internationale recht*, A.A.M. Stols, 's-Gravenhage, 1947.

Naipaul, V.S., *De terugkeer van Eva Perón*, Atlas, Amsterdam 1995 (1980)

Posner, Gerald L., **Ware**, John, *Mengele: The Complete Story*, McGraw-Hill, New York, 1986.

Oppenheim, L., *International Law: A Treatise,* 7th Edition, edited by H. Lauterpacht, Longmans Green & Co. 2 vols. Volume. II, Londen, 1948.

Rüter, C.F., 'De Bijzondere Rechtspleging - symbool of alibi?', in: *Ars Aequi, Juridisch studentenblad XXI 7*, juli/augustus, Nijmegen, 1972.

Saerens, Lieven, *Vreemdelingen in een wereldstad: een geschiedenis van Antwerpen en zijn joodse bevolking (1880-1944),* Lannoo Uitgeverij, Tielt, 2000.

Sassen, Georgette, *Poncho's, zhanza's y bananen,* De Bezige Bij, Amsterdam, 1959.

Schipper, Paul de, *De Stem*, 29-01-2005, *SS-verslaggever uit Geertruidenberg*

Schippers, Hans, *Zwart en Nationaal Front, Latijns georiënteerd rechts- radicalisme in Nederland (1922 - 1946)*, Stichting Internationaal Instituut voor Sociale Geschiedenis, Amsterdam, 1986.

Seberechts, Frank, *Ieder zijn zwarte, verzet, collaboratie en repressie*, Davidsfonds, Leuven, Perspectief Uitgaven, 1994.

Seberechts, Frank, **Verdoodt**, Frans-Jos, *Leven in twee werelden, Belgische collaborateurs en de diaspora na de Tweede Wereldoorlog*, Davidsfonds Uitgeverij nv, Leuven, 2007.

Schulten, JWM, *De Geschiedenis van de ordedienst, Mythe en werkelijkheid van een verzetsorganisatie,* Sdu Uitgevers, Den Haag, 1998

Serra, Alfredo, *Nazis en las sombras*, Editorial Atlantida, Buenos Aires, Argentina, 2008.

Smedts, Mathieu, **Troost**, C., *De Lange Nacht*, N.V. De Arbeiderspers, Amsterdam, 1965.
Smedts, Mathieu, *Waarheid en Leugen in het Verzet*, Uitgeverij Corrie Zelen, Maasbree, 1978.
Sijes, B.A., *Berechting van Oorlogsmisdadigers*, Stichting Wiesenthalfonds, Van Oorschot, Amsterdam, 1969.
Silverstein, Ken, **Burton Rose**, Daniel, *Private Warriors*, Verso, New York, 2000.
Stangneth, Bettina, *Eichmann in Argentinië, Het onbezorgde leven van een oorlogsmisdadiger*, Uitgeverij Atlas Contact, Amsterdam, 2012 (2011).
Steinacher, Gerald, *Nazis auf der Flucht. Wie Kriegsverbrecher über Italien nach Übersee entkamen*, Stuthen Verlag, Frankfurt, 2008.
Het Verzet van de Nederlandsche Bisschoppen tegen nationaal-socialisme en Duitsche Tyrannie, ingeleid en uitgegeven door Mag. Dr. S. **Stokman**, OFM, Spectrum, Utrecht, augustus 1945.
Repertorium van door Nederland tussen 1813 en 1950 gesloten verdragen, samengesteld door Mr. **Stuyt**, A.M., Staatsdrukkerij, Den Haag, 1953.
Staatsblad van het koninkrijk der Nederlanden 1898, **Ter Algemeene Landsdrukkerij**, 1899 's Gravenhage. no 29.
Tetens, T.H., *Het Nieuwe Duitsland en de oude nazi's*, Forum Boekerij, Den Haag, 1962.
Trousse, P.E., Halewijn, J. van, *Uitlevering en internationale rechtshulp in strafzaken*, Larcier, Brussel, 1970.
'Overzicht van de Bijzondere Rechtspraak (Bijzondere Raad van Cassatie en Bijzondere Gerechtshoven', ed. Mr. J. **Veegens**, NV Uitgevers Maatschappij W.E.

Tjeenk Willink, Zwolle, 1947.
Venema, A., *Schrijvers, uitgevers en hun collaboratie, deel 1, Het systeem*, Arbeiderspers, Amsterdam, 1988.
Venema, A., *Schrijvers, uitgevers & hun collaboratie, De kleine collaboratie, 3a*, Arbeiderspers, Amsterdam, 1990.
Verkijk, Dick, *Radio Hilversum 1940-1945*, Uitgeverij Arbeiderspers, Amsterdam, 1974.
Vijver, Herman van den, *België in de Tweede Wereldoorlog, Deel 8, Het cultureel leven tijdens de bezetting*, Uitgeverij Peckmans, Kapellen, België, 1990.
Weber, Gaby, *El lavado del dinero nazi en Argentina*, editorial Edhasa, Buenos Aires, Argentina, 2005.
Weber, Gaby, *Eichmann wurde noch gebraucht, Der Massenmörder und der kalte Krieg*, Das neue Berlin, 2012.
Wesselius, Jacqueline, **Berends**, Lambiek, *Barbie, Misdadiger tegen de mensheid, een ooggetuigenverslag*, Meulenhof, Amsterdam 1987.
Wever, Bruno de, *Greep naar de macht, Vlaams nationalisme en Nieuwe Orde, het VNV 1933-1945*, Uitgeverij Lannoo, Tielt, 1994.
Wojak, Irmtrud, *Eichmanns memoiren*, Campus Verlag, Frankfurt am Main, 2001
Wojak, Irmtrud, *Fritz Bauer, 1903-1968, Eine Biographie*, Verlag C.H. Beck oHG, München, 2009.
Zaal, Wim, *De herstellers, Lotgevallen van de Nederlandse fascisten,* Uitgeverij Ambo, Utrecht, 1966.
"*De zwarte kameraden, Een geïllustreerde geschiedenis van de NSB*", ed. J. **Zwaan**, Van Holkema & Warendorf, Weesp, 1984.
Zeman, Z.A.B., *De propaganda van de nazi's*, Uitgeversmaatschappij W. de Haan, Hilversum, 1966.

Magazines and papers

Dutch papers/ magazines:
Algemeen Dagblad;Algemeen Nederlandsch Dagblad;Amigoe di Curaçao;Arnhemse Courant; Dagblad voor Noord-Limburg;De Avondster: Katholiek Dagblad;De Linie;De Telegraaf;De Tijd Maasbode;De Uitkijk;De Vlam;De Volkskrant;De Waarheid;De Weg;De Wereldkroniek;Elsevier ;Het Dagblad voor Amersfoort;Het Kompas;Het Nederlands Dagblad;Het Nieuws van de Dag;Het Parool;Het Vaderland: staat en letterkundig nieuwsblad.;Het Vrije Volk ;HP De Tijd;Intermediair; Kijk op Veghel, Stadkrant ;Leeuwarder Courant ;Leidse Courant;Limburgs Dagblad;Nieuwsblad van het Noorden; Nieuw Israëlitisch Weekblad;Nieuwe Tilburgse Courant;Nieuwsblad van het Noorden;Noord Hollands Dagblad;NRC Handelsblad;OP WACHT IN AMSTERDAM;Stadkrant Kijk op Veghel;Trouw;Utrechts Nieuwsblad ;Vrij Nederland

Belgian papers/ magazines
Bormshuis-Broederband; De Nieuwe Standaard; De Standaard; De Morgen; 't Palliterke

British papers
Daily Telegraph;The Guardian;The Independent;The Sunday Times

Canada
Hamilton Spectator

USA
New York Times;Time/Life magazine

German papers/magazines
Berliner Zeitung;Der Spiegel;Der Stern;Die Welt;Die Zeit;Stuttgarter Nachrichten;Süddeutsche Zeitung;taz.die Tagezeitung

Argentinean papers/ magazines
Clarin;Estudios migratorios latinoamericanos; La Nación;La Plata;Página 12;Todo es Historia

Ecuadorian papers
El Comercio;Hoy Ecuador

Spanish papers
El Pais;El Mundo

Israëli papers/magazines
Jewish Political Studies Review;Haaretz

Internet

www.taz.de, codename Uranus, 20-06-2011, by Phillippe Gessler

http://dare.uva.nl/document/116970 : Luisterspelen op de radio, A.P.A.M. van der Logt, 2008.

www.derechomilitar.info: casos para el estudio (III) El proceso Barbie, by Miguel Alía Plana.

http://www.interpol.int/Wanted-Persons/(wanted_id)/1999-29998 Robert Sassen

http://www.raremilitaria.com/sassen_001.htm : internet biography SS Sonderführer Alfons Sassen van Elsloo

http://www.refworld.org/docid/3df4be0610.html   :
(Robert Sassen)

Freedom of Information Act (foia): Declassified Nazi War Crimes Disclosure Act (CIA files):

http://www.foia.cia.gov/sites/default/files/document_conversions/1705143/SCHWEND,%20FRITZ_0128.pdf

http://www.foia.cia.gov/sites/default/files/document_conversions/1705143/SCHWEND,%20FRITZ_0146.pdf

http://www.foia.cia.gov/sites/default/files/document_conversions/1705143/LEERS,%20JOHANNES%20VON_0019.pdf

http://www.foia.cia.gov/sites/default/files/document_conversions/1705143/MENGELE,%20JOSEF%20%20%20VOL.%202_0069.pdf

http://www.foia.cia.gov/sites/default/files/document_conversions/1705143/BARBIE,%20KLAUS%20%20(DI)%20%20VOL.%201_0097.pdf

http://www.foia.cia.gov/sites/default/files/document_conversions/1705143/BARBIE,%20KLAUS%20%20%20VOL.%201_0033.pdf

http://www.foia.cia.gov/sites/default/files/document_conversions/1705143/BARBIE,%20KLAUS%20%20(DI)%20%20VOL.%201_0045.pdf

Audio
"Eichmann wusste natürlich sehr viel". Gabriele **Weber** im Gespräch mit Dirk-Oliver Heckmann, 5 april 2011

Gabriele (Gaby) **Weber**, "Radio broadcast 04-03-2011, The Abduction Legend or how Eichmann came to Jerusalem?"

Gabriele Weber, documentary "Disinformation-the wanted historical lie of the Mossad":
https://www.youtube.com/watch?v=0569i90Gpuo

Index

Abel, Wilhem Friedrich, 287
Acre Goméz, Luis, 237
Akkermans, Otto, 74
Argentina, 64, 85, 97, 98, 109, 114, 116, 119 - 121, 126, 128, 130, 132, 134 - 136, 139, 223, 241, 245, 251
A-Schule-West Seehof, Zorgvliet, 186, 221, 225, 289
Augstein, Rudolf, 113

Bakhoven, W.P., 104
Banzer, Hugo, 236
Barbie, Klaus, 123, 129, 132, 137, 138, 149, 154, 155, 234.-.239, 244, 245, 246, 248, 276, 291, 292
Barrientos Ortuño, René, 234, 291
Basti, Abel, 275
Beisel, 58, 182
Belgium, 18, 19, 21, 24, 25, 27, 28, 33, 34, 49, 77 - 93, 121, 122, 135, 137, 174, 204, 205, 207, 212, 224, 246, 269
Berends, Anthony, 179, 287
Besselink, A.J.P., 202, 204, 206, 207, 288
Black, Ian, 127
Blaskowitz, J.A., 76, 268
Blero, P, 287
Blumenthal, 49
BND, 117, 118, 120, 122, 123, 129, 130, 132, 137, 141, 155, 232, 233, 235, 191, 294
Bockaert, Amaat, 97, 99
Bolivia, 129, 131, 132, 137, 139, 233 - 238, 245, 246, 282, 291

Boot, 70, 191
Borginon, Hendrik, 28, 264
Borms, August, 28
Breyer, Karl, 95 - 97, 102 - 105, 145
Brilman, M.P., 249
Bucker, Elisabeth, 84
Buenos Aires, 97, 110-114, 116 -118, 120, 121, 125, 132, 137, 139, 141
Bulang, W, 66, 72, 90, 187, 189, 192, 193, 194, 201, 268, 279, 285
Bündnis 90/ Die Grünen, 279
Burk, Rudolf, 222, 226, 260, 290

Camarasa, Jorge, 134
Cammaert, A.P.M., 266
CAPRI, 112, 116, 117, 130, 274, 276, 281
Casparini, Juan, 276
Chambers, M.C., 72
Che Guevara, Ernesto, 233, 236
Chile, 131, 132, 140, 235, 245, 249
CIA, 120, 123, 134, 138, 149 - 153, 165, 166, 236, 252
Conijn, Eddy, 70, 71, 101, 185, 191, 192, 197, 213
Conijn, Fritz, 47, 48, 55, 70, 79, 100, 267
Conijn, Valentine, 47, 49, 136
Crabbendam, J.G., 217, 286, 288
Creijghton SJ, 94, 106

D'Alquin, Günther, 40, 57
Daels, Frans, 18, 28, 97
Damrau, Hans, 59, 89, 287
De Beaufort, L, 139

De Bie, Pierre
Colaris, 47, 49, 70, 71, 86, 191, 192, 205, 213, 285
De Blécourt, L, 100
De Bruyn, Jeanne, 50
De Jong, Cardinal, 74
De Jong, I.P., 198
De Jong, P.A.L., 206
De Jong, Roel, 193, 201
De Lentdecker, Louis, 120
De Vries, Vitus, 30, 31
De Waarheid, 45, 95, 99, 104, 105, 195
De Wilde, Maurice, 135
Degrelle, Léon, 245, 273
Delbaere, André, 135, 137
Delbaere, Elsje, 137
Delwalde, Leo, 136
Der Adler, 109, 235
Des Tombe, J.W.M., 201
Desselman, Otto, 33, 265
Desseyn, Jef, 41, 45, 181
Dinactie, 246, 247, 248, 294
Dittmar, W, 53, 56, 59, 62
Dole, May, 108
Dollmann, Eugen, 133
Domingo Mingolla, Antonio, 134, 137, 139, 237
Douliez, Yvonne, 205
Douthwaits, R, 193
Drück, Walter, 130, 131
Durán Ballén, Sixto, 296

Ecuador, 132, 140, 217, 219, 221, 223, 226, 228 - 230, 232, 239, 241, 243, 245, 247, 248, 251, 252, 253, 293
Ehlert, Fritz Otto, 276, 278
Eichmann, Adolf, 63, 107, 116, 117, 118, 119, 123, 124, 125, 126, 127, 276, 277
Eichmann, Vera, 276, 279
Einthoven, Louis, 201, 288
Elias, B.J., 231

Elias, Piet, 47
Elle, Kurt, 196
Espinal Mendoza, Ramón, 229
Estrada, Horacio, 296
Estrella, 129, 235
Eximorg, 97, 98, 99, 105, 108

Fabini, Klaus, 110
Febres Cordero, León, 247
Fernau, Joachim, 58, 89, 267
Fisette, Paula, 27, 39, 60, 113, 176, 196, 264
Fort Blauwkapel, 69, 72, 74 - 78, 80, 81, 211
Fort Honsdijk, 74
Foulkes, C, 76
Freiherr von Merck, Karl, 112
Frencken, J, 47
Freude, Ludiwg, 112
Freude, Rudolfo, 110
Fritsch, Eberhard, 111, 117, 120, 274
Frondizi, Arturo, 120
Fuldner, Horst, 116, 130, 276, 281

Gageling, Marinus, 64
Galland, Adolf, 112
Galo Plaza, 229
Galtieri, Leopoldo, 283
García Meza, Luis, 138, 139, 237
Gehlen, Reinhard, 118, 123, 132, 276
Gerardo Enriquez, 229
Germany, 18, 21, 30, 40, 44, 45, 51, 58, 60, 62, 68, 81, 84, 105, 106, 122, 123, 125, 129, 132, 133, 135, 141, 173, 174, 177, 178, 190, 194, 195, 202, 207, 211, 212, 219, 222, 232, 245
Giskes, H, 268
Godefroy, Jan, 97, 101
Goebbels, Josef, 15, 29, 266
Goedhart, J.D.G., 227

Gonzales de la Vega, Edgberto, 296
Gueiler Tejada, Lidia, 138, 237

Haagn, Erwin, 61, 268, 289
Harel, Isser, 127
Haremaker, N, 113, 273
Hauptmann Otto, 62, 63
Heijtink, 56, 58
Hermann, Kai, 135, 138, 154, 155, 160, 173, 190, 232, 239
Hermann, Lothar, 280
Hermans, Ward, 26
Herreweghe, Edward, 18, 83
Hildesheim, 84, 178, 179, 211, 222
Hitchcock, Alfred, 119, 277
Holdert, Hakki, 53, 63, 69, 191
Hollants, Achille, 110
Holterhof, 179, 183
Hoogesteijn, Thea, 49
Höttl, Wilhelm, 119, 277
Hoy, 162 - 165, 294
Hulmann, Hans, 265

Janssen, Jack, 97, 102, 104, 108
Jaspin, Arend, 47
Junker, Werner, 118, 279

Karel, Cornelis, 196
Kaszo, Andre, 78, 79, 80
Keers, Wolter, 199
Kerken, H, 85
Kiesewetter, 268
Kipp, Abraham, 277
Klompe, Huib, 191
Knolle, Friedrich, 221, 224, 225
Kops, Reinhard, 112
Kruithof, L.C., 39
Kuitenbrouwer, Henk, 94
Kuitenbrouwer, Louis, 68, 94, 105, 191

La Coruña, 214, 215, 216, 218, 219, 231
Lages, Willy, 49, 56
Lagrou, René, 26, 28, 97, 109
Lammers, J.J., 206, 207, 208, 219, 288
Lange, Herman, 65, 66, 67, 180, 185, 189, 285
Lasnaud, Jean Bernard, 253, 296
Lauryssens, Stan, 15, 32, 92, 96, 108, 114, 127, 134
Le Beau, Jean, 88
LeClerq, Staf, 25
Lehembre, Edgar, 24, 26, 264
Ley, Raymond, 141
Ligthart SJ, Cor, 95, 96, 107
Lindeijer SJ, Marc, 107
Lo Verde, G., 223
Lonardi, Eduardo, 116
Löns, 119
Lopez Rega, José, 276
Lowey Ball, Jan, 48, 270

Mampuys, 287
Martens, Adrian, 18
Martines, Martin
Pax, 204
Menem, Carlos, 252, 253, 296
Menge, Dieter, 119
Mengele, Josef, 117, 127, 128, 130, 153, 276, 277
Merex, 129, 131, 132, 134, 137, 233, 235, 282, 291, 292
Mertens, Anthony, 17, 46, 47, 48, 49, 52, 55, 64, 70, 71, 72, 77, 78, 83, 90 - 95, 97, 99 - 106, 108, 119, 136, 183, 185, 192, 205, 213, 267, 277
Mertig, Robert, 117
Mertins, Georg, 129 - 131, 291
Meyer, Willem, 110
Meza, Luis, 138, 139
Mingolla, Antonio, 134, 137, 139, 152

Miranda del Ebro, 87
Möhnke, W, 116
Molina Gómez, J, 116
Monteiro, M.E., 212
Montgomery, B, 268
Morris, Benny, 127
Moscardó Ituarte, José, 217, 219, 231
Mossad, 124, 125, 128, 134, 142
Müller – Ludwig, Frederico, 278

Naipaul, V.S., 115
Nannen, Henri, 122, 125, 280
Naumann, Werner, 112
Neubert, Fritz, 112
Ney, Ludwig, 116
Nijs, Joseph, 84, 85, 92, 205
Nitsch, Richard, 47
Nys, Jean, 91

Oelschlägel, Herbert, 48, 49
Olij, Jan, 271
Opdebeeck, Edward, 96, 98, 99, 102, 107, 110, 272, 274

Payne, Phil, 120, 124
Paz Estenssoro, Victor, 234
Peeters, Louis, 136, 137, 229, 291
Perón Duarte, Evita, 114
Perón, Juan, 111, 114, 116, 117, 121, 283
Persijn, Albert "Pim", 83, 84, 88, 271
Peru, 131, 132, 140, 220, 235, 245, 252
Pobierzym, Pedro, 277
Pons, Willy, 266
Poppe, Leo, 128, 130
Posner, Gerald, 128
Priebke, Erich, 148, 276
Prince Bernhard, 173, 199, 201, 268, 275
Pröbsting, Helmut, 224, 225, 267, 289

Protze, Richard, 173, 179, 180, 182, 184, 185, 186, 187
Rajakowitsch, Erich, 117
Rauff, Walter, 132, 134, 235, 276, 291, 294
Rauter, Hanns Albin, 38, 57, 58, 61, 62
Ravenswaaij, 27
Regan, Ronald, 247, 295
Reichelt, Paul, 268
Reulen, A, 47
Richter, R, 275
Rincke, 265
Riphagen, Andries, 283
Romein, J.B., 108
Rommel, Erwin, 42
Rosendo Ordonez, 229
Rudel, Hans Ulrich, 112, 114, 117, 123, 130, 133, 149, 235, 281 - 283, 291, 294

Sanders, Wim, 71, 86, 101, 102, 187, 191 - 200, 202, 222, 285, 287
Saporiti, Piero, 124
Sassen DO, Willem, 288
Sassen O.P, Jan, 11
Sassen O.P, Willem, 12
Sassen SJ, Ferdinand, 12, 16
Sassen van Bavel, Johanna, 11, 41, 69, 122, 179, 285
Sassen, Ad, 23, 27, 32, 35, 94
Sassen, F
daughter of Wim, 116
Sassen, Ferdinand Karel Rudolf Clemens, 194
Sassen, Francisca, 33, 69, 75, 122, 141, 210, 213, 214, 222, 284, 288
Sassen, Georgette, 33, 38, 63, 136, 159, 290, 291
Sassen, Godelieve, 36, 129
Sassen, Hadewych, 111
Sassen, Jan, 11, 21, 22, 25, 26,

27, 32, 41, 69, 143, 178, 180, 184
son of Alfons, 251, 295
Sassen, Johanna, 32, 69, 284
Sassen, Maria, 17, 18, 23, 24, 25, 33, 69, 157, 179, 186, 188, 189, 221 - 230, 264, 265, 289, 290
Sassen, Robert, 140, 251, 252, 253, 295, 296
Sassen, Saskia, 88, 98, 134, 140, 273, 274, 282, 284
Scharrer, Henri, 49, 266, 267, 270
Schermerhorn, W, 204, 217, 231
Schild, Hans, 67, 183, 185, 187, 190, 191
Schneider Captain, 109, 110, 119
Schneider, Antje, 110
Schneider, Inge, 110
Schoorens, Frans, 98
Schramm, Werner, 66, 67, 80, 190, 193, 269
Schwend, Friedrich, 130 - 132, 139, 150, 152, 234, 235, 284
Senan Moynihan, 108
Servatius, Robert, 126
Siles Zuazo, Hernán, 237
Six, Alfred, 265
Six, P, 201
Skorpion West, 58, 59, 62, 67, 73, 74, 122
Skorzeny, Otto, 114, 117, 128, 129, 131 - 134, 155, 233, 245, 273, 280, 282, 286, 287, 291
Skrodzki, Helene, 179, 185
Smekens, Willem, 109, 110
Smit, Gabriel, 94, 184, 188, 190
Sondermann, Gerben, 114
Spain, 46, 71, 73, 78 - 84 - 87, 106, 110, 129, 132, 135, 192, 202, 212 - 215, 219, 231, 233, 241, 243

Speleers, Reimond, 18
Spierings, Kees, 94
Stakenborg, J.H.W., 179
Stangneth, Bettina, 118, 279
Stassen, Nic, 98, 99
Stern, 122, 125, 138, 173, 190, 239, 240, 244, 245, 246, 247
Sternberg, H, 38, 58, 59, 60, 269
Steyr-Daimler-Puch, 135, 137, 138, 236, 240, 247
Stroessner, Alfredo, 134
Student, Kurt, 58, 61, 268
Suárez, Roberto, 138, 152
Sulzberger, C.L., 132

Tank, Kurt, 115, 276, 282
Taubert, E, 62
Ten Berg, Heyst, 26
Thole, Karel, 94
Time-Life, 64, 117, 121, 125, 127, 277
Tonneman, Corstiaan, 63
Torres Herbozo, 253

Van Asch van Wijck, 218
Van Breugel, Anton, 35
Van de Wiele, Jef, 33
Van Dedem, A, 103
Van den Hemel, Eduard, 25
Van den Hout, Willy, 61, 63, 64
Van der Poel, Albertus, 19
Van der Randen, A.J.A., 103
Van der Randen, Wiel, 93, 95, 96, 98, 100, 103, 108
Van der Stad, H.J., 22
Van der Voort, Miep, 72, 73, 77, 83, 84, 85, 86, 88, 98, 101, 110, 111, 113, 134, 188, 192, 205, 273, 282
Van der Voort, Jan, 271
Van der Voort, Peter, 271
Van der Wiel, A.P., 16, 228
Van Gestel SJ, 106
Van Hoek, Kees, 108

Van Kilsdonk SJ, Jan, 272
Van Kooten, Beb, 217
Van Overveldt, Leo, 110
Van Pelt, P., 88, 208
Van Puyenbroek, Harry, 97
Van Severen, Joris, 264
Van Thillo, Renaat, 98
Van Tilt, Roelf, 141
Van Voorst tot Voorst, F, 90, 102, 210
Van Voorst tot Voorst, T.J.G., 207
Verschaeve, Cyriel, 28, 176
Videla, Jorge, 135
Vive Carajo, Alfaro, 295
Von der Goltz, Michael, 167 - 172, 233, 240, 244, 250, 291, 293
Von Feldmann, A., 179
Von Leers, Johann, 112
Von Oven, Wilfred, 112
Von Reichenau, Walther, 31
Voskuil, Johannes, 267

Wagemans, T.M., 185
War, John, 128
Weber, Gaby, 114, 120, 123, 125, 141, 279, 280, 284, 309
Weidemann, Hans, 267
Weidenbach, Helmut, 222, 284, 260
Westendorp, Edo, 91, 100, 206, 207, 208, 209, 288

Yardin Milord, Ton, 48

Zuazo, Hernán, 138